Towards Teaching in Public

Towards Teaching in Public

Reshaping the Modern University

Edited by
Mike Neary, Howard Stevenson
and Les Bell

Foreword by
Mary Stuart

continuum

Continuum International Publishing Group

The Tower Building	80 Maiden Lane
11 York Road	Suite 704
London SE1 7NX	New York NY 10038

www.continuumbooks.com

British Library Cataloguing-in-Publication Data
A catalogue record for this book is available from the British Library.

ISBN: 978-1-4411-2479-1 (hardcover)
      978-1-4411-4395-2 (PDF)

Library of Congress Cataloging-in-Publication Data
Towards teaching in public : reshaping the modern university/edited by Mike Neary, Howard Stevenson, and Les Bell.
   p. cm.
Summary: "Explores the concept of teaching in public, a debate seeking to defend the university as a publicly funded institution, based on progressive public values"–Provided by publisher.
ISBN 978-1-4411-2479-1 (hardback) – ISBN 978-1-4411-4395-2 (ebook (pdf))
1. College teaching–Great Britain. 2. Education, Higher–Aims and objectives–Great Britain. 3. Educational change–Great Britain. I. Neary, Mike, 1956- II. Stevenson, Howard, 1963- III. Bell, Les, 1942-LB2331.T59 2012
378.1'250941–dc23   2011032191

Typeset by Deanta Global Publishing Services, Chennai, India
Printed and bound in Great Britain

Contents

Part Three: Teaching as a Public Activity (Editor: Mike Neary)

Notes on Contributors

Julian Beckton is a teaching and learning co-ordinator at the Centre for Educational Research and Development at the University of Lincoln, UK. He worked in academic libraries for a number of years before moving into the field of educational development. He has been involved in a number of projects including the integration of personal development planning into university curricula, the development and support of Virtual Learning Environments and the introduction of plagiarism management software. Research interests include the role of educational development units, academic freedom and innovative uses of technology in education.

Les Bell is professor of educational leadership at the University of Lincoln, UK, and Emeritus Professor of educational management at the University of Leicester, UK. He taught in both primary and secondary schools and joined Coventry College of Education before its merger with the University of Warwick, UK. In 1994, Les became director of the School of Education and Community Studies at Liverpool John Moores University, UK. He was appointed to the chair of educational management at Leicester in 1999, directing the International Doctorate of Education. He has written extensively on educational management and leadership. Recent books include *Perspectives on Educational Management and Leadership* (2007) (Continuum) and *The Principles of Educational Leadership and Management* (2010) (Sage), with Tony Bush and David Middleton.

Karin Crawford is a principal teaching fellow and faculty director of teaching and learning at the University of Lincoln, UK. Karin's research interests and publications span both pedagogic-related research and health and social care subject-related research. Karin is principally interested in using qualitative, narrative approaches to enable the views and voices of individuals to influence our understanding of academic practice and life-long learning. She has written several books and articles on professional development and enhancing teaching and learning in higher education.

Andy Hagyard has worked at the University of Lincoln, UK, since 1995, for the last ten years as a learning and teaching co-ordinator. As part of this role he is involved in moves to develop research-engaged teaching and learning across the institution. He also acts as co-ordinator for the Student as Producer project. He has a particular interest in institutional strategies to develop effective learning practices and is on the steering group of the Association for Learning Development in Higher Education (ALDinHE).

Aileen Morris is a principal teaching fellow and leads the PGCE Higher Education Teaching and Learning programme at the University of Lincoln, UK. Aileen taught in further education across a range of programmes and led curriculum and programme teams. In 1997, she joined De Montfort University, UK, supporting students in the research, planning and production of degree work and teaching on the PGCE/Cert Ed Post-Compulsory Learning and Teaching programme. She has a special interest in the challenges facing students in higher education who have been identified as dyslexic. Her current research interests are in the higher education learning experiences of students from under-represented groups, teacher identity and the professional development of staff in HE teaching.

Mike Neary is the dean of teaching and learning at the University of Lincoln, UK. His duties include being the director of the Centre for Educational Research and Development as well as the director of the Graduate School. Before taking up his current post in 2007 he taught sociology at the University of Warwick, UK. His recent research has focused on the academic labour process and the student experience and he has written extensively on teaching and learning in higher education. He received a national award for his teaching in 2007 from the Higher Education Academy, UK.

Howard Stevenson is professor of education at the University of Lincoln, UK. He was previously Senior Lecturer at the University of Leicester, UK, in the Centre for Educational Leadership and Management. He is now Deputy Director of the Centre for Educational Research and Development at the University of Lincoln. His research and publishing interests relate to the development and formulation of educational policy processes in both schools and post compulsory education. He is the author, with Bob Carter and Rowena Passy, of *Industrial Relations in Education: Transforming the School Workforce* (Routledge 2010).

Angela Thody is emeritus professor of education at the University of Lincoln, UK, and a Senior Fellow of the Higher Education Academy, UK. She specializes in methods of research writing and lecturing and in education leadership and its history. In these fields she has written five books, edited and contributed to further five books and authored over 50 articles in professional and academic journals and numerous chapters and research reports. She has been a professor at Lincoln since 1996, having previously held posts at Leicester, Luton, De Montfort and Open Universities, UK.

Sue Watling is learning and teaching co-ordinator in the Centre for Educational Research and Development, University of Lincoln, UK, supporting staff in the development of online learning opportunities and inclusive practice with digital data. Sue is leading the 'Getting Started' project which provides online transition support for students before enrolment. Her research interests include digital exclusion as a critique of the social model of disability and she has published on the subject of digital exclusion in relation to social work education and practice and disability and society. Sue is a fellow of the Higher Education Academy (HEA), UK, member of the Association for Learning Development in Higher Education (ALDinHE), UK, and holds Certified Membership of the Association for Learning Technology (CMALT), UK, as a learning technologist.

Joss Winn is a senior lecturer in the University of Lincoln's Centre for Educational Research and Development. In 2009, he led Chemistry.FM, a JISC/HEA funded Open Educational Resources project. Previously, he helped establish the university's open access research repository and continues to work on a number of projects relating to the Academic Commons. His current research interests focus on a critical study of the influence of cybernetics in educational theory and management. Joss has an MA in Film Archiving from the University of East Anglia, UK, and an MA in Buddhist Studies from the University of Michigan, USA. Previously, he worked at Amnesty International and the BFI National Film and Television Archive, UK.

Foreword

This book has grown out of the discussions, debates and thinking among colleagues at the University of Lincoln and elsewhere. It is deeply informed by current concerns about the purpose of higher education, which has always been a fertile ground for theorists. This is because it is not a simple matter to define the purpose of the ever-changing but deeply rooted 'project', that is, higher education. The book focuses on teaching in higher education and in this foreword I want to contextualize this debate on teaching and the public in higher education in the wider context of the debate about the purpose of higher education by exploring three key issues.

 (i) Debates about fees have obscured higher education's responsibility to the public good of higher education and in particular the relationship between tutor and student
 (ii) In the context of an information rich global society where knowledge(s) are no longer owned by an elite in higher education, the value of higher education's knowledge and research in society has to change
(iii) As long as we do not set out and win the arguments and provide evidence of the value of higher education, universities and their potential students will not get the support of wider society, limiting the future advance of higher level learning across society.

The debate about the impact of fees has been a significant feature of higher education policy in England since the Dearing Report (NCIHE 1997). In particular, higher education (HE) has increasingly been defined through the fee level for undergraduate students in the UK. The introduction of fees in 1998 would, it was argued, change the relationship between tutors and students. In 2003, when fee levels were increased from about £1,000 a year to £3,000 a year, again there were cries that this would affect the relationship between tutors and students and again this has been a significant concern about the new system to be introduced in 2012.

As someone who cut her teeth on teaching part-time students (and having been a part-time Open University student myself) I have no problem with the idea of fees and see no reason why students (or perhaps more importantly, graduates) should not contribute to the cost of their study. However, whatever we feel about the fee system we have become captured by a discourse focusing on consumerism, which needs to be recognized as a part of the HE landscape but as only one element within it. If we examined the issues properly, we would recognize that students do and will always consume knowledge, that is part of their role as learners, but we must require them to be discerning consumers, able to distinguish and challenge knowledge in an active fashion.

Equally important is the need for students, along with their tutors, to be creative producers of knowledge. Producing has always been central to learning at a higher level. We are not concerned with repeating what is in books, on the Internet or from lecturers but rather with an engagement that enables the student to find insights and re-interpretations, which advance understanding for them. These two elements are vital to a successful HE engagement between tutors and students. However, because we have been captured by the consumer rights debate we have not been able to articulate the ideal relationship between tutor and student. The point must be how universities ensure that the benefit of higher education is not just focused on a one-on-one interaction but rather on ensuring that questions of service and social development remain central to the higher education project.

Secondly, higher education has itself been challenged by a changing world. As globalization with its instant and extensive information provision has developed, higher education's place as 'the' provider of knowledge has declined. As Scott points out:

> The new knowledge economy, with its proliferation of symbolic and expert knowledge(s), 'hard' and 'soft' knowledge, has tended to subvert these comfortable categories. The result for universities is a radical enlargement, a stretching, of our missions (which, of course, represents a real challenge in terms of governance and management). (Scott 2008: 5)

Equally, Readings saw the challenge in 1996: 'it is no longer clear what the place of the University is within society nor what the exact nature of that society is' (Readings 1996: 4). This challenge for higher education is to explore how we can engage with a different set of concerns and a different environment to equip ourselves and our students to be successful citizens in this globalized world where knowledge is owned by many, not by a few.

Higher education has always been about the development rather than the transmission of knowledge, which has been the domain of school education. This means that in a world where others are also creating knowledge, our mission, as Scott suggests above, is stretched. This is also important for public engagement, engagement with other knowledge creators. It is central to making public what we do and is part of the democratization of HE. It also suggests that value of the research and knowledge we produce has to be open to scrutiny by others as well as our own community. This, as Readings (1996) argues, creates a new sort of HE for the future that is even more engaged and public than the civic ideal of universities in the nineteenth century.

Finally, the need to re-define our public engagement has never been more crucial. It is not just at the level of student–tutor relationships but at the very heart of our overall purpose, that of knowledge creation, where society is in transition and flux and where the nature of knowledge itself is less certain. As such higher education offers something of particular value to society as we can together in public engage with the very nature of our future development. This means that higher education cannot simply be of value just to our students (a private good which creates through transition a better future for the individual) but because the higher education project is essentially about the advancement of society we can and must seek to develop and create a wider debate about this public good for higher education. Higher education has not been very good at defending its role as a public good, not least because we have to acknowledge the notion of 'public' and 'the public good' is itself problematic. We have to ask which public, and whose good, and examine how this translates into our teaching, especially when universities are still seen as removed from the world around them.

Universities are part of the infrastructure that creates new social realities; they are the shapers of individual lives as well as communities and societies. The mission remains the same but has to be transformed in changing social conditions. The heart of this change requires much wider and deeper engagement with our communities and publics. Hence a book on the public good of higher education, 'teaching in public', is very timely. These debates and discussions are vital if we are to ensure that higher education as a project continues to remain healthy and fit for changing purposes in our society.

Professor Mary Stuart
Vice-Chancellor, University of Lincoln
Lincoln, May 2011

Acknowledgements

The editors would like to express their thanks to Penny Brown of Good Impressions (www.good-impressions.net) for her excellent copy editing and proof reading at every stage of this book, from proposal to final manuscript. Her contribution has been immense. We are also grateful to Jill Hubbard and Bev Potterton for their continued administrative support. They play an important part in helping to make the Centre for Educational Research and Development function effectively on a day-to-day basis.

We are also indebted to Professor Mary Stuart, Vice-Chancellor of the University of Lincoln, for writing the Foreword which clearly and succinctly sets the scene for this book.

Our thanks are due to Peter Hoare, advisor on historic and research libraries, and to the librarians and services of the Bromley House Subscription Library, Nottingham, who gave willingly of their time to provide Angela Thody with additional material for Chapter 2.

The project described in Chapter 4 was made possible by the enthusiasm and hard work of the student consultants and colleagues across the University of Lincoln; their receptiveness and willingness to participate in this work has been very much appreciated. Appreciation also goes to colleagues in Missouri State University and Brigham Young University, USA whose work and support was instrumental in the early stages of the project.

Finally, we want to thank all our colleagues at CERD for their co-operation in working so hard to produce this book and to meet the final deadline.

Les Bell
Mike Neary
Howard Stevenson

Part One

Education as a Public Good

(Edited by Les Bell)

All the contributors to this volume work in, or are associated with, the Centre for Educational Research and Development (CERD) at the University of Lincoln. The book sets out to explore one of the key issues that underpin the current debate about the nature of higher education in the United Kingdom – the tension between public and private provision. The starting point for this volume is that there is a balance to be struck between the public and the private. In the current crisis facing higher education, there is a significant imbalance in favour of the private. The notion of higher education as a public good fails to feature significantly in current policy debates. The argument here is that higher education is and should remain essentially a public good and should not be shaped primarily by the demands of human capital, marketization and privatization. It is argued here that the concept of 'Teaching in Public' and the notion of public generally need to be re-established as central principles in the philosophical rationale for the provision of higher education. This volume explores some of the ways in which teaching in public can transcend traditional notions of teaching as a private, privatized and marketized activity based largely, if not entirely, on the exigencies of human capital and eschewing the notion of higher education as a public good.

This first section introduces the key features of the concept of teaching in public and shows how it has emerged as a theme in higher education policy. Teaching in public presents a challenge to some of the current themes in higher education policy by raising questions in four significant areas. These are as follows:

Higher education as a public good – this challenges the marketization and commodification of higher education and asks how far is it possible to promote equality through higher education by using extended and open access, student choice and the scholarship of teaching and learning.

The learning landscape – teaching as a public space, which raises questions about the benefits of re-thinking the classroom as a public space and how far might this link to developments in pedagogy. This was the central theme of Bell *et al.* (2009) and forms the background for the argument in this volume.

The student/teacher nexus – the students as the first public and as producer through student participation in curriculum development, jointly exploring pedagogies. This theme raises questions about the nature and purpose of the relationship between lecturer and student and also challenges the notion of student as consumer and lecturer as provider.

Teaching as a public activity – the extent to which the wider community can engage with teaching and learning within universities both through traditional means such as attendance at public lectures and through alternative forms of access that can be facilitated through information technology and other developments within the public media. Teaching as public activity can be seen to have a profound impact on the relationship between teachers, students and the higher education curriculum.

Any debate about the nature and future of higher education needs to be located within a conceptual and historical context. In Chapter 1, Neary and Morris set out the conceptual framework for this debate by tracing the tensions between the privatization of British universities and the attempts to defend the importance of public in the provision of higher education. They argue that teaching in public provides a conceptual framework within which teaching in classrooms and the collaboration between student and teacher can be located within the wider debate about the nature and purposes of higher education and about the relationship between higher education and the state. They argue that university classrooms should be places where teaching is inspirational and meanings and ideas are reconstructed and challenged through public debate, which transcends the mere acquisition of skills and competences. The challenge for higher education in the face of the current emphasis on the private is to make public the multiple ways of thinking and to deconstruct the perception of student as consumer and teaching as a simple array of competences.

If Neary and Morris provide the conceptual framework for this debate, the other two chapters in this section provide the historical context. In Chapter 2, Thody shows how the origins of and rationale for the current debate surrounding the public and the private in higher education and the concept of teaching in public emerged in the nineteenth century as part of the various social interest groups as they engaged with the promotion of various aspects of higher learning in England. She traces the emergence of the public–private debate in the nineteenth century as different interest groups responded to the needs of different publics, including women and the working classes. She argues that these sought to provide an appropriate curriculum, in relevant institutional forms, for their members. Thody also explores the ways in which public engagement in higher education, for example, through miners' institutes, co-operatives and municipal libraries, together with the newly emerging civic university colleges, developed different perceptions of the meaning, purpose and appropriate curriculum and forms of delivery of higher education.

In Chapter 3, Bell examines how such public engagement in higher education developed in the twentieth century. He argues that, although the public–private debate was evident in the first half of the century, governments tended to adopt an almost *laissez faire* approach to the development of universities. By the end of the twentieth century, this relationship had changed and much of higher education provision can be seen to have been shaped by the tensions between public and private. Although universities are now regarded as central to many aspects of state policy, the state has tended to become a consumer of higher education rather than a provider albeit within a framework of state regulation. Such state regulation and control has forced universities to focus on key features of the private, such as marketization, commercialization of knowledge production and the student as consumer, at the expense of higher education as a public good.

Chapter 1

Teaching in Public: Reshaping the University

Mike Neary and Aileen Morris

Introduction

Higher education is in crisis in the United Kingdom and around the world. The manifestations of the crisis are funding cuts to universities and student protests in response to these government spending restrictions. What underpins this crisis is a controversy about the meaning and purpose of higher education that tends to polarize around the concepts of private and public forms of higher education. In this volume, we attempt to engage with this controversy, but in a way that avoids what is often a sterile and ultimately fruitless debate between notions of the private and the public. Our starting point is that higher education is a fundamental public good that needs to be maintained, but we are concerned that this concept seems unable to defend itself against the claims made by those who wish to privatize the university sector. There is, therefore, a need to transcend this debate and search for an alternative perspective that is both radical and hopeful.

The argument of the book is that the notion of public needs to be reclaimed and redefined as part of a progressive political project based on the rejuvenation of higher education. This argument will be sustained by grounding the philosophical notion of the university in the everyday working collaborations between teachers and students across a range of pedagogical practices. The chapters in this volume provide accounts and analyses of these collaborations, and they give insights into how such activities are trying to forge new notions of the public in higher education. The volume concludes by setting out an alternative conception of higher education with a focus on the traditions of critical political economy, rather than the oversimplified 'private versus public' debate, to make the case for the university as a central feature of the knowing society.

The Privatized University

Since the 1980s, the driving organizational principles for higher education, both in the United Kingdom and around the world, have been privatization and commercialization, based on the imperatives of economic efficiencies and effectiveness in a marketized society (Finlayson and Hayward 2010, Stevenson and Bell 2009). This has been defined in the academic literature variously as 'academic capitalism' (Slaughter and Leslie 1997), the 'death' (Evans 2004) and 'ruination' of universities (Readings 1996). It has been described as part of a process where knowledge is economized: '*homo academicus* is replaced by *homo economicus*' (Lock and Lorenz 2007), where scholarship becomes 'knowledge capitalism' (Leadbeater 2000), with higher education institutions recast as 'profit centres' (Callinicos 2006) and the 'enterprise university' (Shattock 2009). This commercialization and marketization, it has been argued, runs counter to the main academic project of higher education; or, in other words, it 'make you fick, innit' (Allen and Ainley 2007).

This attempt to consolidate the privatization of British universities forms part of a much broader attempt by governments to reinstate the ideology of market-led social development following the near collapse of the world financial system in 2008–2009 (Amin 2009, Archer 2009, Foster and Magdoff 2009, Brenner and Probsting 2008, Elliott and Atkinson 2008, Gamble 2009, Mason 2009, Shutt 2010). This project of privatization and commercialization has intensified in the recent period in Britain and elsewhere (Lambert 2003, Willetts 2010, Fejes 2005, Brunkhorst 2006, Alonso 2003), taking on a number of familiar forms. For undergraduates, it has meant recasting the student as consumer through charging tuition fees and an increasing emphasis on facilitating student choice, driven by the concept of the student experience. At the root of this lies the attempt to reduce the rationale of a university education to that of graduate employability (Harvey 2004). While the positive effects are that universities put considerable effort into securing successful careers for their alumni, there remain problems of student unemployment and under-employment and growing issues of student debt and poverty. There are also significant consequences for curriculum development as a risk-averse culture emerges within a system underpinned by benchmark comparisons and league tables (TUC/NUS 2006, Naidoo 2003, Epstein and Boden 2006, McCulloch 2009).

For staff, this process has been driven by a number of interrelated processes, including the introduction of wrap-around ubiquitous teaching and learning technologies, often leading to the automization, intensification and casualization of intellectual labour (Noble 2001, De Angelis and Harvie 2009, Levidow 2002, Callinicos 2006, Nelson and Watt 2004), as well as the ongoing pressure on academics to favour research at the expense of teaching, exemplified in the United Kingdom by the RAE/REF (Research Assessment Exercise/Research Excellence Framework) (Callinicos 2006). These processes have done nothing to dismantle the dysfunctionality that lies at the core of a university education: the relationship between teaching and research (Healey and Jenkins 2009). At the institutional level, academics are subjected to new forms of managerialism, which have been plagiarized from the corporate world and are underpinned by the concept of 'excellence' (Waterman and Peters 1982, Readings 1996), the cult of auditing (Power 1999) and market managerialism (McKibbin 2006), with a corresponding fetishization of notions of leadership (Callinicos 2006) and quality (Morley 2003).

Across the university sector, new forms of privatized higher education have emerged: not just the University of Buckingham but now the BPP College of Professional Studies (BPP Holdings 2011), with others to follow. At the same time, fundamental changes are being introduced to the ways in which universities are funded (Callinicos 2006), and there is a regression from a unified mass higher education system to the potential re-creation of elite provision within the system (Willetts 2010). This process has been greatly accelerated in the United Kingdom by the publication and government acceptance of the Browne Report (2010), which sets out proposals for university funding in terms of government support and the level of fees that undergraduate students should be charged. The key issues are that student fees will be trebled; there will no government funds for teaching in the Arts, Humanities and Social Sciences, with government funds for teaching targeted on Science, Technology, Engineering and Maths (STEM) subjects; and more private sector provision will be encouraged. Under the proposed new system, funding will follow the student, so that courses provided will be based on anticipated student–consumer demand. The concept of student as consumer is given further emphasis by insisting universities publish information relating to courses, levels of student satisfaction, employability statistics and rates of salary on leaving university so that, it is claimed, students can make better informed decisions about where to study for their undergraduate degree. While these reforms are welcomed by some parts of the English sector, particularly the elite universities, they have raised very high levels of public protest from students and academics (McQuillan 2010). These forms of mainstream opposition demand 'a belief in the public realm, publicly funded institutions, the idea of the university, and a belief in the necessity of critical thought' (McQuillan 2010).

Defending the Public University

In the face of this process, many academics have criticized such rampant privatization. Deem *et al.* (2007), for example, have argued against the introduction of New Public Management and bemoaned the demise of Weber's ethic of civic responsibility and its replacement by the ethos of private accumulation. Similarly, Fuller (2001) seeks to recover the original idea of the university by reconvening it under the notion of civic republicanism. This approach is mirrored in Nixon's (2011) attempt to re-imagine the public in terms of what he describes as present and future trajectories: the social, the civic and the cosmopolitanism, inside and outside the curriculum. Delanty (2001) also wants to recover the university as a public space, by which he means democratizing the ways in which knowledge is produced with reference to notions of technological and cultural citizenship. While Ball (2007) argues that claims for the effectiveness of the public sector are a romantic fiction, he does maintain that the move towards a marketized system of education has led to hybrid forms of management, and that there is a need to think differently about higher education before it is too late. The strength of these accounts is their willingness to engage with the concept of publicness and seek to define general principles for action, but their limitation is that they offer no practical examples of what these alternatives might look like for academics in ways that connect with their everyday teaching practice.

A more grounded approach to defending the concept of the public in higher education can be found in the work of Burawoy (2007) and McLean (2008). Burawoy is interested exclusively with teaching sociology in a model he refers to as Public Sociology, which means that his discipline engages with issues of public concern so as to reinstate the notion of the university as a public good. For Burawoy, the notion of public resides inside as well as outside the university, and students should be seen not as a constraint on professional careers but as an academic's 'first public' (Burawoy 2005a: 322). McLean (2008) makes a strong connection between progressive forms of pedagogy in practice and the philosophical idea of the university. She argues that the current crisis in higher education does provide the opportunity for creating forms of teaching that derive their values from intellectualizing pedagogic activity, by means of fusing epistemology, ontology, political science, philosophy, ethics, politics and sociology. This is based on a progressive moral commitment to active citizenship in a democratic society, linked to the prioritizing of urgent ethical and political emergencies. McLean argues that all of this should be framed in a discussion about the meaning and purpose of higher education: 'the idea of the university' (McLean 2008: 161). The strength of this work is that it makes a link between teaching in the classroom and collaborations between students and teacher with a more expansive debate about the nature and meaning of higher education. These pragmatic and practical approaches by Burawoy and McLean, in the context of a progressive politicized project for higher education, provide the framework and the grounding that underpin both this book and the concept of teaching in public.

The Teacher in Focus

Teaching in public brings the teacher back into focus. An unintended outcome of the concentration on the notion of 'student as consumer', leading to an obsession with student-centredness and the student experience in higher education, has been the diminution of the role of the teacher. The authors in this volume agree that

> It is time to swing the pendulum back to teachers, not as 'lone sages on the stage' but to strongly position them with their students, and educational researchers and developers, as partners in an inquiry into disciplinary concerns . . . a restoration of dignity for academics and a promising reconfiguration of research relationships between students, academics, educational researchers and developers. (Cousin 2008: 269)

Contributors to this book agree that when we look back on our own education, it is the teachers who made a deep and positive impression on us as students that we remember. They, more often than not, were teachers who enthused, encouraged, challenged and stimulated us to learn and think differently about their subject and, at the best of times, altered our world view as a result. We do not look back on our education and think: 'I met that competence'; 'I demonstrated that skill'; 'I learned that fact'. 'Good teaching' and 'good teachers' come in many forms (Standish 2005: 65), and universities have, to some extent, been able to resist the reduction of HE teaching to a set of narrow technical skills and closely described competences:

And there can be no recipe, for so much depends upon the teacher's judgement: in interacting with the class, in constructing and delivering the lecture, in responding to the rhythms of the occasion . . . So much depends on good timing . . . There is no single way in which this is done well. (Standish 2005: 65)

Just as universities are places where diversity, it is now acknowledged, exists within the student body, the same is true of the academic body. This is not just about gender, social background or ethnicity but also about academic discipline, role, orientation to practice and tenure, for example. Teachers in higher education are members of multiple communities within and beyond the institutional base. Working with both students and colleagues, there are opportunities for teachers to make public the moral and ethical base of their professionalism, which will challenge performative notions of what it is to be a good teacher in higher education. As Walker puts it:

What kind of academics and teachers, then, are we, or can we now be? What are our educational purposes and values as teachers in higher education? How might we 'do' critical forms of professionalism and reconstruct professional identities under changing conditions of higher education? (Walker 2001: 2)

The challenge is to bring out into the open and make public, with our students, the multiple ways of thinking and being within the world and how, in the critical spirit, they can be part of a collaborative and 'self-critical community, one in which the participants share with and support each other, in their own struggles towards authenticity. The private becomes semi-public; the struggles intersect' (Barnett 2007: 161). In order to work against the construction of students as consumers of the higher education product (the degree) and draw students into the intellectual community that is higher education, there needs to be openness about our own beliefs, values, limitations and uncertainties so that students can add their voice to the conversation and start to explore how power over learning can become power with learners (Kreisberg 1992).

Universities provide a place where ideas can and should be challenged and subverted. The space that is higher education, and its place in society, is still an important public sphere for contestation and struggle (Walker 2001), where university classrooms are 'whirlpools containing the contradictory crosscurrents of struggles for material superiority and ideological legitimacy that exist in the world outside' (Brookfield 1995: 9) and meanings, identities and ideas are challenged and reconstructed (Walker 2001). As such, they are places where discussion and dissent are welcomed and where students can be initiated into a conversation where they learn to recognize the moral and intellectual norms that fit with this form of critical discursivity (Oakeshott 1989).

Thus, we can enter into the dialogue with students that Burawoy (2007) describes above and where university teachers draw students into learning that becomes an intense engagement with what is studied (Standish 2005). Students then become our first public (Burawoy 2007) and the relationships that we form with them become critical in terms of a collective resistance to 'the economy of exchange and satisfaction' (Standish 2005: 57) in higher education teaching.

Making Teaching Public: Sharing What We Do

All the contributors to this volume work in or are associated with CERD. The chapters that follow offer an insight into the work in which they are involved. They illustrate some of the ways in which CERD's work seeks to articulate and apply the ideas presented in this book. CERD is not a monolithic entity and those who work in the Centre hold a diverse range of views. While all are committed to making our teaching public, there exist different perspectives as to what this may mean, or what it might look like in practice. In this volume, we do not claim a unanimity of view in relation to some of the core arguments presented here. Nor do those who work in the Centre claim to have a blueprint for others to follow. Rather, these contributions represent a range of perspectives from a group of people who work in higher education and who are seeking to make sense of their practice within the current crisis in higher education. The notion of teaching in public is not one that has been fully formed, but one that is constantly being formed and re-formed. It is through this process of collectively critiquing the work in which we are engaged that our shared sense of teaching in public emerges and evolves.

Teaching in public brings teachers into focus through their close collaborative work with their students. In Chapter 4, Crawford reports on an innovative approach to collaboration between teacher and student, the Student Consultants on Teaching Scheme, providing one example of the student as first public. She writes about the way in which undergraduate students were recruited, supported and trained as consultants to provide teachers with feedback on identified aspects of their academic practice. In this way, students and teachers act as partners or co-producers in learning, creating a process of joint enquiry. This approach is democratic to its core, focusing on students as academic citizens with civic responsibility, and altering the power balance between student and teacher; a process in which teachers enter into a dialogue with students underpinned by notions of intellectual intimacy. She frames this in a context based on principles of rights, responsibilities and governance, rather than the higher education sector's preoccupation with managerialist notions of quality assurance and enhancement.

Hagyard and Watling, in Chapter 5, find ways to reclaim the public university by creating projects where students work with academics on real research projects that are linked to issues of concern outside the academy. This project is not just a teaching and learning activity. It is part of a wider debate about the meaning and purpose of higher education. It raises fundamental questions about the role of the university as a site for the critical contestation of meaning as well as for the cultural contradictions that have arisen from recent conflicts between the interests of the state and market forces. In this way, academics and students contribute to the public discourse, transcending their own communities of expertise. The focus for this chapter is the Undergraduate Research Opportunities Scheme (UROS) at the University of Lincoln, where students receive bursaries to work alongside their teachers in the co-production of knowledge. Among the most significant outcomes of this project are the ways in which it confirmed research in this area in terms of the quality of the learning experience that arises from these collaborations and the extent to which students were able to disseminate their work to audiences outside the university. However, a limitation of these programmes is that they are restricted through funding to limited numbers of students. The chapter goes on to describe ways in which the University of Lincoln is attempting to embed these radical schemes by integrating undergraduate research activity at all levels of the undergraduate curriculum through the notion of 'Student as Producer'.

Watling, in Chapter 6, explores the notion of teaching in public through the ways in which digitalized technologies connect with the student experience of learning. For Watling, the notion of public is discussed in terms of access and inclusion. Again, this issue is not simply about practice in the classroom, but involves a critical analysis of both the contradictions and debates between the state and market as regulatory factors and the conditions for participation in the public sphere. She argues that rather than simply providing enhanced opportunities for learning, the digital revolution in higher education is in danger of simply creating new versions of the existing inequalities and exclusions that already create marginalized and disadvantaged groups across society, in a new form of digital discrimination. She refers to this group as a new 'invisible public'. The focus is on the development of e-Learning policy and practice in relation to digital discrimination. She finds that provision for enhancing access and inclusion has failed due to its focus on the issue of disability rather than finding ways to support diversity. To address this issue, the university of the future will have to be reconstituted as a public space within which virtual learning is based on the principles of social justice, in a way that recognizes design, digital inclusion and accessibility as key features of its provision.

Morris and Stevenson, in Chapter 7, explore further the theme of co-operative working, this time between teacher and teacher, based on a review programme of teacher observation. The focus of their chapter is how to overcome the managerialist tendencies within universities through a genuinely collaborative model of teacher observation, or peer review, in a way that is transformatory and offers the prospect of much more meaningful professional and personal development. A key issue that emerged from this research is that observations are most useful when the review process is owned by the participants, rather than conducted as a bureaucratic managerial exercise. The issue of ownership provides ways for teachers to reclaim their teaching and go beyond the institutional frameworks in which they currently function. This sense of ownership extends to opening up their work to fellow teachers so as to encourage a more rigorous critique, based on a reconstructed notion of teaching and learning and the purpose of higher education. They argue that their model provides the opportunity for teachers to create an intellectualized discourse based on critical theoretical positions that teachers have developed, and in so doing expose what they refer to as the 'quack accountability' of the market for the sham that it is.

In Chapter 8, Beckton explores the way in which the use of technology in teaching has tended to make teaching less public and more privatized. His argument is also framed in the context of critical political economy and the historical development of machinery to intensify the capitalist labour process. Beckton's argument is that despite the appeal of digital devices, the logic of their production is to enhance the production of surplus value and to intensify work. He draws inspiration for how we might respond to this problem from the Luddites, a nineteenth-century movement of British textile workers who sabotaged new mechanized looms that, they felt, were destroying their jobs and way of life. His response is not to advocate the destruction of new technologies but to develop new ways of teaching in public, around the principle of sharing. He describes two particular ongoing examples in universities: using Wikipedia as a critical forum for students' work and the notion of the Academic Commons.

The theme of the relationship between technology and work is continued in Chapter 9 where Winn explores it in the context of critical political economy. The focus of this chapter is Open Educational Resources (OER) and the extent to which these constitute a radical new form of public education or teaching in public. His conclusion is that Open Education is not a new form of teaching in public because it concentrates on the freedom of things rather than the freedom of people. The basis of his argument is that although OER create new learning resources made available, free of charge, outside the university, these resources are produced by academics employed as part of a capitalist labour process, in universities that are increasingly driven by the logic of production of surplus value. Winn argues that in order to create a genuinely open and emancipated form of teaching in public, it is necessary to create a new form of social wealth. This is to be based not on the commodified form of things, to be appropriated by consumers in accordance with the capitalist law of value, but rather on knowledge at the level of society, to be re-appropriated by the people who produced it.

The Idea of the University

A debate about the future of higher education needs to be located within a historical context. It is only possible to understand the present, and to speculate the future, by understanding the past. Thody, in Chapter 2, provides an account of the way in which the concept of teaching in public emerged in the nineteenth century as a variety of social interest groups engaged with the promotion of various aspects of higher education in England. Thody shows how these social interest groups responded to the needs of different publics, significantly women and the working classes. She demonstrates the way in which each group, depending on its own values and principles, sought to provide an appropriate curriculum in relevant institutional forms and cites as examples the miners' institutes, co-operatives and municipal libraries, each with its own interpretation of the meaning and purpose of higher education. These meanings rehearse many of the issues that still form the core of debates about higher education and the relationship between public and private provision in higher education today. Such issues include whether higher education should be vocational or be intrinsically valued for its own sake, and whether education is about containment and control, or if it has the potential to be emancipatory.

Bell, in Chapter 3, shows how the themes identified by Thody were instrumental in the shaping of higher education throughout the twentieth century, especially the tensions between public and private provision. He charts the expansion and development of higher education in England and notes the increasingly intrusive nature of state control as participation in higher education is widened in response to government policy, with its growing emphasis on commercialization and marketization. The key issue for Bell is the extent to which universities are now regarded as an important aspect of state policy, funded and directed to achieve specific economic outcomes that can be regulated and controlled. Bell shows us that this new economic imperative exacerbates the debate about the meaning of higher education and the extent to which universities should be commercially orientated or focused on contributing to a greater public good.

Both these chapters highlight the importance of analysing the role of the state in order to develop an understanding of higher education and its growth. In the nineteenth century, as Thody explains, in the absence of state funding, alternative forms of higher education were established by different interest groups based on the needs of particular publics. The question remains to what extent, with the changes to state funding and pressure to widen participation in the twenty-first century, new alternative and radical forms of provision might emerge. The other issue relating to the state, as Bell highlights, is that the changes in funding are accompanied by more state regulation. It remains to be seen how far this regulation and control forces universities to become even more focused on the student as consumer and on commercial and business imperatives.

The final chapter of the book draws all of this together, through a further historical elaboration of the development of the modern university, set in the context of a debate about the relationship between the state and the market. The basis of the argument is that the private and the public are the basic principles of liberal market society and, in that sense, are not antithetical. In order to re-conceive the notion of the public good, it is necessary to transcend the confines of liberal thought in ways that offer real alternatives to the university as it is currently constituted. The most challenging alternative to the liberal notion of private and public is found in debates that integrate economic theory with political theories of the state. The final chapter engages with writers who have attempted to fuse theories of the state with economics and the ways in which these ideas are used to reconceptualize the notions of private and public in educational terms. The chapter draws out the strengths and limits of these approaches but argues that alternative and more radical ideas of what we mean by 'public' might be better developed by drawing on the traditions of critical political economy and linking these theoretical approaches with the historical development of the modern European university. All this leads to the conclusion that it is necessary to develop a new concept of 'public' and, therefore, teaching in public, based on a notion of the knowing society rather than the knowledge economy.

This volume does not offer any solutions but points out ways in which it is possible to contribute to the creation of a new critical discourse through which teachers might counteract the apparently overwhelming project to privatize higher education. While there is much progressive pedagogical practice going on at Lincoln and in universities elsewhere, there is still much work that needs to be done.

Chapter 2

Teaching in Public: Revolution as Evolution in Nineteenth-Century Higher Education

Angela Thody

Introduction

The story of the Oxford scholar poor,
Of pregnant parts and quick inventive brain,
Who, tired of knocking at preferment's door,
One summer-morn forsook
His friends, and went to learn the gipsy-lore,
And roam'd the world with that wild brotherhood,
And came, as most men deem'd, to little good,
But came to Oxford and his friends no more.

Matthew Arnold, *The Scholar Gypsy, 1853*

Nineteenth-century higher education developments can be viewed as origins and rationales for the twentieth and twenty-first centuries' debates about universities as contributors to public social, economic and political needs. These are this book's *raison d'être*, as discussed by Mike Neary and Aileen Morris in Chapter 1. This chapter aims to identify how research, thought and action during and since the nineteenth century have followed the arguments between those supporting policies defining higher education as a private good for very restricted publics and those reconfiguring it as a national good for much wider audiences. These debates were those illustrated by Matthew Arnold with his tale of the poor, and therefore effectively debarred, Oxford gypsy scholar.

Following a note on the context of the analysis, the expansion of higher education for new publics is discussed, since the nineteenth century's contribution to this seems to be underestimated. Secondly, a section on curricula for new publics relates higher education's responses to the theme we now describe as the 'student as consumer', where demands for a vocational education relevant to industry were met and paid for by student fees or private donations. What has been overlooked is that universities were always vocationally relevant, as this section of the chapter will argue, but our understanding of 'vocational' has changed. Finally, an examination of teaching for new publics debates lecturing, group work, libraries, technological developments and their impacts on academic labour.

Arnold's poem used a seventeenth-century failure to critique early nineteenth-century Oxford University, which was then a finishing school for a few hundred gentlemen who neither studied much nor took examinations (Wodehouse 1925, Walsh 2009). Equally small numbers 'read' seriously for their degrees (McCord and Perdue 2007), the sole route to qualify as a minister of religion, with desultory assistance from privately paid tutors. College fellows hardly bothered to lead learning and professors did minimal lecturing (Huber 1843, Simon 1960). Students were all upper class and had to be Anglicans. All studied classical languages, mainly with philosophy or theology. This applied also to England's only other university, Cambridge, which also taught some mathematics. Thus, what little higher education teaching existed was done in private, almost entirely as tutorials for very restricted publics and at the only two early nineteenth-century English universities, collectively termed Oxbridge.

By 1900 – revolution! Higher education 'publics' included all denominations, those needing a vocational route to various middle-class professions or support for the necessary learning for the industrial growth of England, those who were unable to attend universities full time, women, even very underprivileged middle-class women, lower middle-class artisans (Pashley 1968) and a first few working-class students entering via scholarships. Had he been alive in 1900, Arnold's scholar gypsy would have prepared through free libraries, Working Men's Clubs and University Settlements and enrolled at the newly founded Ruskin College Oxford, the first university college for working people, where he would learn to both criticize and reform established institutions (Mansbridge 1920).

Despite this revolution, nineteenth-century achievements seem denigrated in both contemporary and subsequent literature. Teaching was merely lecturing, 'publics' were only middle class and higher education was reported as closed to the working classes either from their lack of aspirations or by deliberate obstruction for fear that enhancing their knowledge would help foment violent revolution (Vincent 1981). Efforts to bring higher education to wider publics in the mid-nineteenth century were often regarded as being based on outmoded moral and religious beliefs that became overridden by Darwinism; in other cases, attempts to reach wider publics were derided as misguided intentions to inculcate in the working classes the *mores* of those more fortunately placed (Goldman 1995). The few revisionist views of these criticisms note the value to the upper working classes and lower middle classes of initiatives such as university extension lectures (Laurent 1984). Some praise higher education's admission of women, while emphasizing that the women were not working class. Writers report university reforms, emerging civic university colleges, growing library access and mechanics' institutes' lectures, but there always appears to be a subtext: all failed to provide suitable teaching and access for the working classes. The middle classes seem almost to be accused of 'hijacking' provision not meant for them, deliberately buttressing ascendancy over the working classes as their educational agendas diverged from the 1830s (Simon 1960, McCulloch 2010); even their genteel suburbanity was mocked for providing a less suitable audience for lectures than the urban working classes (Jepson 1973, citing contemporary sources).

Such denigration underestimates the achievements of nineteenth-century higher education in expanding social class access and evolving teaching in public, both in curricula and andragogy. In 1800, the middle classes largely lacked higher educational opportunity. That they pressed for, and took advantage of, what was offered seems to be worth celebrating. The middle classes evolved as the new public but then played 'a remarkable role as intellectual advisors to the mid-Victorian trade union movement' later creating links with the British Labour Party (Goldman 1995) and thus furthering expansion of university publics from 1900.

The Context of the Analysis

A 'historical dimension for bringing contextual understanding to enrich contemporary research' (Silver 2007: 535) is particularly lacking in higher education's reconstructions of social relations (Goodman and Grosvenor 2009) and is much needed for the nineteenth century (Gardner 2007). The challenge of attempting this here is sourcing evidence from across more than 200 years to allow for writers' differing times and philosophical stances. Interpretations varied from the earliest sources onwards. Some, for example, glowingly described workers with 'a keen appreciation of education' studying Latin, Greek, logic and civil knowledge (Mansbridge 1920: 3–4, proselytizing for a workers' educational association); others noted labourers who took little interest 'in their own mental improvement' (Solly 1867: 267, proselytizing for the improvement of teaching in working men's clubs).

Such positional variations can be significant in influencing authors' viewpoints and arguments, so readers should be aware of this author's position.

She is a middle-class female academic of nineteenth-century working-class origins with a grandfather for whom Harrison's epithet of 'cobbler-philosopher' (1971: 2) is appropriate. At that time, the middle classes would have been 'of independent means . . . professionals . . . factory owners . . . in commerce, shop keepers' (Turner 1966: 49). Her parents benefited from twentieth-century socialism's scholarship ladder and she followed with a state-funded, free education. Socialism's influence continued through her first research supervisor, Brian Simon, seminal communist interpreter of labour education history as a struggle lost by the working classes (Simon 1960, McCulloch 2010). Only recently, having veered towards post-modernist deconstruction, has she begun to consider a middle-class view of the nineteenth century, as in this chapter.

Since no generalist history of nineteenth-century higher education could be located, sources specific to each aspect discussed here were used. Some of these detailed the administrative growth of higher education and are used where relevant to the argument rather than as a chronological review. Nineteenth-century forms of higher education obviously encompassed the universities, but, beyond that, arguments have raged over whether or not any, some or all other developments could be termed higher education at a time when few people had even secondary schooling. Many people were, however, considered to be well-educated, articulate and literate, even without elementary education (Simon 1960). This latter judgement seems supported by the advanced topics offered by various forms of university outreach and non-university efforts at higher education and by the demand for these (Harrison 1961, Jepson 1973, Stephens and Roderick 1983, Walsh 2009), so these have also been included here as higher education.

Expanding Higher Education Publics

This section first explores the development of universities in the nineteenth century and secondly considers efforts to provide higher education independently of the university sector.

Universities and Higher Education

Between the 1850s and 1890s, Oxbridge granted access to all denominations, women and the middle classes. These social changes were not of Oxbridge's own making but were either the outcome of government commissions and legislation (Goldman 1995, Vernon 2001) or a forced response to new publics from England's industrial growth (Walsh 2009). These new, liberal middle-class publics presented 'the full cry against the state of university learning' (Simon 1960: 91) led by Thomas Arnold, later reforming headmaster of Rugby school (and father of the poet whose work opened this chapter) and John Newman (later Cardinal), supporter of social exclusivity (Simon 1960). Oxbridge's corruption and sloth prevented it reforming itself (Vernon 2001) but public hostility demanded total change (Huber 1843). More temperately, the 1850 government commission, subsequent motions and legislation, which forced the reforms, suggested, *inter alia*, ways to admit a wider middle-class audience through fairer competition for scholarships and decreasing the costs of university attendance (Simon 1960), themes reiterated in the twentieth century by Robbins (Committee on Higher Education 1963) and Dearing (NCIHE 1997) Reports (see Chapter 3). Oxbridge responded partly because, like those trying to change them, the ancient universities realized their national significance as public institutions and desired to retain this authority (Goldman 1995).

Despite reforms, Oxbridge's middle-class entry grew very gradually; landowning and clerical backgrounds and careers continued to constitute the majority of the intake and output over most of the nineteenth century, though the majority declined from over 90 per cent to around 60 per cent (Sanderson 1991). Women's admission to the ancient universities in the 1870s also proceeded slowly: the first Cambridge group was only five. The women were not strident feminists but rather timid (Goldman 1995). Women pioneers seemed conscious that it was enough to have entered the portals and did not want to disturb society too much for fear of losing privileges. Male chauvinism was rife; rioting ensued in 1897 against Oxford awarding degrees to women (Robinson 2009). Oxbridge did not proactively seek women's admission but was pushed by external pressures. These reforms gave to the newly extending higher education publics a continuing belief in the importance of universities to the nation's economic growth and to the education of its political leadership (Jones 1977).

Leadership by Oxbridge men can be seen in the idealism of late nineteenth-century university settlements, of which the largest was Oxford's Toynbee Hall in London. Oxbridge women's colleges established their own women's settlement; female student residents at Toynbee were banned since this might 'frighten the ablest university men away' (Meacham 1987: 47). Glasgow and Manchester Universities also established settlements and Cambridge University provided funds for similar developments.

Settlements comprised small groups of volunteer recent graduates living temporarily in inner-city communities to share their educational advantages with working-class publics who would never attend universities. The graduates learnt experientially, the locals received lectures on higher education topics, shared sports and social activities with leading undergraduates from a 'higher life . . . [and were] wise counsellors' (Simon 1974: 79). Short summer residences were arranged for some inner-city children at Oxford to acquaint them with university life (Briggs and Macartney 1984), a now common twenty-first century approach.

As a first attempt at university outreach the settlements, although small, can be seen as ancestors of late twentieth-century developments such as the Open University, access courses to allow unqualified students university entrance, acceptance of mature students' abilities to learn, residential courses, social engineering through preferential treatment of those from inadequate inner-city schools and formally organized volunteer activities by today's students. Initially, however, the settlements attracted strongly opposing assessments of their teaching and the publics they reached (Goldman 1995).

Some assessed the settlements as being more about social reform than higher education, though the lectures presented clearly fell within higher education's remit (Meacham 1987). Simon regarded them as 'neo-feudal . . . appeal[ing] more to the lower middle class than the workers' (Simon 1974: 78, 85). Toynbee's founder admitted it had not brought the classes together as hoped (Meacham 1987). The majority of audiences were 'schoolmasters, schoolmistresses and clerks – a familiar clientele in the history of adult education' (Briggs and Macartney 1984: 29) but from the perspective of this chapter's argument, this was to be both expected and welcomed. Indeed Barnett, Toynbee's founder, considered 'the foremen, clerks, board-school teachers [were]. . . as much in need of improvement as were the very poor' (Meacham 1987: 59); the same groups also accessed the new university extension classes.

University extension classes met requests for higher education from those unlikely to attend universities full time. Oxford and Cambridge were persuaded to allow such classes by arguments they would help further establish the universities as national public institutions (Goldman 1995). The classes were not financially supported by the universities but had to be self-funding from student fees (an early instance of academic capitalism). The lecturers received no university salaries and the meagre university financial support went to an organizer. Some employers subsidized courses, such as colliery owners in Durham where classes included mining technology and also literature. Other funds came from local co-operative societies and from London's City companies. On the whole, though, university extension classes embodied 'the long tradition of assistance by university people in a private capacity, in adult education activities of various kinds' (Kelly 1992: 218).

Demand for university extension classes was generated by the efforts of groups such as Christian Socialists who trialled libraries, reading rooms and cultural lectures from the mid-nineteenth century (Sanderson 1991) and from scientific lectures pioneered by Durham and London universities earlier in the century (Kelly 1992). These initiatives merged into the part-time day and evening courses provided by Oxford, Cambridge, Victoria (the amalgam of northern higher education providers which later became Manchester University) and London universities in the early 1870s, rapidly expanding to about 60,000 students annually by the late 1890s. Durham's five centres alone brought around 1,300 workers to political economic studies. Extension courses lasted six or 12 weeks, culminating in examinations of university honours standard (Kelly 1992); Cambridge offered the same fare as its full time courses, Oxford a more general education (Goldman 1995).

It has been claimed that workers were in the minority, with the lower middle classes predominating (Harrison 1971, Simon 1974), but Kelly (1992) describes this absence of workers as a myth, because fees were deliberately kept low. Certainly, initial demand for such classes came from labourers (Goldman 1995, citing contemporary sources) and the extension movement always aimed to admit anyone denied access to full time university studies (Jepson 1973). Oxford's early classes were for 'superior artisans . . . [and] young men engaged in business [who had left school at 15] but who a few years later found they had still a great deal to learn' (Goldman 1995: 32). Pupil–teachers seized the extension opportunities, which prompted the *Leicester Journal* to ask what was the point of these teachers gaining higher education when they were only teaching elementary subjects (Gill 1968). Secondary school teachers also attended Oxbridge summer schools as part of the extension movement.

Middle-class women, particularly, gained access to higher education through extension classes before they were allowed to attend universities full time:

> little flocks of gentlewomen were emerging from the parlour, and scuttling their way to talks in public rooms by gentleman academics . . . Ladies' Educational Associations were formed, with local committees, to arrange and publicise courses; . . . peripatetic professors were engaged from London, Oxford, Cambridge, and Durham. (Robinson 2009: 39)

Organizations such as the North of England Council for Promoting the Higher Education of Women used extension provision. Genteel lady governesses provided an audience for London's extension classes. Classes focused on women's needs, despite emanating from 'strongholds of masculine privilege' (Kelly 1992: 227, 228), which did not necessarily appreciate the success of extension for women's education (Goldman 1995), for success, it was judged to be, both at the time and since (Jepson 1973).

Extension classes' legacy is their impact upon popular thought about the universal right to access, and gain from, higher education (Mansbridge 1920) and about offering many different routes to access. Extension movements were copied successfully in the then British colonies by Sydney University and others (Sumner 1990) and provided antecedents for England's twentieth-century civic universities, which had their origins in the nineteenth century (Jepson 1973, Kelly 1992, Walsh 2009).

London and Durham universities spearheaded higher education developments up to 1850 (though Durham was mainly a pale imitation of Oxbridge) while Birmingham, Newcastle and others started colleges in the same period. Manchester's colleges grouped themselves as the first university college of the new federal Victoria University in 1880. Liverpool launched a university college in 1884, as had Southampton in 1862, Bristol in 1876 and Nottingham in 1881 *inter alia*. These civic initiatives were graduating only small numbers by 1900, and all remained colleges until after 1900, but their impact on accessibility was huge. From their inception, men of all denominations were admitted and the middle classes could afford the fees. Women were allowed entry to lectures (the first two females at London in 1832, unofficially), were later permitted to be awarded degrees (from the mid-1870s) and formed the majority of non-resident students in some of the new university colleges (Robinson 2009). The whole development emphasized the importance of universities, helped by London's being the first civic development and so naturally acquiring the same national significance as Oxbridge (Vernon 2001).

Inspiration for university-level education in towns other than Oxbridge came from 'local enthusiasts rather than official intervention' (McCord and Purdue 2007: 376). The Weberian civic responsibility of local pride propelled motley collections of medical colleges, mechanics' institutes, extension classes and local libraries into what eventually became the twentieth century's civic universities, helped by some government grants. There is dispute about whether this funding was as important as that provided locally (Vernon 2001) but Treasury grants were awarded as a result of local petitioning (Vernon 2001, Radcliffe 2006).

While the satirical magazine *Punch* congratulated Durham in 1895 on awarding degrees to women, on the basis of it increasing the likelihood of attracting both male and female undergraduates, 'Fortunate Tutors! Lucky Dons! Happy Durham!' (Robinson 2009: 54), women students did not have it easy in the civic universities. To prove serious intent, they had to demonstrate hard work to tutors and families; local people made fun of women students; they were kept apart from the male students in lectures and at meals; they were subject to much personal regulation for fear of scandal; they had to prove they could physiologically cope with the rigours of studying; many worried that women's education devalued degrees (Robinson 2009). Despite this, 'the experiment in providing higher education for women proved surprisingly successful' (Barnes 1994: 46) according to male academics of the time, with women as likely as men to complete graduation and proceed to careers.

As well as the new female publics, the civic university colleges firmly established the locally emergent middle classes with new industrial wealth as their entrants. This was a reaction to Oxbridge's continued cultural and political dominance; the civics gave 'space, both dimensionally and culturally to the values of the new industrial middle classes', sometimes quite literally in destroying local working-class housing to build the universities (Marks 2005: 619–20). This trend appears to have continued in civic universities' twentieth-century developments (see Chapter 3).

Other Providers of Emergent Higher Education

Even those of the upper classes who realized that nineteenth-century higher education might alter social patterns saw this role as independent of the universities (Silver 2007). Simultaneously, the working and middle classes confidently developed their own versions of higher education, so desirous were they of 'self-education and self-improvement' (Baggs 2006: 170). These showed that increasingly wider publics could both cope with and benefit from university-level studies and even displace existing elites:

> It helped materially to develop, from among . . . the workers, men who were able to comprehend and master the most advanced political and social thinking of the time; men capable of acting on . . . their knowledge and so of leading the nascent working-class movement at both the local and national level. (Simon 1960: 180–1)

This section reviews the 'hubbub of semi-institutionalised educational and investigative activity' (Gardner 2007: 295) that developed outside the control of both state and universities. This hubbub's apogee came in the third quarter of the nineteenth century, waning as the new education local authorities' Higher Grade Board Schools absorbed technical education, and the universities absorbed higher education by the end of the century. Was this when democratization of higher education was first displaced – the beginnings of a self-help movement, which the twenty-first century is trying to revive – albeit renamed – in the student-as-producer movement?

Disagreements about whether or not the legacy of the nineteenth century included democratization are encapsulated in opinions from two authors, each from different rationales:

> It has been said . . . education will reduce the rates . . . it will [empty] the prisons . . . will enable our workmen to hold their own in competition with other nations, but I don't believe . . . the working men of England want education on any one of these grounds . . . they want it because it will make them better, happier and wiser men. (Thomas Burt, first working-class MP, speaking in Parliament, 1875, cited in Creighton 1902: 38)

So far as can be traced, there has never been such a general movement on the part of the people towards education (Mansbridge 1902: 2).

All agree that there were many educational movements outside universities, such as co-operative societies, working men's clubs, mechanics' institutes, literary and philosophical societies and adult education classes. Different writers' philosophies, however, produce very different opinions on whether or not these movements constituted higher education; whether they were, or were not, indicative of refusals to accept other classes' hegemony and whether they forwarded or repressed the working classes.

Co-operative societies, originally set up to provide fairly priced food for the working classes, all included instruction for mutual improvement in their constitutions (Simon 1960). Funds for this came from the surplus on their other activities (Mansbridge 1902) and such educational provision continues today, though classified mainly as adult leisure classes. A co-operative for twenty-first century higher education (the Social Science Centre) was launched in Lincoln in 2011 by academics from the local university, though it is not a formal part of that university's provision. The nineteenth-century co-operatives provided facilities for higher education by gradually developing more libraries than were provided by civic authorities; working men established reading rooms above pubs conveniently adjacent to their residential areas; miners' institutes had libraries. All these changed in contents, size and use during the century, but few appeared to contain much serious literature and 'books by Marx, Engels, Bakunin and Tolstoy' looked as if they were never borrowed (Baggs 2006: 171, 178).

Efforts by working men's clubs were criticized by a contemporary working-class leader for failing to achieve educational aims (Solly 1867). In contrast, Simon (1974) considers working men's own initiatives were very successful, citing the London Working Men's College, large numbers of artisans reading free books and journals in coffee-houses, the 'intellectual hot beds' of the Chartist Halls of Science, all developed as an 'outright rejection . . . of . . . education . . . sponsored by the middle-classes' (Simon 1974: 230, 231, 244). An outstanding example of this type of self-help was the People's College in Sheffield, 1842–79, financed and organized by workers (though established on a middle-class clergyman's initiative), hence rather Spartan in conditions but providing higher education in, *inter alia*, Latin, Greek, logic and civil knowledge (Mansbridge 1902).

Despite disagreements about the objectives and effectiveness of working-class self-help higher education movements, to them is owed the genesis of ideas now generally accepted as part of extending the publics in education. Solly (who was the National Secretary of the Working Men's Clubs) suggested that clubs should provide scholarships to working men's colleges or develop a Central Industrial College enabling men to combine work and study (the aims of both Ruskin College, Oxford, in 1899 and the Open University from the 1960s). University extension was also developed as a way to assist working-class self-help and provided an impetus for founding the early twentieth-century Workers' Educational Association (Mansbridge 1902).

Mechanics' institutes began in 1800s Glasgow led by a Dr Birkbeck, whose name is immortalized in London University's Birkbeck College, which still specializes in evening higher education. The origins of Birkbeck can be traced in England to Claxton's working-class mechanics' institute, which operated from 1817–20 (Vincent 1981) and, supplanted by the 1823 London Mechanics' Institute, was rapidly followed in the next three years by another 100 around the country, almost all supported financially by the upper classes but controlled by their predominantly working-class members (Chamberlin 1996). By 1859, there were around 700 mechanics' institutes in England, with membership 'into hundreds of thousands' (Ratcliffe 2006: 362).

These institutes extended the publics' ability to obtain at least some higher education by offering evening lectures, some from university professors, on such topics as electricity, optics, geology, chemistry and political economy (Robinson 2009), all rated as advanced sciences (Laurent 1984). The lectures reinforced beliefs in the value of extension classes and the abilities of wider groups to cope with higher education, even though the intellectual standards demanded in the classes declined in the later years (Mansbridge 1902).

Beyond these achievements, there is the usual dispute about which publics benefited the most. Mechanics' institutes are almost universally rated as middle class, founded to offer education for the working classes but instead providing education for the middle classes (Stephens and Roderick 1983). As such, they are variously described either as exemplars of Christian kindness and social conscience, enabling working-class aspirations (Turner 1966), or as organs of social and political repression (Chamberlin 1996, citing contemporary judgements), which led to the working classes eventually setting up their own opposition mechanics' institutes (Simon 1960). Recollect, however, that 'mechanics' were at the time defined as highly trained workmen (Chamberlin 1996); these and other middle classes were as much in need of opportunities for higher education as were the working classes. The upper middle classes put money and energy into founding the institutes. They appear to have been supported by all middle-class groups and used by the lower middle classes and higher paid working classes as a route upwards (Turner 1966, Inkster 1976).

The legacy of mechanics' institutes was a demand for more higher education leading to the foundation of the civic university colleges, even though the latter mainly omitted to incorporate these institutes (Walsh 2009). Institutes were then deflected into providing technical education before largely disappearing at the end of the nineteenth century. They were arguably at the origin of early twentieth-century municipal technical colleges and so of polytechnic higher education in the 1970s. Significantly, based on neglected evidence from the mid- to late-nineteenth century, institutes' achievements have been reassessed: 'the scientific education offered through Mechanics' Institutes was used by the working classes for their own purposes . . . the development of an alternative social and economic philosophy . . . [which] fostered the growth of evolutionary socialism' (Laurent 1984: 586). They thus achieved the same as Oxbridge: the higher education of future political elites.

Working towards the same ends was the adult education movement, offering elementary education. Their enrolments declined once compulsory elementary education began in the last 30 years of the nineteenth century, so adult education classes moved to higher education topics. Thus were founded the evening institutes of the twentieth century, some of which grew into universities themselves (Wodehouse 1925).

Literary and philosophical societies began in the late eighteenth century and were overtly founded and run by and for the middle classes:

> Most of the leading citizens in provincial towns had not attended university, and so sought for a substitute education within the literary and philosophical societies, whilst those who had attended a university often showed a desire for further education. (Stephens and Roderick 1983: 17)

Nonetheless, they provided special sessions for the working classes which were deemed successful but were mainly a valuable route for the middle classes 'to come to terms with the newly emerging industrial society of which they found themselves a bemused part' (Stephenson 1983: 36). Caught between the upper classes at Oxbridge and the working classes' elementary education, the literary and philosophical societies were a way for the middle classes to gain access to higher education before the Oxbridge reforms and the founding of the new universities (Gardner 2007). Many learned societies were formed for the same reasons but their versions of higher education seemed pitched at too advanced a level; some lectures were reported as understood only by experienced engineers or scientists (Roderick 1972).

The products of all these middle-class higher education initiatives achieved their own advancement but also became those who, in the latter half of the nineteenth century, were the prime movers for compulsory and free elementary education for the working classes (Simon 1960) and for higher education through such bodies as the Workers' Educational Association (see Chapter 3).

Curricula for New Publics

Oxbridge reforms initially reinstated teaching as the universities' prime function, evolving Jowett's effective personal tutorial system (Simon 1960: 297). The professorial system, with its emphasis on seeking new knowledge through research, was seen as antithetical to this, even heretical or revolutionary (Goldman 1995). The civic university colleges, however, adopted the professorial model with lectures on relevant degree topics from those researching them. Although Oxbridge quickly followed suit, arguments about whether the primary role of universities is research or teaching have still not been settled (Goldman 1995). The notion of the undergraduate student as researcher, which is emerging in the twenty-first century, may well unite the two.

Oxbridge and the new civic universities seemed to embody distinct curricular traditions. Oxbridge emphasized knowledge for its own sake (Creighton 1902: 104) as the basis for all gentlemanly education and intellectual activity; from this emanated classical and liberal approaches for the established upper classes with the aim of public service. Even university extension lectures were broadly based on the liberal or humane curriculum with only a little technical education (Kelly 1992). The principal university settlement, Toynbee Hall, prided itself on providing a general higher education, rather than vocational or professional (Briggs and Macartney 1984). Concern about this curricular tradition was expressed during the mid-century reform movements for Oxbridge; 'England [will] recede as a manufacturing nation unless her industrial population becomes more conversant with science than they are now' (Roderick 1972: 42, citing Sir Leon Playfairs' speech after the 1851 Great Exhibition).

Picking up on this, the new civic university colleges leant towards utilitarian vocationalism. Their curricula emphasized subjects necessary to national economic growth, to the skills needed for the emerging commercial professions (Creighton 1902) and to a belief in the importance of new understandings, of which Darwinism was the most dominant. These subjects were also popular with other providers of higher education such as London University's Science Department, extension lectures and Liverpool's Mechanics' Institute (Roderick 1972).

The differences between the curricular traditions were not however as great as they appeared. Both emerged from the Enlightenment. Oxbridge's traditional curriculum was utilitarian career training for leaders of social, political and ecclesiastical establishments (Goldman 1995, Scott 2006). In addition, Oxbridge, in order to meet criticisms of its narrowness (Huber 1843), added the 'vocational' disciplines of pure and applied sciences, mining engineering, political economy, experimental physics, modern languages and extended mathematics (McCord and Purdue 2007). The aim of this broadening of the curriculum was to avoid losing students from the newly-wealthy industrial backgrounds to such university foundations as Birmingham, whose founding money was conditional on its teaching sciences (Walsh 2009).

The putative civic universities, meanwhile, provided liberal education in order to be considered as real university providers. They too provided career training for the ruling classes by 'civilis[ing] recruits from the industrialists' camp'; traditional curricula had primacy (Simon 1960: 298). Government commissions that examined the new civic institutions' suitability for university college status encouraged this. The commissions' membership was Oxbridge dominated, so funds for civic higher education developments were directed to 'a version of university education for those who could not go to the real ones' (Vernon 2001: 261). They were 'not to endow technical education but to promote academic subjects' (Vernon 2001: 252); money for scientific, medical, engineering and musical education had to come from fees or local supporters. Modern languages received government funds because they had literary and philosophical curricula, not grammar or linguistics. Otherwise, government funding was minimal, thus legitimating by its absence what the universities themselves chose to do (Walsh 2009). Local aristocrats helped fund the early professorial chairs in philosophy, classics and other liberal humanities and arts that were at the new civic institutions (Walsh 2009).

Despite its importance in a 'country which was the self-proclaimed workshop of the world' (Walsh 2009: 129), technology was neglected by most universities, although there is a 1860s' account of London, Glasgow and Dublin Universities' colleges efficiently teaching technical education (Roderick 1972). Most technical education developed outside the university sector in technical colleges, incorporated eventually, towards the end of the twentieth century, as the post-1992 universities.

By 1900, overlapping curricular traditions mirrored the binary policy of the late twentieth century, discussed below in Chapter 3. By the early 1970s, it was the polytechnics that had to include liberal education to acquire university status from the Council for National Academic Awards, whose members were from the established universities. Meanwhile, the established universities added polytechnic specialisms to their offerings to avoid losing students in such new disciplines as business, media and performing arts (Pratt 1997).

Teaching for the New Publics

Oxbridge's pre-1860s' teaching was much criticized but was nonetheless their *raison d'être*. Desire to research would 'betray . . . a certain restlessness of mind' and Oxford was advised to 'pension-off professors' in order to progress (Goldman 1995: 579, citing contemporary sources). Professors' public lectures (the 'public' meaning Oxbridge students) were delivered irrespective of relevance to students' degrees. An amended professorial model, with lectures on degree topics, was adopted as the new university colleges emerged. Oxbridge retained its private tutorial teaching, though it was done by the least of the universities' staff (Hewitt 2006), contributing to the legacy of denigrating teaching which is only changing slightly in universities in the current century.

Inside and outside universities, teaching in public was ubiquitously lecturing (Stephens and Roderick 1983). Arguments raged about its success and failure for all social classes (Thirlwall 1850, Solly 1867, Goldman 1995). Opinion leans cautiously to the effectiveness of lectures; oratory was prized; competing methods of learning and of cheap local entertainment were few; people were 'ravenous for mental stimulation' from the new sciences and eager to learn about technology to support the economy (Chamberlin 1996: 47). Lectures were enlivened with artefacts, demonstrations and visual materials and introduced and divided by choirs and recitations (Solly 1867). Interest in improving the 'didactic art' of lecturing grew (Fitch 1883), an art that could also be used for nefarious purposes, as at least some of the middle-class women enrolling as full-time students in the late nineteenth century could testify. Some professors refused to lecture to them at all; others were bad-tempered or deliberately lethargic (Robinson 2009).

Discussion groups emerged as students casually extended university outreach lectures by questioning presenters; these became formalized into post-lecture sessions 'for more intensive study' (Simon 1974: 86). Dialogues were intended for the reading rooms of working men's clubs. One of their leaders criticized these for frivolous chatting and suggested that educated men might drop in to start discussions, carrying perhaps a 'bullocks eye [which] may be dissected and a highly amusing evening may be the result' (Solly 1867: 261). With a different perspective, Simon reports that 'the Sheffield Constitutional Society, which is said to have numbered 2,000 well-behaved men, most of them of the lower sort of workmen' met regularly for class discussions (1960: 182). Toynbee Hall added Thursday Smoking Conferences to provide a more relaxed learning atmosphere (Briggs and Macartney 1984). These were part of their plan to teach only 'groups small enough to allow for some sort of exchange between teacher and pupil' but when 500 came to lectures, this plan became unworkable (Meacham 1987: 51).

It is to university extension and the emergence of the civic universities that we owe the systemization of lecturing, as middle-class local enthusiasts 'organised, planned and publicised courses' offering weekly classes, printed syllabi, continuous assessment with essays and final examinations, increasing attendance from 6,000 to 20,000 in the five years to 1890 (Goldman 1995: 61, 62). These might today be criticized as the first formalization of students' relinquishing of responsibility for their own learning. Cambridge ran mainly 12-week certification extension courses, regarded as the minimum time for effective education, but often both Cambridge and Oxford had to offer 6-week, cheaper programmes that were regarded as superficial, though there is little evidence to prove this definitively. Some extension centres had lengthy lives with large, middle-class audiences; others languished in superficiality (Jepson 1973), dependent on lecturers' varying abilities (Hervey 1855).

Extension lecturers' skills were honed by their varying audiences, middle-class women by day and upper working classes in the evenings; lecturers needed to be good speakers, able to empathize with their listeners. 'Ordinary people [met] leading figures in the internal life of universities . . . many of them destined to eminence in the life of the nation' (Kelly 1992: 237). This seems to meet the demands of a contemporary commentator, pleading for actual Oxbridge lecturers to give external lectures and suggesting that professorial rank might be offered in return (Hervey 1855).

Railways and cheap printing were technological developments affecting teaching for new publics. University extension lectures were

> a product of the railway age . . . the lecturers sent out from Oxford travelled the country, moving from one extension centre to another on a weekly or fortnightly circuit, a train timetable in every pocket, staying overnight in the homes of members of the local extension committee. (Goldman 1995: 63)

Such committees were invariably middle class and no doubt benefited from personal communion with their overnight guests. Fortunately, social and political missionary zeal inspired many lecturers (Goldman 1995) to cope with this nineteenth-century example of mobile intensification of academic labour.

Decreases in printing costs widely disseminated 'useful knowledge . . . a crucial component of the middle-class language of reform' (Vincent 1981: 136), alternatively viewed as a way to keep the working classes in their places (Simon 1960). Its most obvious manifestation was through the Society for the Diffusion of Useful Knowledge (SDUK), established in 1826 by almost the same men who launched London University contiguously, and with the same aim, to dismantle hurdles in the education system. According to a historian of adult education, SDUK's publications proved valuable to many efforts to extend higher education (Vincent 1981). Conversely, SDUK was dismissed by a Labour historian as of no 'real use to the working class political struggle' (Simon 1960: 229), unlike the Sheffield Constitutional Society who republished *The Rights of Man* priced at only 6d (2½p) (Simon 1960). Whatever political stance one adopts, 'cheap mass-produced books, newspapers, popular magazines and journals . . . tracts and pamphlets were everywhere. Cheapness allowed many working-class readers to buy printed material' (Baggs 2006: 170), whether these were mere entertainment (Simon 1960) or Chartist revolutionary periodicals providing history, political geography and economics (Slossom 1967). Overall, cheaper printing was one basis for democratizing higher education.

The development of libraries was another significant advance which facilitated access to personal higher education for all classes, such access having previously been restricted to the very rich with private libraries. The 'people's university' was the term used to describe the municipal libraries, supported by local taxation, established from the 1850s (Black 2006). The term can, however, equally be applied to the many types of nineteenth-century libraries, even to Oxbridge whose libraries began the century as custodial only. By 1900, students could use their universities' libraries; professors and researchers could even borrow books (Hoare 2006: 323). All the civic university colleges had integral libraries (not always the norm in other countries) representing the nineteenth-century values of 'liberalism . . . utilitarianism and idealism' (Black 2006: 29). Subscription libraries prided themselves on their scholarly collections (Forster and Bell 2006). Manchester's public library had 280,000 volumes including rich special collections, whereas the local college had 60,000. It is not surprising therefore to find some evidence of collaboration between town and gown in library facilities (Hoare 2010).

As with other higher education developments, there are unresolved disputes, both about the numbers and classes who used the libraries (Innes 2006) and the extent of libraries' scholarly collections compared with lighter works and fiction. Not disputed is that all the higher education providers discussed above had a library, ranging from silent rooms in middle-class Athenaeums dusted with busts of classical antiquities to libraries established by operatives themselves where working men's committees chose political and theological works, as well as those embracing history, science and literature (Hoare 2003). Democratically, members' choices also led the stock for subscription libraries (Forster and Bell 2006). For miners' institutes, co-operatives, literary and philosophical societies, extension classes and settlements, a library was a *sine qua non*, but it had to be an open and accessible library. Even with cheaper printing, books would still have been a major cost, certainly for working- and lower middle-class households, so libraries would have been their main sources for literature (Baggs 2006), despite most libraries charging at least small fees (Innes 2006). Without these developments to enable self-learning, there might have been no twenty-first century student as producer (Neary 2010) or research-led teaching. Changes in nineteenth-century library provision made new forms of higher education learning possible.

Discussion groups, entertaining lectures, systemized learning pro- grammes, libraries, cheap printing and the railways all allowed new nine- teenth-century publics to access higher education and participate in it actively. These andragogical and technological developments were the cau- tious beginning of the change to students as co-creators of their own learning, a theme that is elaborated on by Crawford in Chapter 4 and by Beckton in Chapter 8. It is unlikely, however, that the eventual direction of all these advances towards abolition of concepts of teachers and learners (Chapter 9) would have been envisaged in the nineteenth century.

Conclusion

By 1900, 'no single idea of the university had triumphed or can even be discerned' (Goldman 1995: 589). For some, universities were buttresses of conspiratorial middle-class power; for others, the middle classes opened up roads for the twentieth-century working classes through 'cross cultural transformation' (Digby and Searby 1981: 25). University education began to be viewed as a desirable good for all classes and for national develop- ment, opinions that are now simply considered unarguable assumptions. How to realize these assumptions in the twenty-first century is the topic for this book.

Graduate employment was an intended output of nineteenth-century higher education. Men attended; social, religious, political, and later eco- nomic leaders emerged. Women joined; better wives, mothers and volun- tary workers emerged (Barnes 1994: 36). Jobs are different now but the instrumentality is not. Liberal, classical education was not only inherently worthy but had a vocational relevance. It was joined by what we now deem more economically orientated curricula late in the century and the two streams coexisted till the late twentieth century. Now, though, it appears that the wider conceptualization is missing. Will the student-as-producer movement bring back the intellectual exercise?

Nineteenth-century teaching methods, printing and libraries remain as bases of university education today; virtual e-ways are the new railways, likewise making higher education teaching in public accessible for much greater numbers than ever before. Widening access to teaching resources continues today as an aim of university educators. A twenty-first century scholar gypsy would be linked into such free websites as iTunes University (launched in 2007 for individual universities to set up their own sites with their best lectures as podcasts) or to Academic Earth (2011) that offers, it is claimed, online courses from the world's top scholars (Weissenstein 2010). This assumes, of course, that our scholar gypsy is computer literate; as Watling (Chapter 6) shows, without this, potential students will be as invisible as some authorities believe the nineteenth-century working classes were in higher education.

To the nineteenth century we owe the notion of universities moving into the social world; university extension classes, settlements and the small civic university colleges may seem minor developments now, but at that time they represented major new understandings. Privatization can be noted in current efforts from outside existing universities to set up competing higher education institutions. Do we now try to ignore, defeat, control, coexist with or absorb the twenty-first century versions of these (all techniques piloted in the nineteenth century)?

In making changes during the nineteenth century, higher education responded to society rather than 'pursuing social change' (Silver 2007: 535); as Bell's analysis in the following chapter shows, they continued to do so in the twentieth century. Initially, nineteenth-century 'society' meant private funders, student fees and members' subscriptions (all versions of the student as consumer); only Oxbridge had sufficient wealth to ignore its teaching and public responsibilities. Later, the first state grants began our acceptance of governments' power to turn higher education to democratically mandated interpretations of national economic need and social engineering. The importance of these grants to university survival became firmly established in the next century while grass-roots higher education movements, without such funding, either disappeared or became marginalized, as Bell demonstrates in Chapter 3. The early years of the twenty-first century see significant reductions in this funding; will ways be found now to revive self-help higher education?

Chapter 3

Teaching in Public: Participation and Access in Twentieth-Century Higher Education

Les Bell

Introduction

Universities are complex organizations that evolve over time in response to both the internal challenges and the external environment: 'They can grow and thrive. They may even reproduce, creating new campuses or begetting new institutions . . . They may also be starved and die' (Boggs 2010: 1). In the twentieth century, universities became increasingly subject to the exigencies of government policy. As Neary and Morris argue in Chapter 1, educational policy in England and Wales, and especially policy pertaining to higher education, has been shaped by the conflict between those who advocate that education should be regarded as a public good, resourced from public funds, and those who claim that education should be regarded as part of the human capital provision that society makes and, as such, should be treated as a private commodity.

These two positions are based on different understandings of social action (Coleman 1997). The former argues that the behaviour of individuals is influenced by social rules, norms and obligations and based on a sense of a society that is wider than themselves. Here, higher education is a public good, intrinsically valuable for both the individual and the society. This view leads to policies intended to extend access, widen participation and maximize student choice. The latter position sees people as having goals that are independently arrived at and wholly self-interested. The extension of this view is that education is a private commodity, the availability of which should be controlled by market forces or the requirements of human capital at any given time. This consumerization of higher education and commodification of knowledge generates policies based on managerialism, quality control and accountability. Teaching in public argues that universities, by their very nature, should be firmly located in the public domain in such a way as to provide a counterbalance to the private world defined by utility and self-interest (McSherry 2001). Hence, teaching in public seeks to address this public/private dichotomy and to find new ways of supporting higher education as a public good.

Thody, in Chapter 2, points out that this dichotomy was evident in arguments about the nature and purpose of education as long ago as 1875 when Burt (cited in Creighton 1902) argued that self-improvement provided a more powerful reason for extending educational provision than did any reference to enabling industry to compete more effectively with other nations. Thody goes on to explore how higher education in the nineteenth century was shaped by the debate about provision and access, particularly as it affected women who tended to be excluded from universities and as it impacted upon those who were unable to pay for access to universities. Teaching in public is presented in this volume as a significant part of those debates as it offers both a critique of the argument in favour of education as a private commodity and a way to present higher education as a public good.

It has been argued that teaching is like dry ice: it evaporates at classroom temperature unless lecturers take the initiative to go public (Shulman 2005). Teaching in public in the context of twentieth and twenty-first century higher education seeks to prevent such evaporation by exploring key themes and posing significant questions and challenges. The concept has already been outlined in the Introduction to Part 1 of this book, and it can be seen that teaching in public raises broad questions, including the learning landscape and teaching as a public space; students as the first public and as producers through student participation in curriculum development; the relationship between lecturer and student and open access and the role of IT. The concept challenges the marketization and commodification of higher education and asks how far is it possible to promote equality through higher education. It raises questions about the extent to which the wider community can engage with teaching and learning within universities. Thus, teaching in public, by posing such questions, presents higher education policy as an arena within which a contested process between groups with competing values and differential access to power seeks to form and shape policy in their own interests and, in so doing, raises issues about the changing role of the state in the provision of higher education (Stevenson and Bell 2009). In the last three chapters of this book, such issues are explored in detail. This chapter explores the relationship between higher education and the state in the context of the expansion of higher education throughout the twentieth century.

Higher Education Expansion

Although the main focus here is on higher education in universities, it must be acknowledged that similar provision elsewhere has had a significant impact on the themes that shape the teaching in public agenda. The contribution made to opening up the boundaries of higher education by the Co-operative Society, mechanics' institutes, miners' institutes and working men's clubs has already been acknowledged in the previous chapter. As the twentieth century dawned, the Workers' Educational Association (WEA) continued the process of extending access to and widening participation in education and, in so doing, enhancing the access of women to education (Munby 2003). Even here, however, there were tensions about the purposes of education that anticipated debates still to come – social purpose or social control; personal benefit or societal advancement (Coles 2003) – while Goldman (2003) also notes that the tension between the advancement of the individual and the wider implications for society has been one of the recurring themes within the WEA movement. To extend a point made by Tatton (2003) in his analysis of this dichotomy within the WEA, when education is driven by the concerns of business and commerce, the emphasis is on people as they are, but when education is seen as a public good, the focus is on people as they may become. This crystallizes the argument about the provision of higher education and locates teaching in public firmly in the camp of those who wish to see people develop as individuals.

At the same time as the WEA was emerging as a significant provider of more widely accessible education, the civic university movement was challenging the hegemony of the traditional English universities. Six universities, Birmingham (1900) Liverpool (1903), Leeds and Manchester (1904), Sheffield (1905) and Bristol (1909) were among the first of these civic universities and were regarded by the ancient universities as arriviste, the term 'redbrick' often being applied to them. To their number was added Reading, which received its charter in 1926 and was the only university to be established between in the inter-war years (University of Reading 2011). Civic universities were largely established as a result of local ambition and patronage. As was shown in Chapter 2, some developed from colleges founded by individuals, others from colleges formed as a result of local pressures, but all were founded to provide higher education for the middle classes in large urban areas and to enhance the skills of those who did not have access to traditional universities (Ratcliffe 2006). Their impact on widening participation was significant since men of all denominations were admitted, the middle classes could afford the fees and women were allowed entry to lectures and were later permitted to be awarded degrees (Robinson 2009). This development can, nevertheless, be seen as the middle classes reaping the benefit from the foundations laid by working-class groups and institutions, since civic universities tended to attract a largely middle-class student population. As Simon (1994) points out, by the last decade of the twentieth century, the class differential in access to higher education had changed little over the previous 40 years.

Although civic universities were funded both through local patronage and from central government resources, they were largely left to develop themselves as institutions of higher education and could focus on the importance of the educative process rather than being overly concerned with specific outcomes, unlike many of those institutions that achieved university status towards the end of the century. Eastwood (2009) has argued that the redbrick universities were founded to enhance learning and transform people within their communities and beyond. There is no doubt that the number of students increased. In 1900, there were 19,000 full-time students (Committee on Higher Education 1963: Table 3), and by the early 1920s, there were fewer than 40,000 students, increasing to around 50,000 by the early 1930s, numbers remaining stable until the expansion in the post-1945 period (Sanderson 1972). By 1962, there were 216,000 students in full-time higher education (Committee on Higher Education 1963: Table 3). The civic universities played a major role in this expansion. To the extent that they provided greater access to higher education, the civic universities can be seen as expanding access and participation although, as Halsey (1997) points out, in spite of state scholarships and local education authority grants, social class and gender remained the largest barriers to the equitable distribution of access to higher education. However, many of these civic universities provided adult education courses that were available to those who were not full-time students, sometimes teaching these courses off campus and thus moving teaching more into the public domain.

The largest of these civic universities, the University of London, made an even more significant impact on teaching in public not only because it provided access to higher education to students from less affluent backgrounds but also because of its external degree programme, chartered in 1858, making the University of London the first university to offer distance learning degrees to students. By 1908, there were over 4,000 students registered (London University 2010). Enrolment increased steadily in the first half of the twentieth century, and during the Second World War, there was a further increase in enrolments from members of the armed forces stationed abroad as well as those imprisoned in German prisoner of war camps. They were sent study materials by mail, and at specified intervals sat examinations in the camps. Almost 11,000 exams were taken at 88 camps between 1940 and 1945. Though the failure rate was high, substantial numbers of soldiers earned degrees while imprisoned. With the advent of inexpensive airmail services after the war the number of external students taking University of London courses increased dramatically and, by 2008, more than 40,000 students across 180 countries were enrolled (London University 2008).

In many ways, as civic universities were becoming established, universities were protected from significant political influence, giving them opportunities to strike their own balance between the public and the private (Shattock and Berdahl 1985). It was clear by 1919, when the University Grants Committee (UGC) was created, that there was

> the need for some new and effective mechanism for channelling funds to universities which had suffered severely through neglect and lack of government funding during the war. The UGC was created from above by politicians . . . not by pressure from below by universities . . . It was primarily a mechanism for resource allocation . . . it was not a planning body. (Shattock and Berdahl 1985: 173)

Planning and development remained an institutional function rather than something undertaken by the UGC, which tended to act as a buffer between the universities and the government, thus leaving universities free to shape their own provision, to make individual policy decisions in a way that was largely free from political intervention and to determine for themselves the extent to which participation and access should be public or private. During and after the Second World War, this began to change and the UGC was required to take on a wider role. By the second half of the twentieth century, as well as administering university funding from the government, the UGC was increasingly concerned with the development of universities, the location, nature and extent of the expansion that was underway in order to

> Increase greatly the number of students qualified for university matriculation . . . the UGC also endorsed a major expansion in the number of universities . . . The UGC took the lead in bringing to the government's attention the need to create more universities and was extremely active in selecting the sites for new universities. (Shattock and Berdahl 1985: 175)

However, as Shattock and Berdahl (1985) point out, the UGC still took the view that the initiative for initiating change within the sector remained with universities and not the UGC, which tended to distance itself from the growing debate about access, participation and the needs of society. The UGC largely ignored the public–private debate, but its successor, the Higher Education Funding Council for England (HEFCE), found itself dealing with many of the tensions generated by that policy debate.

The Era of Robbins

The gradual expansion of university provision during the immediate post-war period was predicated on both economic and social grounds, although it was clear that the public was more influential than the private:

> Social and economic values thus dominated the original educational and institutional assumptions. In 1950, the universities were untouchable because it was assumed that they should best be allowed to have their own ideals of excellence and their own ways to contribute to the social good. This would be enough accountability. (Kogan 1975: 198)

Higher education began to change significantly in the late 1940s, as more universities were created. Exeter, Keele, Leicester, Nottingham and Southampton – all received charters (Kogan 1975). By the end of the 1950s, it became clear that gradual expansion was not going to yield the growth that was required, largely because universities raised their entry requirements to cope with increased demand, rather than accommodating larger groups of students within the existing infrastructure. This resulted in the establishment of the Committee on Higher Education to inquire into the future development of the sector. Its report, commonly referred to as the Robbins Report after its chairman Lord Robbins, was published in 1963. This report stated that 'all young persons qualified by ability and attainment to pursue a full-time course in higher education should have the opportunity to do so' (Committee on Higher Education 1963: 49). This reflection provided a guide for the development of the British higher education system for the next three decades, but in the process of achieving this widening of participation and access, the private–public debate intensified.

Although these policy developments appeared to be justified mainly on social or egalitarian grounds, some economists argued that education should be seen as an investment with expansionist education policies being justified on the grounds of providing competitive advantage in world markets (Kogan 1975). The argument about how far higher education should be seen as a private commodity contribution to the economy, and to what extent it should be justified on the basis of egalitarianism and personal freedom, was clearly evident in the Robbins Report (Committee on Higher Education 1963). The Robbins Report led to the establishment of the so-called plate glass universities, notably the universities of East Anglia, Kent, Lancaster, Stirling, Sussex, York and Warwick (Beloff 1968). These new universities were established as a consequence of the need to cope with the growing pressure for university places and the widening of participation in higher education. The Robbins Committee appeared to establish social demand as the firm imperative guiding admission to higher education. In a major part of the report, however, it was argued that expansion was based primarily on human capital rather than egalitarian or social justice considerations. The development and diffusion of skills was a primary objective in higher education, especially in view of a growing need to maintain competitive advantage (Committee on Higher Education 1963). However, although the Committee approvingly quoted the classical economists, it did not develop the argument of these same writers that where an educational institution is made more dependent for its funds on fees paid directly out of the customers' pocket, more competition between suppliers will result (West 1963). This argument was pursued post-Robbins by economists such as Peston (1975) who wanted universities to be regarded as 'multi-product institutions. Some of these products may be generated more cheaply by large departments . . . More obvious examples of the efficiency of large-scale operations lie in lectures, examination setting and libraries' (Peston 1975: 193).

Peston (1975) went on to point out that there was little if any competition between universities, hence there was no significant driving force that would force university administrators to re-examine the efficiency and effectiveness of existing practices, in the way that businesses might re-evaluate their activities in the face of competition. This argument about the efficacy of the private sector model was to emerge more strongly in the last decade of the twentieth century but by then higher education would have expanded further and the very nature of university education would have been challenged.

This challenge was exemplified by the establishment of the Open University (OU) in 1969, which moved the notion of teaching higher education in public to a different level. The OU was founded on the basis of inclusiveness and the widening of participation in higher education to include those who were unable to study full time (Open University 2011). Within three years of its foundation in 1969, the OU had 40,000 part-time, mainly mature undergraduate students who had jobs and often family commitments and who were being given the opportunity to obtain a degree using a credit/module system via distance learning. By 2011, there were over 250,000 students enrolled, including more than 20,000 students studying overseas (Open University 2011). The popularity of the Open University and its rate of success seriously challenge the idea, formerly widespread, that there is a limited pool of ability in any one country. Furthermore, its programmes are delivered by distance learning and most of the material was made publicly available to anyone who was interested through libraries, radio, iTunes U and television, although its late night, course-based programmes on BBC2 stopped in 2006. Nevertheless, the OpenLearn site still gives public access to hundreds of course materials and, with the BBC, it now co-produces mainstream television and radio programmes such as Rough Science (six series between 2000 and 2005) and Coast (started in 2005 and now on its fifth series). These changes were driven by the need to cope with the growing pressure for university places and the widening of participation in higher education following the Robbins Report (Committee on Higher Education 1963), aimed at bringing the results of academic study to a wider public in an accessible form.

The non-university sector of further and higher education, almost entirely under local authority control, was emerging as a powerful force in competition with universities. By the mid-1970s, there were 30 university-status polytechnics offering degrees that were validated by the Council for National Academic Awards (CNAA). They were seen as 'providing a network of educational provision for any citizen who cares to avail himself of it from the age of sixteen to retirement' (Kogan 1975: 186). These polytechnics, many of them emerging from technical colleges and already as big as average-sized universities, were based on a tradition of public provision and service and were concerned with the practical application of knowledge while, at the same time, espousing the scholarly values associated with universities. The paradox of the emerging polytechnics, therefore, was that although they emphasized the public element of higher educational provision, they were also driven by the private demand for skilled labour.

Challenges were also emerging to the principles derived from the Robbins Committee that appeared to underpin the provision of university places. The basic principle that university places should be provided for those who were qualified seemed to be enshrined in the policy that shaped higher education (Fulton 1981). In spite of this, however, access to higher education and widening participation was acknowledged as a fundamental issue:

> We have little difficulty in accepting as a point of departure the guiding principle proposed by Fulton . . . We are less certain about the terms on which each kind of course should be available. To assert that facilities should be available is not the same as saying that they should be paid for exclusively out of public funds. Yet if public funds are not available, access remains a chimera for most people. (Williams and Blackstone 1983: 22)

The question was, of course, 'If not public funds, then what?' Implied in the answer to this question is a further challenge to universities – about their very nature and purpose.

It became evident in the three decades following the Robbins-driven expansion that there were two distinctly different views about the purposes of universities. On the one hand was the idealistic view of the self-motivated, self-regulated community of disinterested scholars, teaching and research-ing without external direction or control, where higher education was per-ceived as a public good At the other extreme was the utilitarian view of justification by measurable results, or output, in terms of trained and com-pliant employees where higher education was to meet the requirements of the labour market (Broers 2005). Gombrich (2000) has argued that two distinct aspects of the commodification of higher education can be identi-fied. The first is based on the belief that free markets and economic priori-ties should determine policy, while the second involves the continued increase of state intervention in the structure and funding of higher educa-tion institutions. Both aspects, however, generated an increased emphasis on the private rather than on the public in higher education.

Dearing and Beyond

By the beginning of the 1990s the approach to higher education based on marketization and commodification was in the ascendancy. Polytechnics and some colleges of higher education were given university status under the Further and Higher Education Act (DES 1992) and to coincide with this, a new, more proactive funding agency for universities was estab-lished: the Higher Education Funding Council for England (HEFCE). This body was to allocate funding to both pre-1992 and post-1992 universities, a responsibility since extended to colleges subsequently granted university status. Thus, the binary system was, to all intents and purposes, abolished. Such changes were clearly significant and far-reaching. Nevertheless, the period between 1992 and 1997 was characterized by retrenchment in both the statutory and the post-compulsory sectors, most graphically illustrated in higher education by a cap on undergraduate recruitment and significant reductions in unit cost per student spending in the sector. Higher education was, to a large extent, becoming cost and market driven, reflecting the managerial approaches adopted in the private sector.

The brief of HEFCE was far wider than the allocation of funding between institutions and included assessing the quality of teaching and research in the institutions that it funded (HEFCE 2006a). Quality assessment became part of the managerial discourse within universities. As Deem (2001) points out, this discourse is derived from the application of techniques, values and practices derived from the private sector of the economy. It emphasizes competition between cost centres within universities and the establishment of internal markets and the monitoring of efficiency and effectiveness through appraisal and the measurement of performance, perhaps with the intention of explicitly changing the culture and values of universities and changing them to mirror more closely those found in private sector organizations.

At the same time as this managerialist, private sector discourse was emerging, HEFCE was tasked with expanding participation in higher education:

Widening access and improving participation in higher education are a crucial part of our mission and form one of our strategic aims. Our aim is to promote and provide the opportunity of successful participation in higher education to everyone who can benefit from it. This is vital for social justice and economic competitiveness. (HEFCE 2006b: 1)

This statement conveniently glosses over the tensions between expanding participation and access to higher education on the grounds of it being a public good or justifying such expansion through treating higher education as a private commodity between the public and the private in the provision of higher education.

These tensions can, however, be identified starkly in the education policy of the New Labour government, which took office in 1997. This tension in policy was evident in that government's commitment to expand higher education, but to achieve this by introducing student fees for tuition costs. Expansion was in part advanced as an equity argument, and a discourse related to widening participation was developed later. However, the case for expansion was also an economic one, based on the need to increase the nation's skills base. At the same time, the decision to introduce student fees revealed further policy tensions. Critics have argued that fees disproportionately deter those from low-income backgrounds who are likely to be more debt-averse; this would mitigate against widening participation. It is further argued that fees undermine the universalist principle of the welfare state and transform the student into little more than a consumer in the market place (Stevenson and Bell 2009).

The new government responded to these complex issues by commissioning Sir Ron Dearing to present a 20-year vision for the development of higher education. The intention was to frame the discourse shaping higher education policy and thereby set the parameters within which higher education policy would be developed in the coming years. Dearing's report (NCIHE 1997) highlighted the central contribution that higher education should make to meet the needs of an adaptable, sustainable, knowledge-based economy while enabling individuals to develop their capabilities to the highest potential levels throughout life, so that they grow intellectually, are well equipped for work, can contribute effectively to society and achieve personal fulfilment. Thus, in many respects, the Dearing Report signalled a shift in emphasis within higher education by recognizing its pivotal role in contributing to commercial success in a globalized economy while also acknowledging traditional role of the university and the importance of widening participation still further.

This shift in emphasis has produced a reconfiguration of higher education in the first decade of the twenty-first century in which the state has taken an increasingly dominant role in framing the environment in which higher education institutions function, such that strategic government direction and regulation remain important. At the same time, however, the government is becoming increasingly uncoupled from higher education as a provider and may more appropriately be seen as a purchaser. This reflects the view of higher education as a private rather than a public good (Taylor 1999). This shift is further emphasized by the move to a 'consumer pays' system and the growth of private sector institutions. At the same time, universities are also encouraged to be autonomous and free-standing in a competitive and entrepreneurial marketplace and are under increasing pressure to fund their own expansion, whether by private sector funding for research, payment for traded consultancy services or income derived from student fees (Stevenson and Bell 2009). Hence, there is an increasing drift away from the concept of public, towards the notion of private in higher education provision. Teaching in public sets out to counter this policy shift by placing greater emphasis on the inherently beneficial aspects of higher education rather than on its instrumental and human capital-driven features.

Conclusion

Higher education provision has expanded throughout the twentieth century. There have been three key stages in this expansion: the establishment of the civic universities in the first decade heralded widening participation in higher education, especially for the middle classes, within institutions that were locally based, partly locally funded and had a commitment to both the public and the private aspects of higher education. This trend continued in the late 1940s and early 1950s but was given greater impetus after the Robbins Report (1963). Although participation and many of the other public features of higher education, including teaching in public at the Open University, were significant, the importance of the private became an increasingly key feature. It was no co-incidence that one of the plate glass universities was termed *Warwick University Limited* (Thompson 1971). The final stage was marked by the emergence of polytechnics and their elevation to university status, which increased the importance of the public through widening participation still further, as well as through their links to much older establishments such as mechanics' institutes. One of the post-1992 universities claims to be able to trace its origins back to a Mechanics' School of Arts formed in 1825 (LJMU 2010). At the same time, however, these institutions, with their emphasis on vocationalism and business links, have proved to be at least as privately driven as their chartered counterparts.

After the incorporation of polytechnics in 1992, the public–private balance became an even more significant issue within higher educational policy-making. The Dearing Report (NCIHE 1997) and subsequent government documents (DfEE 1998, DfES 2003) highlight the determination of the Labour government to implement both funding and governance regimes for higher education based on consumerism, typified by the introduction of tuition fees and quality control mechanisms at the expense of the public aspects of higher education (Naidoo and Jamieson 2006). It was apparent that

Government policy is seeking to change, fundamentally, the terms on which teaching and learning take place in higher education . . . the impact

could be ... profound ... In relation to consumerism, these changes
could have an effect on some of the key constituents of higher education
including; the professional identities of academics; the curriculum and
teaching; the nature and outcomes of student learning. (Naidoo and
Jamieson 2006: 876)

At the same time, higher education provision is shifting from an elite to a
mass higher education system. There is no doubt that higher education has
extended access and widened participation beyond those boundaries that
existed before the Robbins Report. As Halsey (2006) notes, there were
more university lecturers at the end of the twentieth century than there
were students in the early 1950s. Such expansion has had its price, though,
since the contemporary rationale for higher education 'is frequently nar-
rowed on to problems of efficient and economic means towards the ends of
innovation and the formation of "human capital"' (Halsey 2006: 856).

Part Two

The Student–Teacher Nexus

(Edited by Howard Stevenson)

The aim of this volume is to present and explore the different ways in which those working in higher education can make their teaching public by transcending traditional notions of teaching as a private, and privatized, activity and ensuring that the teaching and learning process is made both more open and more democratic. The concept of teaching in public presented here offers a number of forms by which these objectives may be achieved, but the chapters in this section are born out of a recognition that the lecturer's first public is always the student (Burawoy 2005a).

Much has been written about the changed nature of the teacher–student relationship at a time when universities have been compelled to adopt increasingly marketized practices. Within the United Kingdom, the introduction of tuition fees represented a major development in this trajectory, encouraging students to see themselves as paying customers engaged in a market exchange. However, the concept of higher education as an exchange relationship goes much beyond the payment of fees and is reinforced by the myriad ways in which market forms are reproduced through market testing, which are then used to construct league tables and target-setting. All of these pressures are likely to be accelerated as the recommendations of the Browne Report (2010) into higher education funding are translated into policy. Browne's analysis is predicated on a neo-liberal critique of public education, in which it is argued that universities have hitherto been protected from the discipline of market forces, and that so-called improvement will only be driven by increasing market pressures within the system. Central to this argument is the notion of the student as consumer, empowered by more information and more choice, but with higher expectations as a consequence of paying considerably higher fees, all of which marks a significant change in the relationship between the state and higher education.

It is likely therefore that this latest phase of 'academic capitalism' (Slaughter and Leslie, 1997) will accelerate the deleterious consequences of HE marketization already witnessed. The notion of the student as consumer will be exacerbated as a university education is reduced to a cost-benefit analysis in which fees paid are evaluated against future earnings and labour market advantage. These pressures will be powerful, but the outcomes are not certain. The influence of such pressures renders it all the more necessary to analyze the future and identify the opportunities for challenging dominant discourses. Current policy developments simply intensify the need to locate the spaces in which progressive practices can be developed, and in which the values of teaching as a public activity, and higher education as a public good, can be asserted. The challenge for those working in higher education is to move beyond critique and to work within the spaces for action and agency. Chapters in this section offer practical insights into where such opportunities might lie.

Crawford, in Chapter 4, presents work on an important project in which students were supported to take on a role as consultants to the teaching process. Students Consulting on Teaching (SCOTs) sought to engage students in new and more meaningful ways in a dialogue with teachers about teaching. The project represents a repudiation of more traditional forms of teaching feedback, but it is also innovative insofar as it involves students from outside of their subject working with lecturers in other subjects and disciplines. Crawford highlights the complex and contested ways in which many of these issues play out in practice. Students were encouraged to work with lecturers to provide a specific student's eye view on an agreed aspect of the lecturer's teaching practice. Such an approach had the potential to be either reinforcing of managerialist agendas, or appearing tokenistic to genuine student involvement. Crawford's account of the project demonstrates how these issues were negotiated and offers a useful insight into how a project can begin to challenge traditional notions of the student–teacher relationship. She challenges us to consider how the power relationship between student and teacher might be transformed. While we may reject the bogus nature of the student empowered as a consumer, it is also important to recognize and challenge the unacceptable face of much existing practice in which traditional notions of teacher as expert are used to reinforce unequal power relations.

In Chapter 5, Hagyard and Watling report on a particular project at the University of Lincoln designed to provide undergraduate students with the opportunity to engage with academic staff on a specific research project. The Undergraduate Research Opportunities Scheme (UROS) was deliberately intended to reconnect the undergraduate experience with a Humboldtian conception of university education in which learning takes place through a synthesis of both teaching and research. Engagement in real research is not seen as the preserve of postgraduate research students but could become core to the experience of all students. Hagyard and Watling describe how the scheme operated, the benefits that appeared to emerge from it and the shifts in culture that began to flow from this relatively limited project. They also indicate how this experience has been used to inform a much wider project in which the principles of research-based learning as central to the undergraduate experience have begun to be embedded much more widely within the undergraduate curriculum.

These chapters share a concern with re-balancing the relationship between lecturers and students in the teaching process. There is a recognition that this is inevitably problematic, but that developing the notion of students as co-constructors of knowledge can begin to challenge the dominant discourse of the student as consumer. In the final chapter in this section, Watling notes the importance of recognizing the diversity of the student body when considering how students experience and engage with teaching. Chapter 6 focuses on the impact of digital technologies on learning, and we are reminded not to accept uncritically the idea that technology necessarily makes teaching more accessible. Rather than making teaching public, many students can experience the reverse, as teaching is presented in ways that make it difficult, or indeed impossible, to access. At a time when it is commonplace to talk of the student experience, Watling demonstrates that there is no such monolithic experience. It is not possible to talk about making teaching public, without also making it accessible – and that requires a commitment to reflecting diverse needs and the logic and complexity of students' experiences.

Chapter 4

Rethinking the Student–Teacher Nexus: Students as Consultants on Teaching in Higher Education

Karin Crawford

Introduction

This chapter explores a progressive project, implemented in the actuality of teaching and learning at classroom level in a post-1992 university. In the process, it challenges the 'technical-rational constructions of university pedagogy' embedded in the 'new public management' approaches to quality assurance in higher education (McLean 2008: 40). These exemplify the private approach to university education discussed in Chapters 1 and 3. Here it is argued that commonly used, often managerialist performance-led approaches to gaining feedback on the student experience, such as central end-of-module evaluations and large surveys, are at best impersonal, untimely and ineffective and at worst de-skilling and devaluing of professional practice in higher education. This chapter examines an innovative alternative, a collaborative approach to harnessing the student experience through engagement in the philosophies of democratic professional practice, teaching in public, repositioning the student–teacher relationship and recognizing students as university teachers' 'first public' (Burawoy 2005b: 7). This practical example captured the essence of teaching in public, situating students in partnership with teachers as it empowered them to participate in the enhancement of teaching and the joint exploration of pedagogies. Students were employed as pedagogic consultants, offering a student perspective on specific episodes of teaching and learning, redefining the nature of accountability and making teaching and access to knowledge transparent and public. It engaged students as academic citizens with civic responsibility and offered a fresh approach to Burawoy's (2005b) concept of service learning. Moreover, the example set out in this chapter transformed the relationship and power balance between student and teacher, recognizing the student as another expert and producer in the joint endeavour to address the collective challenges and aspirations of knowledge production.

Before documenting the details of the project, the chapter conceptualizes the issues by drawing on existing literature to expose current practices. Further to this alternative possibilities are examined, inspired by evidence from creative examples embedded in professional practices beyond higher education. The example project is then outlined prior to a more detailed exploration of the opportunities and challenges that became apparent from the project evaluation. The intention of this chapter is not to suggest that this is the only way to do it, but rather to offer a reflective account of a progressive teaching practice and the issues and possibilities it raises.

Conceptualizing the Issues

In setting out to conceptualize the issues that are being challenged and addressed in this chapter, this section draws on the existing literature to expose three core concerns: managerialist modes of accountability, notions of student voice and complexities of power balance in the student–teacher relationship.

Managerialist Modes of Accountability

In the United Kingdom, government policy drivers such as the White Paper *The Future of Higher Education* (DfES 2003) are infused with an overt, pervasive managerialist discourse (Crawford 2009). These approaches to management, which reflect business models (Delanty 2001), have been recognized as being in conflict with what many see as the traditional values of 'collegiality, trust and professional discretion' (Deem 1998: 52) that characterize academic practice. Moreover, it can be argued that the neo-liberal policies and performance management-led accountability inherent in New Public Management result in what Clegg (2009) regards as a general decline in collegial governance.

In the 2002 Reith Lectures, O'Neill debated the notion of a crisis of trust in the context of current approaches to accountability. This is recognized in higher education where there is a 'complex and changing balance between "trust" and "control"' (Deem *et al.* 2008: 19) with present managerial approaches being indicative of a 'crisis of trust' (McLean 2008: 124). Indeed, the complexity of 'measurability' and demands for evidence can result in only two opposing potential solutions: high levels of trust or strong regulation (Field 2002). Furthermore, it is argued that 'Herculean micro-management' is 'widely experienced . . . as distorting the proper aims of professional practice and indeed as damaging professional pride and integrity' (O'Neill 2002).

The 2003 White Paper describes the enhancement of teaching as 'central to the purpose of higher education' (DfES 2003: 46). There is thus an increasing drive towards 'good-quality teaching for everyone' (DfES 2003: 49) with teachers being accountable for providing a '"quality" academic performance' (McWilliam 2002: 296). This quality is frequently 'assured' using criteria based on calculations of input (for example, module specifications and hours of direct student–teacher contact) and output (for example, student grade achievement and module evaluations). Increasingly, outputs, in the form of the views and experiences of students who have undertaken the relevant course of study, are being seen as useful and informative measures of teaching effectiveness. Hagyard (2009) describes a range of internal and external sources of student feedback including internal module evaluations and external data from the National Student Survey. However, their value in enhancing the quality of teaching and learning is questionable. Research challenges the usefulness of quantitative rating scales, such as those generally used in student module evaluations, as findings (Shevlin *et al.* 2000, Zabaleta 2007) show that they are not a reliable measure of teaching effectiveness: '. . . a significant proportion of the scale's variation is reflecting a personal view of the lecturer in terms of their charisma rather than lecturing ability and module attributes' (Shevlin *et al.* 2000: 402).

This concern may be less of an issue where qualitative comments are also collected. Indeed, while Hagyard acknowledges concerns about the efficacy and validity of large-scale surveys such as the National Student Survey, he argues that there is undeniable value in large data sets and the inclusion of qualitative comments (Hagyard 2009). Yet, these approaches to gaining feedback on the student experience are often untimely, in that usually surveys are administered after the full module or programme of teaching has taken place (Cook-Sather 2009). Thus, while it may be feasible for the teacher to reflect on the outcomes and develop future modes of teaching, it is not possible to enact change for the cohort of students who have provided the information. Further to this, surveys of this type do not reflect contextual depth, are impersonal and can be experienced as de-skilling and devaluing of professional teaching practice.

Such approaches could also be seen as divisive in that they set student and teacher apart, as consumer and provider, rather than bringing students and teachers together in collegiate activity. Additionally, they suggest a very narrow and instrumental interpretation of the student experience rather than embracing 'one which allows intellectual, ethical and social progression at the heart of which is communication with peers and teachers and results in communicative reason' (McLean 2008: 91).

Notions of Student Voice and Participation

All of this raises concern about the authenticity and meaningfulness of current approaches to harnessing the student experience. Arnstein (1969: 216) states that 'the idea of . . . participation is a little like eating spinach: no one is against it in principle because it is good for you'. Yet, while the notion of student voice is much discussed in the literature (Taylor and Robinson 2009, Seale 2009), the whole concept of 'authentic student voice' is contested and open for critique, with evidence that it is both heterogeneous and discursive (Thomson and Gunter 2006), and ill-understood (Seale 2009). Increasingly, student engagement in universities is characterized by representation, commonly by student union officers, on various committees and working groups. Student roles in these forums are often passive and thus questions remain about whether these processes result in change and are successful in shifting the culture and relationships in institutions towards meaningful partnership in a community of scholars.

Education has been described as 'a dialogue between ourselves and students, between students and their own experiences, among students themselves, and finally a dialogue of students with publics beyond the university' (Burawoy 2005b: 9). There is a strong association between notions of student voice and a culture of collaboration and partnership, with partnership being one level in a hierarchy of levels of participation (Arnstein 1969). Arnstein developed a model, the Ladder of Participation, in the context of town planning and community participation. However, as it describes the redistribution of power within social relationships, Arnstein's typology and the messages within it are arguably transferable to a range of contexts, including the student–teacher relationship in higher education.

At the middle level of Arnstein's ladder are *Informing*, *Consultation* and *Placation*, which while offering more control, do so in a tokenistic and meaningless way. At this level, students may be provided with information, they may be asked for their opinions or a small number of key activists may be included in forums and committees, but the reality is that power remains firmly with the teachers and managers. These approaches are more aligned to the concept of student as consumer; they can be seen as tokenistic, being

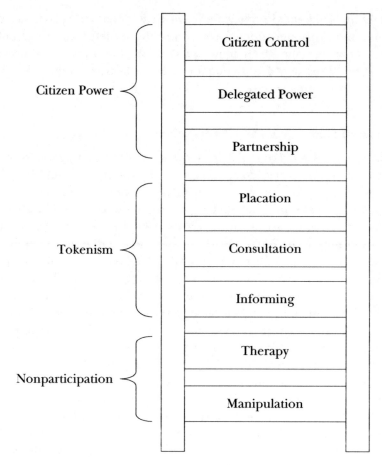

Figure 4.1　Ladder of participation (after Arnstein 1969: 217)

contrived to meet managerialist requirements for student participation and 'sought primarily through insistent imperatives of accountability rather than enduring commitments to democratic agency' (Fielding 2001: 123). Indeed it is argued that, in the context of education in schools, 'the current popularity of student voice can lead to surface compliance' (Rudduck and Fielding 2006: 219).

The upper rungs of Arnstein's ladder illustrate a shift in power, with *Partnership* described as a relationship where decision-making responsibilities are shared and distributed through negotiation (Arnstein 1969). While not originally conceived to reflect practice in higher education, this is potentially a powerful model with which to analyze practice and the experience of the teacher–student relationship. It is, however, not without problems, in that as a model or typology, it is one-dimensional, offering a linear and arguably simplistic conception of relationships in what is now a very complex environment. Thus, it is important that students and teachers enter a dialogue, underpinned by intellectual intimacy, to develop clarity and agreement about the purposes of their joint work, what is possible and the outcomes being sought.

Power balance

Seale (2009) argues that the literature on student voice in higher education fails to address the issues of power, equality and empowerment in relationships between students and teachers. Yet, these issues lie at the heart of the student–teacher nexus and the development of meaningful partnerships (Taylor and Robinson 2009).

Streeting and Wise perceive a more relational, dynamic and ever-shifting power within communities of practice in higher education. They suggest that

> all participants, especially students . . . do have power – and that it can be exercised through their commitment and contribution to their community of practice, as opposed to the exercise of power simply through choice-making, complaint or responding to consultation . . . this might be a better route to strengthening the relationships and fostering the attitudes which must underpin improvements in quality. (Streeting and Wise 2009: 5)

Yet, shifting the balance of power between teachers and students demands that academics recognize every student's potential to contribute analytical and critical thinking (McLean 2008) and are ready 'to be surprised by students' insights and capabilities and not dismissive of their thinking' (Rudduck and Fielding 2006: 227). Study in higher education is but one activity in a student's life; they bring with them a myriad of life experiences, knowledge and self-understanding to share (Burawoy 2005b).

In a desire to democratize knowledge, making our teaching more public, it is not enough to recognize the inequality in power that characterizes the relationship between student and teacher; that recognition must be a catalyst that enables challenge and cultural transformation.

The Potential for a New Way Forward

The discussion in this chapter thus far has depicted the student–teacher nexus in higher education as fraught with challenges related to managerial-ist modes of accountability, contrived notions of student voice and power imbalance. There is a case for radical change. While the ideas and example set out in this chapter are set firmly in the context of teaching and learning in higher education in the United Kingdom, there are opportunities to learn from developing practice in other professional areas such as schools and social work. Arguably these loci of practice operate in similar structural contexts to higher education, including: 'a change of balance of power and control between a greatly increased central administration and diminished professional bodies, reflected in a rarely articulated but powerful system and language of accountability' (Pring 2002: 15).

There are also lessons to be taken from experiences and practice in schools. In an exploration of the literature on student voice, Seale (2009) reports that projects in higher education commonly cite quality enhance-ment and assurance as their purpose, while projects in schools refer to issues of representation, rights and governance. The schools-based research and literature provides evidence of new ways of working arising from a cri-tique of cultures and structures in education. Cook-Sather, for example, has written extensively about student participation in schools in the USA (Cook-Sather 2002, 2008, 2009). She argues that: 'authorizing student perspec-tives introduces into critical conversations the missing perspectives of those who experience daily the effects of existing educational policies-in-practice' (Cook-Sather 2002: 3).

In a later article, Cook-Sather (2009) describes a specific project under-taken in two colleges in the United States. Entitled Students as Learners and Teachers (SaLT), this project placed undergraduate students as observ-ers and pedagogical consultants in classrooms and has many similarities with the approach evaluated in this chapter. Arguing for students to be 'co-constructors' of their education, she suggests that this approach 'can move faculty members from traditional accountability towards shared responsibil-ity' (Cook-Sather 2009: 231–2) achieving a rebalancing of power and responsibility for the development of pedagogical practice.

A range of new terms are emerging in an attempt to describe the chang-ing roles that students occupy, for example, as co-creators of curricula (Bovill 2009: 130), as 'co-constructors' in schools (Cook-Sather 2009: 213) and 'the student as producer' (Neary and Winn 2009: 126). Similar lan-guage can be found in health and social care, in particular, in professional social work, where those who use these services are seen as experts by virtue of their experiences and 'co-producers' in partnership with those who provide services (Hunter and Ritchie 2007: 16). Again here the notion of partnership is coined to describe working together in a collaborative, productive endeavour. Co-production is set out as a philosophy that is particularly relevant to the development of personalization in social care (Hunter and Ritchie 2007); this is reflective of consultation work with students in schools being linked to personalizing the curriculum (Thomson and Gunter 2006).

Contemporary social work, much like higher education, has been significantly shaped by the dominance of managerialism (Beresford 2008). Yet, social work has arguably moved from perceiving participation as a linear process, much as Arnstein's model discussed earlier, to a more radical concept of empowerment and participation within whole systems (Charnley *et al.* 2009). There is then recognition that meaningful participation requires change, which is 'seldom a pain-free process' (Charnley *et al.* 2009: 205). Change is necessary not only in individual practice, but in organizational cultures and structures, so that user views are valued in policy-making, research, evaluation, training and education. Thus, 'organisations cannot "do" participation without changing their own attitudes and structures' (Brown and Barrett 2008: 47). These ideas resonate with the student position in higher education; there is clear transferability of the notions of co-production and partnership, with students as learners in joint inquiry (Freire 1972).

The SCOTs (Students Consulting on Teaching) Project

The project that provides the underpinning empirical data for this discussion is a pioneering practical example based on the reality of teaching and learning in higher education. The general motivation for this progressive development was located in the themes and issues raised in the conceptual discussion above; the need for radical change. Implemented in one school in a new university in England, this innovative, highly successful scheme has the potential to contribute to significant change across the wider landscape of higher education. As part of a large faculty, the school employed 44 teaching staff, including full-time, part-time and hourly paid lecturers. The project empowered undergraduate students from across the school to work in collaboration with teachers to provide meaningful, timely feedback on identified elements of teaching practice. Fundamental to this approach were the notions of active participation and dialogue, which Lodge (2005, cited in Cook-Sather 2009) contrasts with quality control and compliance.

Students were recruited and paid as pedagogical consultants, as students have unique perspectives and are experts on the experience of learning in higher education, while teachers are experts in the disciplinary and educational content. This initiative can be contrasted with peer-observation and review processes, discussed by Morris and Stevenson in Chapter 7, as in this case, students are considered to be the peers in the processes of teaching and learning; as noted by Cook-Sather (2009: 235) 'students see different things'. The student consultants therefore offered a student's-eye perspective of teaching and learning.

Upon request by a teacher, a trained student consultant, who was not a member of that teacher's classes or a student on that programme, met the teacher to negotiate the focus and details of the task (Rudduck and Fielding 2006), which was tailored to the specific teaching session, the needs of the students and the teacher; a process of collegiate co-construction. In this way, activities in the scheme were designed to be teacher driven, with the interaction between the teacher and the student consultant remaining completely confidential. The feedback that teachers received was from an impartial student perspective as the student consultants were not, and had not been, members of that course.

This unique and radical approach to teaching and learning enhancement is rarely found in higher education, with the exception of a handful of colleges and universities in America. The work of two of these American institutions (Missouri State University and Brigham Young University) provided the inspiration for the development of the scheme set out here and, following their approach, the English scheme became known as the SCOTs project (Students Consulting on Teaching).

The project was developed by a cross-university group of representatives, including undergraduate students, the Students' Union, teaching staff, Student Services and Library and Learning Resources. With recognition of the managerialist requirements in the institution, it was readily apparent that the philosophy of the scheme would marry with institutional plans and values. It could be seen to contribute to key objectives as it supported the achievement of articulated targets, such as the drive to develop teaching as a less private and more public act, supporting staff to continuously improve teaching and furthering the scholarship of teaching and learning through working with students to evaluate teaching practice.

Following approval at institutional level, the recruitment process was instigated with the support of Human Resources. A part-time student co-ordinator was appointed along with a team of five undergraduate student consultants representing a range of programmes across the school. With support and engagement from the Students' Union, a desk, computer and office space were identified so that the co-ordinator and the project had a base. A two-day induction training programme was held with the newly appointed student consultants and the co-ordinator. This training was delivered by teaching staff in the school, Library and Learning Resources, Student Union and the Centre for Educational Research and Development. It included areas identified by the Project Development Group such as communication skills, giving and receiving feedback, health and safety, making learning accessible, issues of confidentiality and setting the foundations for team working, the role of the consultant and the purpose of the project.

The part-time student co-ordinator organized, oversaw and monitored the daily running of the project and the allocation of consultants. A project database was established to support on-going co-ordination and the collation of project evaluation information. Further to this, mechanisms were put in place to enable the student consultants to support each other and to collaboratively further develop the project, these included a confidential virtual community discussion forum and regular team meetings facilitated by the student co-ordinator. Awareness-raising materials were developed, including project leaflets, a website, team t-shirts and a project poster. A range of procedural documents supporting the project were collaboratively written by the student consultants during the early phase of the project. These included forms requesting feedback from teachers who had taken advantage of the service, basic policies, a process flowchart and a consultancy prompt list to support the team when working with teaching staff. Teacher participation in the project was encouraging. Ten staff, nearly a quarter of the total, participated and sometimes requested more than one consultation, resulting in over 15 consultations in a six-month period. All of the team of student consultants were involved in undertaking consultancy tasks with teachers across the whole of the school. Thus, all aspects of the project's activities were developed in a collective endeavour.

Project Evaluation

The evaluation of the SCOTs project drew on many of the principles of participatory action research in that it was a reflective, inclusive and participative process (Rogers and Williams 2006). Thus, each element of the project activities was open to critique and scrutiny involving the student consultants at their regular meetings and the wider project development team; this collaborative analysis and reflection led to further actions and development throughout the project. Drawing on evaluation data from participating teachers and student consultants, the following section of this chapter highlights the opportunities and challenges identified through the project evaluation. This discussion of the evaluation of the project addresses the three core concerns raised earlier in the chapter: managerialist modes of accountability, notions of student voice and complexities of power balance in the student–teacher relationship.

Managerialist Modes of Accountability

The overt context of managerialism and bureaucracy in the institution led to some constraints and challenges in the development of the project. For example, despite reassurances of confidentiality and collegiality, some teachers were reluctant to engage with the service as they had concerns about the potential interface with performance-related human resource processes and issues. The crisis of trust (McLean 2008, O'Neill 2002) discussed earlier in this chapter is arguably manifest here through a culture of fear. Further to this, Cook-Sather (2009: 239) argues that 'beliefs and expectations about the value of interdependence and collaboration vary [and thus] competing ideas could come into play'.

Teaching staff who took advantage of the service highlighted the opportunities and strengths of the project, suggesting that the student consultants 'provide[d] a new (independent) insight into the student learning experience' (Teacher A). Teachers identified difficulties with current approaches to gaining information about the student experience of learning and teaching; many of the issues they raised are reflected in the literature discussed earlier in the chapter. In particular, concern about impartiality in feedback, linked to issues of teacher role and power, were clearly evident. By contrast, these teachers saw one of the key strengths of the project as being its ability to offer impartial feedback:

Feedback from students is the ideal for improving lecturer skills, but your own students may have many reasons for not being fully frank. The SCOTs scheme is a fantastic solution to that problem. (Teacher C)

I prefer SCOTs observations to peer observations which can lack impartiality. (Teacher B)

I feel that it is an excellent idea to gain feedback and comment from an impartial student source. (Teacher E)

The SCOTs project demonstrated that it is possible to explore teaching and learning in partnership with students with the aim of enhancing practice. Despite being implemented within a challenging managerial context, many teachers felt that the approach had integrity, allowed for contextual depth and that it valued and intellectualized professional teaching practice.

Notions of Student Voice

With awareness of the dangers of tokenism (Arnstein 1969) and the risk of 'surface compliance' (Rudduck and Fielding 2006: 228), the project set out to foster 'mutual respect, trust and reciprocity' (Rudduck and Fielding 2006: 223). The data shows that student consultants and the teachers they worked with developed a shared climate of confidence, appreciation and openness; arguably student participation took place on the higher rungs of Arnstein's ladder (1969).

The lecturers I worked with were great . . . they asked for my ideas on how best to get the views of their students on some issues. (Student Consultant A)

As discussed earlier, authentic attention to student voice requires the teacher to be genuinely interested in the dialogue with students and their suggestions, with active follow-through (Rudduck and Fielding 2006). In this project, there was evidence that the student consultants felt valued and listened to

At first I was nervous but the lecturer really wanted to hear my thoughts. (Student Consultant C)

I did an observation in a lecture for a lecturer in a different subject to the one I am studying; it was a really useful lecture so I suggested that this lecture should also be given on my programme. . . . [the programme leader on my programme] agreed that this was a good idea and is looking into it. (Student Consultant D)

The student consultants experienced the project as inclusive and empowering as it enhanced the breadth of their learning, enabling them to develop and demonstrate a wider range of skills and knowledge than had hitherto been possible. This expansion of the student role has resonance with the concepts of citizenship and civic capacity; as such, there is reciprocal gain.

Citizenship is associated with responsibility and a commitment to social justice and concern for the greater good, while civic capacity has been defined in the context of higher education as 'the capacity of members of the campus community to access their own and one another's knowledge and experience as they work together to meet individual and common educational goals' (Lesnick and Cook-Sather 2010: 4). The SCOTs project was underpinned by a sense of student academic citizenship as it adopted a democratic and reciprocal approach within which students interacted, collaborated and developed relationships with teachers as colleagues and joint-learners, having equally valid perspectives, views and voices.

Reflecting confidence and genuine interest in the student views, teachers described how participation in the project enriched their 'capacity to reflect on their own practice' (Cook-Sather 2008: 473). Directly addressing the student consultant, an experienced teacher stated, 'I feel confident in your abilities to observe and assess my teaching and valued the feedback you gave'. In similar vein, other teachers stated the following:

> It has given me confidence in my abilities and one or two of the comments from my student consultant have made me think differently about what I do and how I do it. (Teacher A)
>
> They [the student consultants] were clearly able to identify appropriate issues. (Teacher D)

With student engagement in teaching and learning decisions and developments in universities being at best passive and at worst meaningless or even non-existent, the SCOTs project revealed a different approach to hearing the student experience. The project facilitated meaningful student participation and dialogue at the classroom level where, arguably, the most effective changes can take place.

Power Balance

At the heart of this chapter is a re-conceptualization of the relationship between the student and the teacher in higher education; to achieve this, the issue of power imbalance has been considered. While Arnot and Reay (2007: 311) suggest that 'caution [is] needed in assuming that power relations can be changed through the elicitation of student talk', this project set out, through a process of empowerment, dialogue, reflection and collaboration, to explore a way of redressing some of the power issues inherent in the student–teacher nexus. The paradox remains, however, that in order for student consultants to be perceived by teaching staff as being experts, that expertise had to be validated through an explicit and mandatory short training programme which involved teacher representatives in the delivery. As such, the validity of the trained student expert is decided upon and given credibility by the teachers themselves.

Further to this, some teachers suggested that because the student consultant was not studying their subject, they would lack the necessary knowledge to make effective comment on teaching and learning in their specialist area. This perspective could be seen to arise from teachers' strong attachments to disciplinary cultures or, as expressed by Becher and Trowler (2001), 'academic tribes and territories' and the consequent tribalistic behaviours that are not inclusive. Yet, in every consulting episode, the student consultants demonstrated their ability to contribute to the enhancement of effective pedagogical practices, regardless of subject specialism, validating the significance of their input through sharing their unique perspectives on the experience of learning. However, the student consultants were conscious of the issue of power and the challenge they faced in gaining credence and acceptance from teachers:

> . . . hopefully lecturers will see that the student consultants are a tool to benefit/enhance people's learning rather than to criticise/evaluate those imparting the knowledge. (Student Consultant B)

As a consequence of their recognition of this challenge, the student consultants suggested that should a lecturer feel an initial discomfort with teaching in public by having a student consultant in the classroom, more externalized activities could offer an alternative access to the service and perhaps allow for confidence in the partnership to develop. Thus, the student consultants saw potential for expansion in the range of tasks that they undertook. Examples of tasks that were undertaken outside traditional teaching activity included providing a student view of a batch of module evaluations, reviewing a set of open learning materials written for students and facilitating student focus groups' post-module evaluations to allow students to articulate and expand on the structured module evaluation responses.

Furthermore, in reflecting on whether power differences were addressed in the relationships between student consultants and the teachers they worked with, there were concerns that the consultations only allowed for a very short-term relationship, realistically offering only a snapshot view of a particular episode of learning. Some teachers and student consultants

suggested that it would be useful to consider ways in which the allocated
student consultant and teacher might develop their working relationship
further to provide a 'longitudinal' consultation with, for example, tasks
being undertaken at agreed periods throughout the delivery of a module.

While this project was a small short-term study, it demonstrates that it is
possible to work within the managerialist context in which we find ourselves, to explore 'complementary forms of regulation' (Chapter 10), which
may, in turn, influence the wider institutional culture.

Conclusion

This chapter set out to offer a reflective account of why and how we might
rethink the student–teacher nexus within teaching practice in higher education. Rather than recommending one particular approach to reconstruct-
ing the relationships between students and teachers, the chapter has
explored the possibilities and challenges that emerged through an innovative exemplar partnership project. Aspects of this progressive approach will
be transferable into a range of teaching contexts across higher education,
and as such the discussion in this chapter provides the catalyst for reflection
and dialogue about how these concepts may be embraced more widely in
teaching practice in higher education. Three key concerns have underpinned the structure of this chapter, shaping both the conceptualization of
the issues and the evaluation of the exemplar project.

The first of these concerns relates to managerialist modes of accountability, in particular where teaching enhancement and effectiveness are gauged
by quantitative measures that do not reflect context and cannot take account
of learning as a process of dialogical social engagement and joint enterprise. Secondly, the chapter has critiqued notions of student voice in higher
education and argued that there is a need for a shift away from tokenistic
representation towards meaningful partnerships between students and
teachers. Acknowledging and addressing the complexities of the power balance in the student–teacher relationship are central to cultural change and
form the final area of concern addressed in this chapter.

Through an exploration of developing practice in schools, in higher education internationally and in the field of health and social care, different
approaches to empowerment and the status of individuals and their interface with organizations have been shown to offer transferable learning for
practice in higher education. With a focus on active engagement and collaboration, the exemplar project centred on the transformation of the

relationship between teacher and student; arguably offering a way to challenge managerialism through a new kind of democratic professionalism. In contrast to managerialist notions of quantifiable audit, quality control and compliance, the SCOTs project set out to enhance teaching and learning through participation, partnership and an open exchange of ideas. The project developed an approach that repositioned teachers with their students 'as partners in an inquiry into disciplinary concerns' (Cousin 2008: 268); in this case, the concerns of learning and teaching in the disciplines. The challenges and lessons learned have been made explicit so that others may take these ideas forward in their own context, to explore further creative approaches to democratic education.

The Students Consulting on Teaching project was a new way forward, with students and teachers working in partnership and taking shared responsibility in the enhancement of democratic pedagogies. Thus, this work was a potential agent or medium for the transformation of teaching and learning in a university. By re-imagining the student–teacher nexus, challenging the power imbalance and moving 'from traditional accountability to shared responsibility' (Cook-Sather 2009: 231), it becomes possible to perceive a very different way of working, one that genuinely enables student-driven quality, participation and democratic professional practice.

Fielding, in a consideration of schools-based student voice work, cautions against the 'unwitting manipulation often embedded in much of this activity' (Fielding 2001: 123) and argues for a more emancipatory approach, which he calls 'students as researchers'. There is much resonance here with Neary and Winn's (2009) concept of the student as producer and the overarching concept of this book, teaching in public. It is argued in this chapter that a university culture in which students are empowered as equal partners in a community of scholars has, at its core, a democratic, participative and respectful relationship between student and teacher. The concepts explored in this chapter, therefore, not only uphold the notion of teaching in public but also offer a practical teaching-focused approach that is meaningful to teachers in their everyday practice.

Chapter 5

The Student as Scholar: Research and the Undergraduate Student

Andy Hagyard and Sue Watling

Introduction

In the United Kingdom, during the first decade of the twenty-first century, the need to ensure that teaching is informed and enriched by research was identified as one of the national strategic priorities for learning and teaching in higher education (HEFCE 2006c). Significant funds were dedicated to exploring the research/teaching nexus, with a number of institutions developing undergraduate research bursary schemes, which gave students the opportunity to gain authentic research experience and contribute to the research work of the university. The development of these schemes was largely modelled on US experiences and drew heavily on the recommendations of the influential Boyer Commission report (1998).

This chapter explores the findings of ongoing research into the experience of students on the undergraduate research scheme in one UK university, as well as drawing on evidence from similar work being conducted across the higher education sector in the United Kingdom and internationally. One of the key aspects of the concept of teaching in public is to counter the growing consumerist tendency in higher education and recapture the university as an organization for the public good. By engaging students in the research, which is at the heart of the academic endeavour of the university, they begin to perceive themselves as co-producers of knowledge, rather than passive consumers of an educational product. This changing relationship and redefining of the role of the student within the university is central to the concept of teaching in public and addresses the tensions between private and public in higher education, which are discussed in Chapters 1 and 3.

In addition, the chapter focuses on the potentially public nature of student work, as contrasted with the essentially private nature of undergraduate work within a traditional curriculum and explores the student reaction to this. Finally, it considers a range of sustainable strategies to redesign curricula in ways that allow the mainstreaming of undergraduate research, thereby providing research opportunities for all students rather than a selected few in selected institutions.

The Internet has broadened potential opportunities to access existing information and engage in the active construction of new knowledge in a way that was unimaginable 20 years ago. The university of the future is well equipped to support the role of the student as agent of knowledge production and inquiry. Higher education benefits from a wealth of new information technologies, which enable potential communication and collaboration on an international scale. While debate continues as to whether these changes constitute an information revolution or a restructuring of existing social structures in digital disguise (Webster 2002), there is little evidence showing a radical shift in the organization of industrial societies or in their potential future directions. Instead,

> the imperatives of profit, power and control seem as predominant now as they have ever been in the history of capitalist industrialism. The difference lies in the greater range and intensity of their applications . . . not in any change in the principles themselves. (Webster 2002: 266)

Burawoy notes the continuing disempowerment of marginalized social categories: 'Even as the rhetoric of equality and freedom intensifies so sociologists have documented ever-deepening inequality and domination' (Burawoy 2004: 4). It is within this ever-present sphere of social inequalities that Delanty locates the university of the future. This university has a crucial role to play, providing the location for critical contestation of meaning, in particular around the cultural contradictions that have arisen from recent conflicts between the interests of state and market forces (Delanty 1998, 2003). These conflicts are exemplified by the Dearing Report (NCIHE 1997), as discussed in Chapters 3 and 6.

Background

The idea of students and staff working collaboratively in pursuit of the production of knowledge is not new. The first modern European university, established in Berlin in 1815 by Wilhelm von Humboldt, was based around the idea of linking research and teaching as its fundamental pedagogical principle, Humboldt declaring that 'universities should treat learning as not yet wholly solved problems and hence always in research mode' (Humboldt 1970, quoted in Elton 2005: 110).

The subsequent disconnection of research and teaching and the dysfunctional relationship between these two core activities (Neary 2010) was identified by the work of Ernest Boyer (1990). The Boyer Commission in the USA was set up to investigate the changing nature of higher education, and it published, in 1998, a report that was to become a seminal document in the development of undergraduate research. The report acknowledged serious failings in research universities, with thousands of students graduating 'without ever seeing world-famous professors or tasting genuine research . . . and still lacking a coherent body of knowledge and any inkling as to how one piece of information might relate to others'. It recommended that every university should provide 'opportunities to learn through inquiry rather than simple transmission of knowledge'(Boyer Commission 1998: 6–12), that research-based learning should become the standard and that every degree should culminate in a major project to bring together all the research and communications skills that students had developed.

The Higher Education Funding Council for England (HEFCE) echoed the Boyer recommendations in its strategic priorities for learning and teaching. These included the aim of 'ensuring that teaching is informed and enriched by research', with one of the areas where institutions should seek to invest funds being 'students experiencing research, and developing research skills' (HEFCE 2006c: 5). As significant ring-fenced funding was attached to these aims, institutions across the country began exploring a range of strategies to link research and teaching, summarized in the report commissioned by the Higher Education Academy (HEA) (Jenkins and Healey 2005).

At the same time, a number of Centres for Excellence in Teaching and Learning (CETLs) were set up to promote inquiry-based learning and the development of undergraduate research skills. These included the Reinvention Centre based at the Universities of Warwick and Oxford Brookes, the Applied Undergraduate Research Skills CETL at Reading, the Centre for Inquiry-Based Learning in Arts and Social Sciences in Sheffield and the Centre for Excellence in Enquiry-Based Learning in Manchester.

The national strategic emphasis on linking research and teaching, coupled with the availability of significant funds, led many institutions to develop undergraduate research bursary programmes, typically summer schemes where students could apply for bursaries to work alongside staff on research projects. They had become widespread in the USA under the influence of the Boyer Commission report, although they can be traced back to the first scheme implemented at Massachusetts Institute of Technology in 1969 (Cohen and MacVicar 1976). In the United Kingdom, notable institution-wide programmes developed at the Universities of Warwick, Reading and Imperial College London, alongside a number of faculty-based initiatives. The University of Lincoln was one of the first post-1992 institutions to implement an undergraduate research scheme (the UROS scheme described below), with the University of Central Lancashire also making its research intern scheme a major focus of its research-informed teaching strategy.

Evidence of the impact on students of engaging in real research projects is considered in detail below. However, by 2010, the political and pedagogical environment of higher education in the United Kingdom had shifted substantially. The Independent Review of Higher Education Funding and Student Finance – generally referred to as the Browne Report (2010) – heralded a period of economic restraint. The replacement of the ring-fenced Teaching Quality Enhancement Fund (TQEF) with the Teaching Enhancement and Student Success (TESS) fund in 2009 brought an end in many institutions to the guaranteed availability of development funds, while the global economic crisis led to massive cuts in public expenditure, including higher education, and wholesale changes in the way the sector is financed. As a result, the strategy of funding undergraduate research bursary schemes in order to promote linkages between research and teaching was significantly challenged.

There are pedagogical as well as political reasons why bursary schemes need to be reconsidered. Due, at least in part, to the success of such schemes and a growing body of research evidence that highlights their impact on student learning, there is a developing consensus that the benefits of learning through research should be available to all students. Healey and Jenkins (2009) set the tone for much of the debate in their report, which was commissioned by the Higher Education Academy and therefore instrumental in developing national strategy. They argue that 'all students in all higher education institutions should experience learning through, and about, research and enquiry' (Healey and Jenkins 2009: 3) rather than simply providing research opportunities for selected students in selected institutions.

The term mainstreaming is widely used to refer to this process of embedding undergraduate research throughout a programme, a faculty or indeed a whole institution. It represents a significant advance in the status accorded to research-based learning, moving it from the periphery of learning and teaching strategy to a central role in defining the undergraduate curriculum. It has the potential to radically alter the role of the student within the university, moving away from the growing tendency to see them as consumers of education and towards the notion of the student as a researcher, scholar and producer of knowledge, thereby returning the university to its original Humboldtian principles. The potential for this radical reconceptualization of the role of the student will be developed further later in the chapter.

The Impact on the Student of Engaging with Research

Much of the early research into the connections between research and teaching focused on the impact on students of learning to operate in a research-intensive environment, while the much-quoted meta-analysis by Hattie and Marsh (1996) concluded that there was no clear evidence of any mutually beneficial relationship between research and teaching. While this report almost led the UK government to formalize the divide between teaching and research, (DfES 2003) and to designate certain institutions as 'teaching only' universities, opposition from the sector led to a rethink and the decision to focus strategic efforts on better connecting the two activities rather than accentuating the dichotomy.

However, research into the impact on students of engaging in research was noticeably sparse until the last few years. As recently as 2004, Jenkins (2004) concluded that there was very limited evidence of the impact of different forms of research-based learning on student epistemological and intellectual development. Fortunately, the upsurge in interest in undergraduate research in the United Kingdom, which followed the creation of the CETLs in 2005 and the allocation of TQEF funding in 2006, is now producing a significant body of evidence within the United Kingdom to complement what has emerged internationally and in the United States in particular. Blackmore and Cousin's evaluation of a pilot undergraduate scheme at the University of Warwick concluded that students 'learnt much by getting closer to the culture of inquiry in their subject and greatly appreciated playing a role in knowledge production' (Blackmore and Cousin 2003: 24–5), while Levy's (2008) work at the University of Sheffield demonstrated the positive impacts of inquiry and research on first-year undergraduates.

Much of the most compelling evidence comes from the US, often co-ordinated and disseminated through the work of the Council for Undergraduate Research (CUR). The most comprehensive study comes from a team at the University of Colorado at Boulder, who have conducted longitudinal research into the effects of undergraduate research in the sciences. They conclude that the benefits that students describe fit into a series of conceptual categories:

- personal/professional gains
- gains in thinking and working like a scientist
- gains in skills
- demonstrating norms of professional practice and understanding how scientists practice their profession (the 'becoming a scientist' category)
- gains in career clarification
- enhanced career preparation

(Hunter *et al. 2007*)

Evidence from Australia is less conclusive, with Jewell and Brew's report into undergraduate research programmes in Australian universities highlighting the lack of formal evaluation of these programmes. As a result, they conclude that 'the undergraduate experience in these programmes has not been measured' (Jewell and Brew 2010: 18).

However, the majority of the research findings listed above concern research bursary schemes, operating outside the curriculum. When it comes to evaluating the impact of research and inquiry-based learning within the curriculum, much of the difficulty arises from the lack of consensus around the usage and precise meaning of these terms. Spronken-Smith and Walker (2010) make an attempt to identify some commonality of opinion around what constitutes inquiry-based learning, and they identify five core ingredients:

- learning is stimulated by inquiry, that is, driven by questions or problems
- learning is based on a process of constructing knowledge and new understanding
- it is an 'active' approach to learning, involving learning by doing
- a student-centred approach to teaching in which the role of the teacher is to act as facilitator
- a move to self-directed learning

(Spronken-Smith and Walker *2010: 726*)

They then identify various types of inquiry-based learning, according to three important qualifiers: the level of scaffolding (structured, guided or open inquiry), the emphasis of learning (whether learning existing knowledge or building new knowledge) and the scale of the inquiry-based activity (within-class, within-course or whole-course). Spronken-Smith and Walker also adopt Wood and Levy's (2008) distinction between information-oriented and discovery-oriented inquiry. The conclusion of their research study is that inquiry-based learning can strengthen the teaching-research nexus, especially when an open-inquiry approach is used where students generate their own research questions; the focus of learning is discovery-oriented rather than information-oriented, so that teachers are co-learners in the inquiry and where open, discovery-oriented inquiry is introduced early in the curriculum and used as the basis for whole course design.

Students as Researchers: The Undergraduate Research Opportunities Scheme (UROS) at the University of Lincoln

The Undergraduate Research Opportunities Scheme (UROS) was introduced as a pilot scheme at the University of Lincoln in 2007. Using the Teaching Quality Enhancement Fund (TQEF), bursaries of £1,500 were offered to one student in each of the faculties. This gave the opportunity of becoming a paid researcher for the university, working alongside research staff and gaining experience of being producers rather than consumers of knowledge. The pilot was a success, with students reporting both increased research skills and an improved understanding of the research process.

> This project increased my knowledge of some historical sources and of research procedures. It gave me the opportunity to develop further my skills of analysis, critical thinking and interpretation of primary sources and emphasized the importance of project management skills such as the need for a logical approach to research and the importance of accurate note taking. (Student E)
>
> I feel that this project was a valuable experience. The six weeks' research was a welcome intellectual stimulation during the long summer break. It helped me hone my research and project management skills required for my dissertation and it gave me a sample of what part of an academic career may be like. (Student B)

During the next two years, the pilot was extended and over 50 research projects, with student bursaries of £1,500 each granted to single students or small collaborative groups, were funded from the TQEF. Staff were asked to identify existing research projects and invite student applications for placement. Where students had ideas of their own for research projects, they were invited to contact an appropriate member of staff for further discussion. A key feature of UROS was to ensure students were fully supported throughout their research experience. All projects had a member of academic staff in a supervisory role; helping students not only to enhance their own understanding of the research process but also their knowledge of their own discipline.

To gain as broad a range of research opportunities as possible, UROS was widely publicized across the university through posters, leaflets and the University radio station (Siren FM Radio). A launch event, open to staff and students, included presentations from previous UROS students and their supervisors, who spoke with enthusiasm for the scheme. Typical staff comments included the following:

> The scheme has been an excellent opportunity for a student to become involved with a faculty research project. (Staff B)
>
> I found the opportunity to work with a keen undergraduate on a research project a most stimulating one. (Staff C)
>
> The research findings have plugged a number of gaps in my own research in this area. (Staff A)

A feature of UROS was to replicate as far as possible a genuine research experience, starting with the invitation for interested students to fill in a bursary application form. This went before a UROS panel, which included the Dean of Teaching and Learning and the Dean of Research. Some projects involved a single student; some consisted of groups of students who shared the bursary between them. A UROS website was set up for dissemination, and each project was provided with an online blog for reporting and reflection.

A networking event was considered an important part of the scheme, both to maintain cohesion and provide a valuable opportunity for sharing experiences between staff and students. Short information sessions were included, for example, on creating a research poster and setting up a blog. On occasions where projects were close to finishing or completed, they were invited to give a presentation. For example, during the first year, a group from the Lincoln School of Performing Arts used their UROS bursary to research into Victorian melodrama, following the discovery of a rare version of the drama, *Sweeny Todd*. This had already been produced by the Lincoln Performing Arts Centre, and the group were able to give a presentation on their research experience.

At the end of the project, a dissemination event was held. This attracted over 100 people from across the university who met with the students and viewed their research posters before attending a series of student-led presentations. The aim was to provide the students with a replica conference environment where they could gain the experience of participating in a poster display and giving a presentation in a friendly, supportive atmosphere. Typically, the majority of funded projects took part and although presentations were voluntary, over half took the opportunity to present and the majority to create research posters. As part of their UROS experience, students were invited to consider their research findings for submission in Neo, the university's new online, peer-reviewed student journal, aimed at promoting and celebrating student work and giving an opportunity for UROS research outputs to be recognized as professional academic work.

Evaluation and Impact

Evaluation of the UROS student experience was carried out in 2008 through survey and follow-up interviews. 20 out of 39 students (51 per cent) completed the survey, with 6 of these selected for interview. These semi-structured interviews explored students' experiences of UROS and, more fundamentally, whether it had changed their perceptions of research, their role as a student within the university and their relationship with staff. In addition, staff who had acted as UROS supervisors were also sent surveys, which asked them to evaluate the benefits of the scheme to students and to staff. 26 out of 35 staff supervisors (74 per cent) completed the survey.

What is immediately clear from the evaluation is that the participation of undergraduate students in research projects creates advantages for both students and staff. From the students' point of view, they benefit hugely from their involvement in the research work of the university. Students were virtually unanimous in agreeing that they had enhanced both their understanding of their discipline and their research skills, as well as gaining insights into the processes and practices of research, the experience of working effectively with colleagues and staff and the opportunity to improve their employability. Staff, on the other hand, gained the opportunity to work with a keen undergraduate on a research project and in several cases reported that UROS enabled them to undertake small pieces of research and write articles that might not otherwise have been completed.

The following quotations from the evaluations illustrate the impact and effectiveness of UROS:

> Research seems like a much more doable thing now whereas before I wouldn't have thought I could do my own research project. (Student A)

It further backed up my opinions that research is stressful, frustrating yet incredibly interesting and important. (Student D)

I have learned a lot about topics related to my degree subject by doing research and not simply being told about it. (Student G)

Having to contact different people has made me more confident with my communication skills. I felt the theme was incredibly interesting and quite relevant to my work hence considerably aiding my own practice. The report is something I worked hard at thus making me feel I have achieved something of a substantial outcome. (Student C)

The Public Nature of Undergraduate Research

Engaging undergraduate students in research supports the concept of teaching in public primarily by changing the relationship between staff and students and by challenging the growing view of students as consumers. There is, however, a secondary way in which this research engagement develops a sense of public good among students. Research into the student experience of research programmes consistently highlights the impact of engaging in real-world projects and of sharing their work in a public arena. In this way, students begin to perceive themselves as not only producers of knowledge but also producers of the social world they are moving into.

Particularly striking in the evaluations, and the subsequent interviews, was the impact on students of having to present and disseminate their findings publicly. 90 per cent of the students had presented, or were intending to present their findings to a live audience, either internally or externally. 50 per cent had published their findings, with a further 25 per cent considering publication. Internally, a number of UROS students presented their work to research seminars and events within their own departments, while several students were also successful with external dissemination of their research findings. A UROS student and supervisor presented their research findings at the International Conference on Software Maintenance (ICSM) in Beijing (Capiluppi and Knowles 2008). Collaboration between two UROS groups took place on a research paper for the International Conference of Open Source Systems (OSS) in Sweden (Boldyreff *et al.* 2009).

This public aspect of the project featured consistently in students' comments, presenting itself as one of the defining characteristics of the UROS scheme when compared with the typical experience of the undergraduate student. On reflection, this should not be surprising. While research and inquiry are rarely totally absent from the undergraduate curriculum, all too often, it is confined to a final level dissertation or independent project, and even then the student's final work may only ever be read by the student, the supervisor, a second marker and an external examiner. It should not come as a surprise to find that students treat the dissertation as a mechanistic exercise in gaining sufficient credits to meet the requirements of their course.

When asked to describe the principal benefits for students, staff comments repeatedly acknowledged the benefits of engaging in genuine research 'that matters to all concerned' rather than 'simply doing it for the course'. By implication, there is a recognition by staff that a good deal of what is currently termed research in the undergraduate curriculum is artificial and makes no contribution to the creation of new knowledge for the greater public good.

These comments are not of course true of all disciplines. Programmes in Art and Design, Performing Arts and Media Production have a tradition of presenting students' work in degree shows. Programmes in the humanities and social sciences have tended to adopt more traditional approaches to the assessment and presentation of student work, but could learn a great deal from the engagement created among students by having to publicly present the outcomes of their work.

Changing Staff/Student Relationships

Another theme to emerge from the interviews conducted with students was that of the changing relationship between staff and students. One student in particular exemplified this by contrasting UROS with another project that had adopted a much more structured approach to enquiry:

> . . . this time was different . . . I felt like I was working WITH [the member of staff], not working FOR them. (Student C)

The collaborative nature of the projects and the blurring of relational boundaries between staff and students were particularly evident at the UROS dissemination event. A number of staff attending the event commented on the fact that it was not at all clear who were the staff and who were the students, as all had equal status in the joint presentation and dissemination of their research findings.

There is evidence from the student interviews of a fundamental re-conceptualization by students of their role in the university: moving away from a consumerized model of education to one where students see them-selves as collaborators in the creation of knowledge. In her work on thresh-old concepts, Cousin (2010) describes the ontological shift that occurs as students grasp fundamental concepts within their discipline and cross the threshold to 'become' an engineer, a historian or a speaker of French. Although threshold concepts theory is typically applied to learning within the disciplines, Edwards (2011) develops an argument for the identification of generic threshold concepts in terms of learning development. This view is strongly endorsed by the experience of the UROS students, who clearly emerged with a changed sense of themselves as students. UROS demon-strates that engagement in undergraduate research has transformative potential.

Mainstreaming UROS: The Student as Producer

Despite the undeniable success of the UROS scheme and the obvious ben-efits to staff and student participants, it is clearly impossible to give every student a genuine research experience through this scheme alone. Consequently, a range of other strategies need to be considered, and a number of these are documented in various sources (Jenkins *et al.* 2007, Healey and Jenkins 2009).

It can be seen that undergraduate research schemes have been shown to have significant impact on their student participants, but these schemes can only ever be on the periphery of a university's learning and teaching strat-egy. The challenge facing the modern university is to bring undergraduate research into the mainstream, embedding the principles of UROS and pro-viding all students with the opportunity to learn through a process of research, inquiry and discovery.

The University of Lincoln developed and adopted the Student as Producer initiative in response to this challenge. Funded from 2010 to 2013 by the Higher Education Academy as part of its National Teaching Fellowship Scheme projects strand, this project set out to establish research-engaged teaching and learning as the underpinning principle for all curriculum development, becoming the *de facto* learning and teaching strategy of the university. The concept of student as producer (Neary 2010) incorporates the principles of research-based learning, such that students become pro-ducers of knowledge alongside staff. But it extends the ideas to become the organizing principle for the whole university rather than simply a curricu-lum design initiative. Re-conceptualizing students as collaborators in academic endeavour allows them to become engaged in every aspect of the university: participating in curriculum design and review, acting as consultants on teaching to help enhance its quality (as described in Chapter 4) and working alongside staff in pursuit of the production of knowledge.

Student as Producer can be seen as an umbrella term for a range of initiatives designed to radically alter the role of students, their relationships with staff and the very nature of the university itself. Hence, it is more than a curriculum design project. It is a movement that strives for wholesale institutional change, providing a new paradigm within which to consider a whole range of key issues in higher education. At its heart is the concept of learning through discovery, a principle that is identifiable in a range of pedagogies such as problem-based, inquiry-based or research-based learning. However, Student as Producer also incorporates the notion of digital scholarship, recognizing the enabling power of Web 2.0 technologies to support changing relationships between staff and students and facilitate commons-based peer production of knowledge. It also recognizes the use of space and spatiality as an important aspect of the learning landscape (Neary *et al.* 2010). In addition, Student as Producer incorporates the student voice by active engagement of students in the design, delivery and review of their programmes and in assessment and feedback activities. It engages students with the world beyond the university, producing graduates with a stronger sense of social responsibility and better prepared for a world of complexity and uncertainty.

The university should reform itself as 'a site of public discourses' rather than the 'exclusive site of expertise' (Delanty 2003: 81) and, with issues of social equality and justice at its heart, offer an authentic challenge to the influence of the market and claims of academic capitalism. Student as Producer does just this; it offers opportunities for genuine engagement with lived experience of disempowerment and in doing so it challenges the reproduction of market dominance and structures of elitism and privilege. The answer to Burawoy's question 'Do we have to abandon the very idea of the university as a "public" good?' (Burawoy 2004: 7) lies within initiatives such as Student as Producer. It offers undergraduates the exposure to real research, which is informed by unpicking discursive practices and uncovering the constitutive nature of the invisible mechanisms of power and control. Inquiry-based projects within Student as Producer not only support active engagement with the learning process and ensure it is relevant to the student's own purpose, they also reduce hierarchical teaching barriers and enable critical thought and reflection. McLean (2006) calls for the design of teaching and learning activities that connect knowledge with human interests through a theoretical engagement with research. Ensuring teaching and learning engage with research as well as being informed by existing knowledge and practice provides the trajectory through which the core values of academic life are restated and reconnected. Promoting a culture based on argumentation and critique early in the student experience can offer the prerequisite conceptual tools to not only enhance later learning but inform the citizens of the future for more effective participation in the public sphere.

Student as Producer encourages students to be critical and questioning at the start of their university experience. They are shown the world as a dynamic and continual process of becoming rather than a fixed, static reality. In doing so, they will be empowered to be active within the public sphere, engaging with anti-oppressive practices and working towards social justice and change (Freire 1972). McLean (2006) adds her own voice to the supporters of the university of the future, who see it as the site of emancipation and social transformation; 'critical university pedagogy would take up the functions of universities to educate citizens and professionals who can tackle injustices and social problems' (McLean 2006: 39). Universities have the potential to enable the ideal speech conditions identified by Habermas, which are rooted in the life-world where cultural reproduction and social integration take place (Calhoun 1992). McLean (2006) argues that even though higher education has become colonized by managerialist, market driven forces, university pedagogy remains the most appropriate and useful site for querying the *status quo* and supporting the contestation and construction of existing and new knowledge. Student as Producer is one such opportunity for a redesign of the university curriculum to incorporate inquiry-based learning and research partnerships between staff and students designed to challenge the relationships between power and knowledge. As Delanty (1998) argues, universities must recapture a sense of public commitment.

Conclusion

Across the world, undergraduate research schemes such as UROS have proved their worth, and there is growing consensus internationally around the benefits to students of engaging in real research projects, collaborating with staff in the creation of knowledge. At the same time, there is increasing interest in attempts to mainstream undergraduate research, so that all students have the opportunity to learn through and about research and experience the transformative potential of a research-engaged curriculum. Existing undergraduate research schemes are increasingly being seen as templates for extending this type of activity across the whole institution.

Student as Producer offers a radical way forward. The purely pedagogical benefits of inquiry-based, discovery-mode learning can be incorporated into the broader concept of student as producer, redefining the role of the student within the university and within society. Working on real research projects brings student work into the public domain, transforming the student experience and level of engagement and banishing the traditional model of students working privately and independently. More than just producers of knowledge, students also become producers of their social world and the future environment in which they will be living and working. Student as Producer is central to the concept of teaching in public. It recaptures the sense of the university as a public good. At a time of increasing marketization and potential privatization of higher education, it serves as a timely antidote to the growing notion of student as consumer. It not only reinforces the sense of the university as an institution concerned with the creation of knowledge and understanding for the greater good of society, but also strengthens the focus on the public rather than the private in higher education.

Chapter 6

Invisible Publics: Higher Education and Digital Exclusion

Sue Watling

Introduction

Teaching in public involves reducing barriers to access and nowhere is this more appropriate than with the subject of electronic resources and the delivery of virtual learning opportunities. The future of the university, in a time of resurgence of neo-liberal values, the primacy of market forces and an increasing emphasis on private rather than public provision, has become the subject of much debate. Insufficient attention, however, is being paid to the possibility of exclusion, which is the inevitable result of increasing digital pedagogies and practices. This chapter focuses on the role of the university in ensuring equitable access to digital technology. Over the last decade, the possibilities of virtual learning have included opportunities for widening participation, increasing student numbers and opening up world trades in professional and academic expertise, thereby sustaining the globalization of education. This chapter addresses the limitations to these opportunities, in particular the failure to prioritize issues of digital inclusion and the divisive consequences of digital discrimination. The chapter is in two parts: the first examines the adoption of virtual learning within higher education, in particular, the ability of the technology to both enable and deny access. The second looks at the wider implications of this duality when set against the background of an increasingly digital society, and how inclusive practices are failing to have inclusive results.

The chapter begins by revisiting the early potential of Communication and Information Technologies (C&IT) and electronic learning (e-Learning) for higher education, first made explicit in the Dearing Report (NCIHE 1997). Of particular interest are the promises of widening participation and of providing support for a non-traditional student base. The chapter will examine national e-Learning policy for evidence of support for these promises, before exploring in more depth how the divisive potential of the technology depends on the ways in which it is managed and distributed. Informed by research which suggests that digital exclusion follows existing patterns of social exclusion, the chapter examines how issues of access have become almost exclusively associated with disability and how this side-lining has blurred the boundaries of responsibility for ensuring digitally inclusive practice. Examples of digital discrimination demonstrate how a society dominated by virtual ways of working requires equitable digital practices as a key to gaining social citizenship. Unless these are realized, exclusion from digital public spheres may constitute new social categories of silenced and invisible publics. It has been suggested that higher education for the public good has a significant role to play in addressing issues of social exclusion and disempowerment (Burawoy 2005b, Delanty 2003). The chapter concludes by suggesting that the university of the future must be the site of critical debate, in particular, with regard to pioneering equitable online learning environments and championing digital democracy.

The Emergence of e-Learning

In 1963, the Robbins Report supported the expansion of entry to higher education for young people with ability and attainment (Committee on Higher Education 1963). The report informed the creation of the Open University and the establishment of new 'plate glass' institutions. However, during these pre-internet times, the only significant increase in admission of students from non-traditional backgrounds to higher education was into the new city polytechnics. The Dearing Report (NCIHE 1997) revisited the issue of widening participation. It focused on the potential of new C&IT for broadening access and better preparing students for a burgeoning knowledge economy. The proposal was that 50 per cent of all people between the ages of 18 and 30 should have experience of higher education by 2010, and this would be achieved through the possibilities of C&IT for virtual learning. Its transformative power would enable students to become self-directed, benefiting from links to resources at all times and in places of their own choice. Underpinning the rhetoric of widening participation was the anticipation that e-Learning would become a new tradable commodity in a competitive international market. Potential benefits would include opening up lucrative contracts for digital publishers, content creators and providers of educational hardware and software, attracting international students and establishing a world-wide research network through the digitization of academic literature and sharing of virtual knowledge.

This initial enthusiasm for e-Learning was deterministic in scope and promise. Providing access to virtual learning was prioritized; the complexity of adopting new working practices was underestimated. The vision of digital higher education within the Dearing Report failed to acknowledge the existence of cultural capital or the influence of 'social shaping' (Bijker 1989). From the beginning, C&IT was promoted as equitable when, in reality, learning technology privileged those with technical ability and adoption was limited to areas where subject discipline or personal interest was already developing within digital parameters. The divides between analogue and digital practices proved to be more extensive than anticipated, diluting early promises of virtual learning. The Dearing Report had promoted C&IT as a means of reaching those in remote, rural areas or with existing work or care commitments, as well as improving access for students with visual, hearing or motor impairment. The report also recognized that 'disabled students learn in different ways' (NCIHE 1997: 7.40). This explicit recognition of the power of technology to support non-traditional access was commendable but did not go far enough. It failed to recognize how technology did not exist within a vacuum but within a complex social and cultural mix of attitudes and behaviours. It was not only disabled students who learned in different ways; there were wider social determinants of digital access. Gender, age and cultural background all had a potential influence on preferences for learning and online interaction.

Enabling this diversity of access was dependent on inclusive digital design. The transformative power of virtual environments, which the Dearing Report had promised would enable students to become self-directed and interact with teaching and learning content at times and places of their own choice, failed to recognize the unique ability of digital data to be made available in alternative formats. So long as resources were designed in ways which took into account multiple modes of delivery, users had the potential to customize content to suit their own preference; they could, for example, convert text to speech, change print size or adjust colours and contrasts. The inherent flexibility of digital data meant that not only did it suit a range of assistive technologies, it also offered support for other users; for example, text-to-speech software provided a valuable alternative delivery mode for non-native speakers or those with aural preferences for learning. If C&IT were to inform digital engagement with communication, information and active participation in the construction of new knowledge, e-Learning content had to support diversity of access rather than denying it. The Dearing Report had highlighted the potential for digital democracy, but it was left to those developing the adoption of virtual learning to ensure the necessary structures for achieving this were in place. In the next section national e-Learning policy directives will be examined to identify the extent to which this potential became practice.

e-Learning Policy

The *Strategy for eLearning* (HEFCE 2005) was one of the first national guidelines to address the influence of virtual learning upon the higher education sector, and it appeared to dilute some of the early technological determinism evident within the Dearing Report. Instead of viewing C&IT, now referred to as ICT (Information and Communication Technologies), as a panacea for moving higher education forwards, the attention focused on supporting students as independent learners and meeting their needs and aspirations for development. The shift from technology to user was an ideal platform from which to address the diversity of user requirements and to offer strategic direction at a national level. However, HEFCE was an adamant supporter of institutional freedom, insisting that decisions with regard to developing e-Learning strategies would remain the prerogative of individual universities. Students were merged into a homogenous group where the access parameters for virtual learning appeared to be taken for granted. The pattern whereby e-Learning strategy was designed and delivered by those already operating within a narrow range of digital criteria had already been established, resulting in a failure to acknowledge the specific requirements of assistive technologies or the need to prioritize accessible digital content for a diverse range of users. This narrow range of criteria can be usefully described as following an MEE model, where computer access via a Mouse, Eyes and Ears are taken for granted as the dominant modes of working. When this model is privileged, it is followed with the assumption that others operate within similar constraints, and the diversity of ways in which people operate in digital environments is not supported. Individual universities created strategic guidelines which also failed to address the critical issues and, inadvertently, contributed to the embedding of a range of barriers to access which ran contrary to the early promises for widening higher education opportunities.

The revised e-Learning strategy, *Enhancing Teaching and Learning Through the Use of Technology* (HEFCE 2009a), was a response to the rapidly changing nature of digital environments in the first decade of the twenty-first century. The read-only nature of the first phase of the Internet, retrospectively named Web 1.0, had been dominated by web development specialists, and digital environments were designed primarily for access rather than interaction. Web 2.0 was characterized by a move towards increasing user-generated content via multimedia creation and text-editing facilities in programs such as blogs and wikis. The increased availability of video and audio and the collaborative affordances of new Web 2.0 tools offered new potential ways of working and developing virtual teaching and learning resources. A number of external reports had also focused on the use of new ICTs in education, aided in particular by developments in mobile technology (BECTA 2008, UCISA 2008, JISC 2008, JISC 2009a). These reports had offered evidence of how the Internet, in particular, the social networking phenomenon, influenced students entering higher education, and how their increasingly digital lifestyles were changing expectations of university responses to virtual practices. They also suggested a greater need for digital literacy provision in order to support students making sense of the vast array of digital data they were being exposed to. However, HEFCE re-affirmed that while it would continue to support and encourage institutions to use technology to widen access and opportunity, it remained institutions' individual responsibility to identify the specific directions to follow. Any co-ordinated attempt to address the dual ability of the technology to both enable and deny access, or the critical need to support diversity of digital access via alternative delivery modes, remained invisible.

The only support for ensuring access to digital content was within statutory legislation that was enshrined in the Disability Discrimination Act (DfEE 1995). SENDA, the Special Educational Needs Disability Act, (DfEE 2001) made it unlawful to treat a disabled person less favourably than a non-disabled person. This covered access to information, so was applicable to higher education. The Act required individual institutions to be proactive in anticipating cases where students were likely to be substantially disadvantaged and to accept the responsibility for making reasonable adjustments, either through alternative formats or the provision of equivalent experiences. Concepts of 'substantial disadvantage' and 'reasonable adjustment' were vague; the justification being that interpretation depended on individual circumstances. This made it difficult to judge the boundaries for establishing inclusive practice guidelines, in particular, within the development of teaching and learning resources which typically crossed multiple disciplines and specialist subjects. The lack of direction was compounded by the remit of the legislation. Isolating the requirements for accessible content within SENDA associated inclusive practice solely with disability. It made invisible other strands of diversity such as age, gender or cultural background which might influence learning preference and be a determinant of access to digital content.

HEFCE's hands-off approach, allowing freedom for each university to set its own digital agenda, led to a focus on provision of access rather than attention to quality of access and usage practices. Where the need for inclusive practice was recognized at an institutional level, due to SENDA, it continued to be primarily regarded as a service for students in receipt of Disabled Student Allowance (DSA). This narrow perception limited awareness that diversity was about more than making changes for a discrete group, it was a socially responsible example of inclusivity where making changes for some had potential benefit for all. The first document to state that ensuring learning and teaching practices were inclusive of disabled students would enhance the learning opportunities of all students was the Quality Assurance Agency (QAA) revised *Code of Practice for Disabled Students* (QAA 2010). The code provided a useful reminder of the social model of disability, whereby barriers to participation are environmental in origin. It reminded the university of its statutory obligation to identify and remove obstacles. It also called for the direct involvement of disabled students in the design and review of inclusive provision for new programmes, the review/revalidation of existing ones and their methods of assessment, a direct involvement of students that mirrors the SCOTs project described in Chapter 4 and the concept of the Student as Scholar (Chapter 5). The code reiterated the need for institutions' websites, and all other sources of ICT, to be designed according to professional standards of accessibility and states how 'gaining knowledge of these standards should be part of the professional development of relevant staff in the institution' (QAA 2010: 16). Unfortunately, the potential usefulness of this powerful document remained constrained by the focus on disability, which not only suggested limited distribution to areas of the university with remits for disability issues, such as Student Services and Disability Support Units, but also diluted its strength to offer wider strategic direction.

Existing social restrictions such as the influence of age, low income and cultural background, as well as individual preferences for learning, all play a role in determining quantity and quality of access and thereby contribute to the complex nature of digital divides. As the digitization of information increases, the learning curve required to operate with confidence and competence within new twenty-first century digital environments becomes steeper. Costs of participation can also be significant barriers for low income families and individuals. Many existing categories of social marginalization and exclusion are those where new digital exclusions are also frequently to be found (van Dijk 2006, Seale 2009). There was, however, no broadening of diversity beyond the category of disabled students, ensuring that other disadvantaged students remained invisible. Instead, e-Learning directives were limited to maximizing the benefits of ICT across the institution's business activities, suggesting that business models and their underlying agenda had priority over resourcing measures to ensure access for all.

Pressure to use virtual learning environments, in particular, via policies that promised enhancement of the quality of teaching and learning, had led to a melee of contradictory practices. Placing lecture notes online for students with dyslexia was encouraged, but this was also of benefit for those with alternative learning preferences and non-native English speakers, as well as providing reliable catch-up or revision materials. Scant attention was paid to the inclusive design of these documents, often resulting in access barriers being inadvertently put in place by staff, for example, presentation slides with text too small to read effectively or text running across images and blurring visibility. When staff provide content in a single fixed format with no opportunity for the user to customize it to suit their own preference, or no other alternative version, it significantly reduces its usefulness as an aid to teaching and learning. In the decade since the Dearing Report, awareness of the individual responsibility of staff for ensuring inclusion, such as greater attention to text size and formatting, had become disassociated from the core teaching and learning functions of the university. In an increasingly digital environment with multiple modes of digital delivery, inclusive practice was rarely incentivized or given priority. Instead, attention focused on the technical support for the virtual environments rather than on the daily production of digital documents created by staff to support their teaching and learning.

Moving beyond the campus, ample evidence of exclusive digital practices is available within the wider society. Here, the Internet is increasingly being used to support digital lifestyle choices which include online shopping, banking, access to health care and leisure activities plus a broad range of opportunities for social networking and virtual collaboration. The more the Internet supports digital lifestyles, the greater become the divides between those with access and those for whom access is problematic. It is the potential implications of this and the consequences for the university of the future which are addressed in the next section.

Access Enabled – Access Denied

The dual potential of the technology to enable or deny access stems from a broad range of differences in skills and motivation as well as wider determinants such as gender, age, cultural background, disability and learning preference (van Dijk 2006). However, digital educators have continued to support an increasingly narrow gateway of access criteria; one which excludes diversity rather than enables it. There is a vast range of technology available to support digital equity, therefore the majority of barriers to access derive from the failure to design for a diverse range of access criteria rather than restrictions which are technical in origin. As already mentioned, the strength of providing resources in digital format lies in the potential flexibility of digital data to be customized to suit individual user preference. The value of this cannot be stressed enough, as it offers genuine opportunities for digital inclusion. However, issues of inclusive practice have become associated with disability which, while it partially recognizes this value, it misses the wider support digital data offers to a diverse user base. Individuals who are not registered as disabled can also benefit from a range of assistive software, such as text to speech facilities, in order to check the flow of a piece of writing, to practice competence in an additional language or simply because they have a preference for aural learning. The only weakness of digital data is dependency on inclusive design practices. Where such practices are not evident, those who have most to gain from customizing their digital access to suit their own preferences are also those most likely to have that access denied.

> If staff in higher education do not design, develop and support accessible e-Learning materials, then the gap between disabled and non-disabled students will widen and the technology will outstrip it usefulness as a tool that can facilitate access to learning, curricula, independence and empowerment. (Seale 2006: 27)

The gap referred to here is not only about disabled and non-disabled students but is about supporting diversity. Seale (2006) calls for e-Learning material which maximizes opportunities for the technology to enable access. The first step to ensuring digital equity is a clear understanding of the nature of the barriers to be overcome.

The principle of inclusive design informs equitable digital practice. This states that making changes for some creates an improved environment for all. Within the built environment, providing ramps into public buildings not only overcame barriers for wheelchair users, but also improved access for those pushing prams or buggies, shopping trolleys or suitcases on wheels. Removing digital barriers follows the same principle; design that recognizes and caters for a diversity of delivery modes is potentially improving access for all.

Digital barriers have three sequential layers: first the cost of any alternative technology; secondly appropriate training and support and thirdly inaccessible design. Within higher education, cost can be less of an issue; the majority of university computer networks supply a range of assistive programs such as text-to-speech conversion and additional costs for specialist assistive technologies can be met through the Disabled Student Allowance (DSA) or Access to Work scheme. The second stage involves the specialist, non-standard nature of any alternative technologies. Perception of their use as marginal when compared to core practices can result in support being side-lined. ICT helpdesks are frequently ill-equipped to answer queries about the complexities of text-to-speech software, while technical support from manufacturers is not only expensive but can fail to take into account any unique individual set-up, resulting in assistive technology being unable to realize its full potential. The third barrier is the quality of content because, even with the pre-requisite training and support in place, if the digital data has not been designed with diversity in mind, or if it is provided in a single fixed format preventing customization, then access will continue to be denied.

Digital design becomes exclusive when content is fixed in a single format which prevents users from customizing it to suit their own requirements and when this format is problematic. Examples of exclusive digital practices include

- Providing text in a complex font which is difficult to read
- Using the upper case, underline or italic functions for emphasis as these formats can take longer for the brain to process and grasp the meaning; the bold function is preferable
- Fully justifying text, which creates 'rivers' of white space running down the page between unevenly-spaced words
- Audio or video content provided without textual equivalents, which prevents alternative access their content
- Inadequate labelling of digital images which leads to loss of information when viewed via non-visual delivery modes
- Inconsistency of navigation can create confusion if structures change from page to page
- Online module sites demonstrating a conflicting variety of styles
- Interaction requiring a mouse click rather than a key stroke
- Failure to use inbuilt headings and styles for word processed documents, which prevents users from taking advantage of alternative reading layouts.

There are many other examples, but these are common barriers which could be overcome if awareness of inclusive digital practice was given a greater priority. As mentioned earlier, it is common for creators of digital content to assume a narrow range of access criteria rather than being aware of a diverse range of delivery modes. Unfortunately, it remains the case that digital design is primarily taught for the needs of visual users and the Internet continues to develop into an increasingly visual environment, one where style is privileged over substance and appearance over usability. Over the past decade, while the university has adopted multiple digital ways of working and user-generated content has become integral to daily working practice, it has failed to promote inclusive digital practices. One area in particular which is causing increasing access problems within teaching and learning is the adoption of commercial e-resources including e-journal and e-book platforms. While on the one hand they offer wider availability of core texts and their facilities to annotate and extract content are improving, on the other they have complex navigation structures and significant inconsistencies in style. The advantages of providing reading content online are diluted by their general inaccessibility to proprietary screen reading and text narration software. Similar limitations are found within increased use of collaborative online opportunities such as blogs and wikis and with experiments with social networking tools and data management mechanisms like RSS feeds. The value of the technology in supporting diversity has been diluted by policy guidelines which have side-lined the accessibility of digital resources into the disability arena, resulting in digital exclusion remaining a largely invisible discrimination. To investigate this further, it will be useful to pay attention to the wider social background beyond the university and in particular to the contemporary location of disability alongside other determinants of socially inclusive practice.

Invisible Publics

The language, or discursive practices, used to label categories of social exclusion are fluid and changing by nature (Foucault 1980). As a result, these categories can become culturally repositioned in response to external pressures and influences. Underpinning this shifting landscape of identities can be found hierarchical social systems which favour an inequality of resource distribution on the one hand, while promoting explanations for disadvantage on the other (Foucault 1988). Disability studies offer clear examples of this dichotomy. Individuals with physical, sensory or cognitive impairment have been discriminated against historically on the ground of deficit medical diagnosis, a dominant view which remained unchallenged until the late twentieth century and calls for raised awareness of the social nature of barriers to participation. The medical barriers model was replaced with a social model, whereby discrimination was perceived as resulting from society failing to make provision for a broad enough range of difference. In the twenty-first century, it can be useful to apply this barriers model to digital exclusion where, while the technology exists to ensure digital equity, the range of barriers preventing inclusion is non-technical in origin.

There may be a need for a more sophisticated understanding of the ways in which the digital parameters of access reflect broader social inequalities, in particular in new knowledge societies where the redistribution of resources privileges the transfer of digital information. Research into unequal access to ICT within higher education identifies the social groups most likely to be digitally excluded as those already experiencing social exclusion (van Dijk 2006). This aligns with findings from the UK government Digital Participation agenda which describes those most at risk of digital discrimination including older people, those in low income households, people with no formal qualifications, disabled people, new immigrants and those living in geographically remote communities (BIS 2010). The parallels between digital exclusion and groups already marginalized and disadvantaged suggests the potential for digital discrimination may not yet be fully realized. The role of the university, as a producer of the citizens of the future, should include the critical function of identifying and challenging the unequal power structures which afford privilege. This chapter suggests that of particular importance is the need for higher education to address issues of digital exclusion and provide institutional support for equitable digital practice. In order to do this effectively, the structures which support discrimination must be visible and their destruction must be considered to have value. If new digital ways of working are to be made available to all then it is critical that accessible digital practices become fundamental to the university's philosophy. The side-lining of accessibility issues into the disability arena has blurred the boundaries which delineate responsibility for digital inclusion and it is to these blurred boundaries this chapter next turns.

Future Digital Exclusions

Increased adoption of ICT within the university mirrors the broader social shift towards the affordances of the Internet. Fundamental to these new digital practices is their social shaping (Bijker 1989). Not only does inaccessibly designed digital data exclude users who operate outside a narrow range of access criteria, it effectively silences analogue voices by denying them access to the new digital platforms of the public sphere. The university of future must take the lead in offering opportunities for critical debate, in particular addressing issues of social inequality and giving voice to narratives of marginalization and exclusion. In a challenge to market solutions to the financial problems of higher education in the US, Burawoy asks 'Do we have to abandon the very idea of the university as a "public good?"' (Burawoy 2005b: 4). The answer has to be a resounding 'no' and several chapters in this book suggest how students can be empowered to question traditional ways of working. The re-design of teaching and learning within disciplines such as social work already seeks out narratives of exclusion to inform education and practice (SCIE 2004). If higher education is to prepare socially responsible citizens for the future good of society, increased awareness of the consequences of inequitable practices is essential. The lens of digital exclusion has a unique contemporary relevance due to the pervasive nature of the Internet and the dual capacity of the technology to enable and deny access. However, bringing the issues to the surface can be problematic. This is partly due to existing marginalization of publics rendered invisible through lack of participation in public spheres, but also because of the shifting parameters of categories of social exclusion.

Changes in cultural attitudes towards difference can be evidenced by the history of anti-discriminatory legislation designed for the protection of minority or non-traditional groups. It is a comparatively short history which derives from the identity politics movements in the late twentieth century, and gave rise to the first protected categories of gender, race and disability (DfEE 1995). This triad has recently been extended to include age (within the workplace), marriage or civil partnership (within the workplace), sexuality, gender reassignment, pregnancy and faith/religious belief. These are currently 'protected characteristics' against which discrimination directly, indirectly or through association is illegal (DWP 2010). Following in the footsteps of SENDA (DfEE 2001), the Single Equality Act reaffirms the specific association between access to information and disability. It does not make explicit the mass development of digital information over the past decade or its unique power for digital democracy and fails to identify alternative social determinants of access such as age, gender, location or cultural restrictions. However, what the act does is to use language which puts the stress on the individual having difficulty with digital access, rather than the digital environment being incorrectly designed. This is a worrying echo of the medical barriers model whereby disability was perceived as a personal deficit (Oliver 2009). While the Act draws attention to discriminatory practices, the subtle use of language suggests that the individual rather than wider society is the source of these barriers. As such, it fails to challenge broader social attitudes towards social difference. This raises concern for groups at risk of digital exclusion in the future. On the one hand, as can be seen within higher education, the need for inclusive practice with access to information has primarily been associated with the disability arena; on the other, within the wider society, the social category of disability itself is being subsumed into generic equality issues. The risk is that attention to unique identity and the rights necessary for valuing diversity is becoming diluted and, in places, seems to become invisible.

The very word disability has a complex history, which involves social attitudes of fear. Society has traditionally dealt with diversity through incarceration; from the mediaeval Ship of Fools, set afloat to sail permanently on the oceans, to purpose-built Victorian asylums and institutions designed to render impairment invisible (Foucault 1988). It has been mentioned above that contemporary use of the word disability derives from the social barriers model, which called for recognition that individuals did not have disabilities, instead they were disabled by society. As the language of the Single Equality Act suggests, this distinction appears to be fading. It is worth noting that Burawoy, calling for public sociology in the university to 'make visible the invisible' (Burawoy 2005b: 8), lists gender, race and class as categories of marginalization, but fails to mention disability. In an ideal world, examples of absence might suggest that diversity has been recognized and barriers to participation identified and removed. Unfortunately, this does not appear to be the case and this chapter has shown how using a narrow range of access criteria to control digital access is not only reiterating and reinforcing exclusion, it is also rendering it invisible.

Discriminatory Practices

Deal (2007) applied the principles of aversive racism to disability discrimination, suggesting that individuals are not overtly discriminatory but where statutory legislation has reduced instances of blatant discrimination, it gives rise to more subtle forms of prejudice instead. Individuals do not recognize themselves as exhibiting discriminatory behaviours. 'Aversive disablists recognize disablism is bad but do not recognize that they themselves are prejudiced. Likewise, aversive disablism, like aversive racism, is often unintentional' (Deal 2007: 97). The effectiveness of legislation in modifying discriminatory behaviour is limited. The language of prejudice may have changed, with certain words and phrases no longer in current use, but the human problem of being uncomfortable when faced with difference remains. Future advances in challenging the discrimination of minority groups will only be supported if they can be seen to promote the self-interest of the majority, otherwise they will not materialize (Deal 2007). This can be usefully applied to digital exclusion. Individuals already operating effectively within the MEE model do so within a narrow range of access criteria, therefore alterations in habitual ways of working are unlikely where there is no perception of personal benefit. As a result, the inadvertent contribution to oppressive digital practice is not unusual. 'The conscious actions of many individuals daily contribute to maintaining and reproducing oppression, but those people are usually simply doing their jobs or living their lives and do not understand themselves as agents of oppression' (Young 1990: 41–42).

Discrimination derives from lack of knowledge and privileges culturally discursive practice over personal experience. Social labels, when accompanied by attributions of stereotypical behaviour, often have unfortunate connotations with deficit images and traditions. Prejudice based on fear of difference has deep roots, making elimination unlikely and attempts at control through statutory means a tokenistic alternative. Social attitudes towards maintaining discrimination are becoming more sophisticated. For example, Freire (1972) has suggested the use of a 'banking concept' within education where disadvantaged individuals are taught passive acceptance of the world as it is, together with its structural inequalities. This unquestioning acceptance informs a lack of action, thereby condoning and replicating the structures of oppressive practice. Mullaly (2002) examines some of the ways in which citizens are persuaded, at an unconscious level, to comply with and contribute to their marginalization. Dominant groups, and in particular the media distribution of content reinforcing negative categories of the Other, have a powerful impact on personal identity.

These socially constructed differences are then used by the dominant group as the bases and rationale not only for appropriating most of society's resources and political influence but for carrying out acts of prejudice and discrimination against subordinate group members. Such acts can be either conscious and aggressive or more likely today unconscious and aversive. Unconscious and aversive acts of oppression are much more difficult to contravene since, given their nature, they seldom can be legislated against (Mullaly 2002: 70).

Post-structural discourse has also contributed to the social acceptance of oppressive practice. Traditional categories of identity and knowledge have been challenged, giving rise to linguistic games. Social reality is no longer a fixed knowable experience but has morphed into an uncertain landscape, delineated only by the shifting parameters of multiple ways of knowing. The term inclusion, as favoured by politicians, offers an example of the ease with which meaning can be obscured. The definition refers to the bringing together of disparate parts into a whole, in particular with regard to recognizing and valuing diversity. But without making public the specific measures for action necessary to challenge exclusive practices, the word becomes a cultural contradiction (Delanty 2003: 76). Closer examination of policy designed for inclusion reveals reinforcements of existing conditions which results in greater, not less inequality. 'Even as the rhetoric of equality and freedom intensifies so sociologists have documented ever-deepening inequality and domination.' (Burawoy 2005b: 4). The contradiction can be applied to widening participation directives in higher education, whereby promises to broaden access through technology to non-traditional students favoured those who could operate within a narrow range of access criteria. Those with ability but with diverse ways of working were marked out as different and continued to have equitable access denied. Without specific measures for breaking down the barriers of exclusive practice, promises of inclusion will continue to be cancelled out by existing conditions and continue to be at best tokenistic and at worst completely ignored.

The University as a Site of Social Justice

The university of the future is likely to become increasingly reliant on digital ways of working and the production of digital research and knowledge. The reconstitution of the university as public space will require democratization in the way knowledge is produced and disseminated. Universities have invested heavily in networks and infrastructures to enable digital communication, information and the flexible distribution of teaching and learning content. However, this has largely been constrained by a narrow range of access criteria, which fails to take into account the diverse ways in which computers are used and interaction with digital environments is enabled.

Addressing the divisive nature of digital data and the management of digital access should be generic to the future development of all learning landscapes. It has already been argued in Chapters 4 and 5 that an increased focus on the student experience and supporting the concept of students as active producers rather than passive consumers of knowledge encourages critical examination of the relationships between knowledge and power and the discursive practices through which they are mediated. If the university of the future is serious about challenging the restraints of marketization and reforming itself as an institution of the public sphere (Delanty 2003), it has a vital role to play in the education and training of future citizens. This includes addressing issues of social exclusion and marginalization and nowhere is this more important in a digital society than ensuring digital democracy for its public spheres.

McLean (2006) suggests the university adopt a role of emancipation and transformation, with the goals of social justice at its heart, so 'critical university pedagogy would take up the functions of universities to educate citizens and professionals who can tackle injustices and social problems' (McLean 2006: 19). Links between existing categories of social exclusion and individuals most likely to be digitally excluded indicate that access will continue to be denied to those already marginalized and disempowered. Unless the university increases focus on the social inequalities that inform and enable digital participation, it is in danger of reproducing and reiterating external oppression. One way forward is to address the issues directly through generic social justice modules for all first year undergraduate students. These would offer public commitment to the principles of social justice. It would fit well within the parameters of conceptualizing the student as producer rather than consumer and offer a lens for viewing the deeper cultural causes informing structural inequality. Van Dijk (2006) suggests the most conspicuous fact with regard to understanding digital exclusion is that digital divides have not been discussed against 'the background of a general theory of social inequality; other types of inequality or even a concept of human inequality in general' (van Dijk 2006: 212). Doing this would involve critical analysis of the contradictions and debates between state and market as regulatory factors and the conditions for participation in the public sphere.

The university also needs to take steps to ensure equity of digital access on campus. This will initially be more demanding of resources, both in terms of people and finances, and will require personal commitment and motivation. Seale (2009) describes how a higher education built on the theoretical frameworks of inclusion and social justice

demands a commitment to adopting a political stance that actively seeks to challenge discrimination, exclusion and unwillingness to change things. Inclusion and social justice research stems from passionate outrage rather than dispassionate interest. Research underpinned by inclusion and social justice theories cannot be neutral. (Seale 2009: 15)

Research informed by policy and procedure which supports the alleviation of anti-oppressive practice is fundamental to a university of the future that supports public fairness and individual empowerment.

Conclusion

This chapter suggests that digital inclusion is set to become a new, divisive category of social exclusion, the full effects of which might not yet be realized. Individuals denied digital access may constitute the new invisible public of the future, doubly disempowered through barriers to digital lifestyles as well as to a public sphere which makes increasing use of digital platforms for discussion and debate. Awareness of digital exclusion has been marginalized into the disability arena, and while access for users of assistive technology is of critical importance, attention must also be paid to the wider social determinants of digital participation such as age, gender, language and cultural background.

Issues of digital exclusion have to be made public. Citizens who are rendered invisible need to be identified and given a public identity. Without a focused drive towards digital inclusion, the technology that enables access will continue also to deny it and those already marginalized and disadvantaged will be further disempowered.

The university of the future has a critical role to play in addressing these issues and taking positive steps to ensure it does not reproduce and replicate wider social inequalities on campus. All staff and students should have opportunities to engage in effective and rewarding digital practices. Ensuring their confidence and competence, and promoting digitally inclusive ways of working, will ensure that when they move out into wider social spheres they take digitally inclusive ways of working and living with them.

This chapter ends where it began, with the Dearing Report (NCIHE 1997). In spite of criticism that the report is typical of the cultural contradiction of massification and democratization (Delanty 2003), it remains the first document to link the new information and communication technologies with widening participation in higher education for a public previously denied access for multiple reasons, prejudices and beliefs. Setting aside potential political motivation, it is useful to revisit Dearing's conclusion:

'above all, there remains an urgent need for institutions to understand better and respond to the challenges and opportunities of the emerging information age' (NCIHE 1997: 13.57). We should no longer be seduced by the rhetoric of ICT. Instead, attention needs to be paid to the ways in which technology reinforces existing oppressive practice. The university of the future needs to address the challenges and opportunities of its time and play a critical part in ensuring solutions and practices are inclusive and empowering. The greatest challenge of all may be the pervasive influence of the Internet on digital ways of working in the twenty-first century and the uncovering of the potential implications for those for whom access to digital participation is being denied.

Part Three:

Teaching as a Public Activity

(Edited by Mike Neary)

In the final section of this book, the nature of the relationship between higher education and the state is explored more fully. This analysis provides a lens through which to contemplate a version of the concept of public that can be defended against the apparently inevitable onslaught of the private sector and commercialization.

In Chapter 7, Morris and Stevenson are very clear about the importance of teachers going beyond the institutional limits of their current working arrangements. Based on an analysis of a peer-observation scheme, they suggest that the current provision for improving teaching quality is likely to become increasingly characterized by surveillance and sanctions framed around managerialist notions of quality. They argue that observations are most useful when the review process is owned by the participants, rather than conducted as a bureaucratic managerial exercise. The issue of ownership provides ways for teachers to reclaim their teaching and go beyond the institutional frameworks in which they currently function. This sense of ownership extends to opening up their work to fellow teachers so as to encourage a more rigorous critique, based on a reconstructed notion of teaching and learning and the purpose of higher education.

The chapters by Beckton and Winn point to a vocabulary through which this radical discourse might be articulated: critical political economy. Both Beckton and Winn discuss the changes in higher education in terms of the significant social forces that shape the ways in which struggles between notions of the private and public are played out in practice. In Chapter 8, Beckton explores the way in which the use of technology in teaching has tended to make teaching less public and more privatized. His argument is framed in the context of critical political economy and the historical development of machinery to intensify the capitalist labour process. Beckton's argument is that, despite the appeal of digital devices, the logic of their production is to enhance the production of surplus value and to intensify work. His view is that technology has tended to exacerbate the commercialization of the student experience and the working lives of academics. He argues for a labour process based around the concept of sharing, citing the examples of Wikipedia and Academic Commons as ways in which this more collaborative process might be taken forward.

In Chapter 9, Winn examines Open Education Resources (OERs), starting with the Cape Town Open Education Declaration, then exploring one of the major sources of OERs, MIT's OpenCourseWare, locating his analysis within a framework derived from critical political economy. He analyzes, in terms of the labour theory of value, the potential for OERs to become a new pedagogical material. He argues that OERs fail to live up to their progressive potential because they are based on the emancipation of things, rather than the emancipation of labour, or of people. OERs might well be freely distributed but they are made by wage labour rather than free labour, on behalf of higher education institutions for whom generating a monetary surplus is still an overwhelming preoccupation. Winn argues that in order to create a genuinely open and emancipated form of teaching in public it is necessary to create a new form of social wealth. This is to be based not on the commodified form of things, to be appropriated by consumers in accordance with the capitalist law of value, but rather on knowledge at the level of society, to be re-appropriated by the people who produced it.

In the final chapter, Neary synthesizes the ideas and practices discussed in this volume in order to attempt to provide an alternative version of the concept of public within the context of higher education, an alternative that might be able to stand up to the law of value and commercialization. Neary frames this radical discourse within critical political economy and with reference to the law of value. He traces the historical development of the idea of the modern European university – the speculative university – and looks for ways to ground it in the everyday practices of university teachers and their students, some of which are identified in this book. This leads Neary to argue against the current notion of public good framed within the so-called knowledge economy and to argue for a notion of publicness, or teaching in public, based on the idea of a knowing society.

Chapter 7

Making Teaching Public: Cracking Open Professional Practice

Aileen Morris and Howard Stevenson

Introduction

As was shown in the first three chapters of this volume, the history of higher education in England is, at least in part, a history of the tensions between public and private provision. By the end of the twentieth century, the emphasis on private provision was predominant and from the publication of the Dearing Report (NCIHE 1997) onwards there have been calls for the higher education sector to demonstrate the effectiveness of the teaching and student learning experiences that they offer. Within the HE sector, there is no equivalent to the school teacher's Qualified Teacher Status, and the academic's relationship to teaching, as opposed to scholarship, has sometimes been presented as ambivalent. Most recently, the Browne Report (2010) into higher education funding has returned to concerns about teaching quality and, for example, has argued that potential students should be made aware of the proportion of staff, teaching on courses, who possess some form of teaching qualification.

Since the Dearing Report (NCIHE 1997), and the publication of the framework for higher education quality (QAA 2000), the HE sector's response to these concerns has emerged in a variety of forms. Significant developments were the establishment of the Institute for Learning and Teaching in Higher Education, later the Higher Education Academy, and its publication of the UK Professional Standards Framework for teaching and supporting learning in higher education (HEA 2006). HEFCE's introduction of the Teaching Quality Enhancement Fund (HEFCE 2009b) and the embedding of institutional strategies for learning and teaching provided another example of an initiative focused on enhancing teaching and learning quality. At an institutional level, and as part of this drive, many universities adopted some form of teaching observation scheme in which academics engaged in observing and feeding back on each other's practice.

In this chapter, the authors seek to analyse the role of teacher observation in the form in which it has emerged most commonly in the HE sector: peer observation schemes. Such schemes are now common across universities but have often struggled for an identity as they have been viewed as both a valuable opportunity to engage in reflective practice and to further an emphasis on teaching in public and yet one more addition to the armoury of managerial controls linked to private provision. The tensions within these debates will be explored, both through an analysis of the literature relating to peer observation and through an analysis of data collected from staff at the University of Lincoln relating to their experience and perceptions of engaging with peer observation.

Arising from these tensions some have suggested (for example, Gosling and Mason O'Connor 2009: 7) that there is a need to go 'beyond peer observation' and, as a means of understanding and improving teaching, to develop schemes that are more clearly rooted in the philosophies and principles associated with reflective public practice. In this chapter, the authors support much of this analysis but argue that it remains necessarily limited. Principally, this is because the schemes themselves continue to be rooted within an institutional framework concerned with quality, which is often narrowly defined, unclear and not shared in the sense that those who teach and those who monitor the teaching will have different views as to what quality means. Is it quality as value for money; quality as fit for purpose or quality as transforming? (Harvey and Green 1993). More often than not, quality in teaching is more concerned with identifying those who are lacking the necessary skills and approaches: a deficit model of teaching focused on the idea of the bad teacher. The danger is that as the Browne (2010) agenda spreads its tentacles the HE sector will increasingly be drawn into Ofsted-style assessments with, perhaps, results published to help inform student choice. The inevitable consequence will be safe and choreographed teaching, avoiding risk wherever possible. The dead hand of standardization and uniformity will weigh heavy on the system.

The key concern here is that existing forms of peer observation, or peer review, are not sufficiently independent from the institution, howsoever described. They will not, therefore, be able to withstand the power and pervasiveness of the post-Browne quality agenda, reinforced by the discipline of market forces that Browne is determined to unleash. The danger is that academics will internalize the new discourse and adapt their practice accordingly. Peer review systems will not challenge this agenda, but reinforce it.

In this chapter, it will be argued that teachers in higher education must go 'beyond the beyond'. Teachers in higher education need to reclaim their teaching, but to do so they must transcend the institutional frameworks within which they currently function. This requires a transformation of practice in which teaching is reclaimed, not by hiding it from the monitors and the inspectors, but by cracking it wide open to everyone – peers, students and the public. This is not simply a process of making teaching more open; crucially, it involves opening up our teaching to a much more rigorous critique from those involved in the teaching and learning process. It is argued in this chapter that teachers can reclaim their teaching, but only if they let go of it and make teaching and its observation more public.

Teaching Observed – By Whom, How and for What Purpose?

Words are important. They convey meaning in powerful ways, but they also carry dissonance and disputes about meaning. This is certainly the case with regard to the term teaching observation. All teaching is observed in some form since for teaching to take place there needs to be a learner. But, references to teaching observation very seldom include the learner in the process being described. Rather, teaching observation suggests the involvement of another – an individual outside the teacher–learner relationship. The involvement of observers of teaching is nothing new, but what is new is the scale of observation, the complexity of forms and in some cases the consequences of outcomes. This is particularly prevalent in the school and further education sectors where the impact of Ofsted, with its judgements of teaching quality based on grades, combined with performance management requirements, has driven an enormous increase in the scale of observations being undertaken.

Within higher education the rash of observation by numbers has not, thus far, become widely established. The grading of teaching by external observers or the requirement to be observed teaching by a line manager as part of an appraisal or performance management process have not, as yet, become established in UK higher education. It may well be, however, that the Browne Report (2010) represents a step in this direction and it remains to be seen to what extent the clamour for consumer information leads to the introduction of some form of grade for teaching quality and, thus, a rating for not just the individual but perhaps the institution? To date, in higher education teaching, observation has been much more closely associated with processes of peer observation whereby individual institutions generate their own models and policies, and processes tend to be underpinned, at a rhetorical level at least, by commitments to reflection and development. That said, the drive for peer observation has its roots in the same clamour for quality and accountability that has been experienced in the school and FE sector, but has thus far tended to play out very differently in higher education institutions (HEIs). The focus on quality in HEIs became most apparent in the QAA *Handbook on Academic Review* (QAA 2000). Following the QAA's publication of this guidance, HEIs have sought to develop and embed peer observation schemes as a means of not only improving the quality of teaching, but also as a means of being seen to be attentive towards issues of teaching quality; a focus on peer observation systems is frequently part of the process of institutional audit, the principal means by which UK HEIs are evaluated by the QAA.

This brief outline of issues relating to peer observation within HEIs highlights the tensions and contradictions that are a feature of peer observation processes in the university sector. At one level, peer observation schemes tend to espouse commitments to development and reflection; principles of ownership and empowerment are typically cited (Cosh 1999, Hammersley-Fletcher and Orsmond 2004, 2005). At another level, peer observation schemes are rooted in the quality agenda, participation is often mandated (although not always closely monitored) and links to more formal elements of the performativity agenda such as appraisal and the murky world of university merit pay systems remain unclear. Attempts to unpick these contradictory impulses are in part assisted by Gosling's (2005) presentation of three distinct models of peer observation of teaching, an approach that is widely cited and continues to offer a useful framework for analysing peer observation schemes.

The approach most closely aligned to the QAA's demands for quality is referred to as the evaluation model. This is firmly based on a hierarchical approach in which senior and more experienced colleagues undertake the observation of subordinates. The principal purpose is to form a judgement in relation to performance and capability, and the process may be linked directly to key elements of career progression (confirmation of probation, appraisal, applying for promotion). While there may be some potential for constructive feedback and support for improvement, at its most elementary level, the evaluation model turns observation into a test of competence. Judgements are restricted to assessing whether appropriate performance thresholds are being achieved and whether or not teaching is fit for purpose. This model is later described in this chapter as a managerialist model. Gosling (2005) contrasts this with a development model that focuses less on judgements with respect to the meeting of minimum standards and more on identifying the processes necessary to support development. In this model, observations tend to be undertaken by more experienced colleagues or educational developers, and there remains a clear implication that the role of the observer is to impart their expertise for the benefit of the observed as a means of charting a path towards improvement.

The final model presented by Gosling (2005) is identified as the collaborative model. This is principally defined by its rejection of the hierarchical approach common to both the previous models. Observation can be undertaken by colleagues who may have no obvious source of seniority in relation to the observed colleague, indeed they may be junior in status and/or experience to that colleague. A key principle of this approach is that the observee owns the process; they choose the colleague that they wish to act as the observer. In this model, even the term observation becomes contested. Observation implies a largely disconnected relationship between the observer and observee with the former observing, analysing and feeding back. In the collaborative model, the process may be viewed as a more co-operative process in which both participants are engaged in a common endeavour via a professional discussion in researching an element of professional practice. For these reasons, the term review is often used in preference to observation.

The differences highlighted by Gosling's (2005) models point to the limits and potential of peer observation as a process. Debates tend to focus on the tensions within peer observation, between its use as a sophisticated framework to ensure academics' compliance with a quality agenda that they would otherwise resist, and its potential to offer a more radical alternative, one in which professional dialogue relating to professional practice is encouraged between autonomous academics. The question remains whether peer observation promotes genuine staff development 'deeper learning through reflective practice and, thereby, acquisition and development of teaching competencies' (Shortland 2004: 219–20) or serves as a mechanism for ensuring staff compliance and conformity. Similarly, Peel (2005) questions whether peer observation provides only an instrumental way to address technical issues in teaching, or whether it has the potential to act as a more transformatory tool, capable of bringing about genuine personal change and growth. She concludes that peer observation does have such potential provided that it is not seen as a quick fix for problems, but is located within a much broader and longer-term perspective on professional development. Institutions need to be 'explicit about what . . . *peer observation of teaching is intended to achieve, responsible about how it is* resourced and articulate clearly how staff and students may engage with and benefit from the process' (Peel 2005: 501).

Peel (2005) draws on debates relating to structure and agency to evaluate to what extent peer observation of teaching can either confirm the *status quo* or be transformatory. A balance that favours structural influences limits progressive potential; those involved in the process of peer review are subsumed within systems and cultures that compel an adaptation to institutional norms. If, in contrast, there appears to be more scope for agency, then individuals and groups of individuals begin to have more space within which to work in potentially transformatory ways. Our argument in this chapter is that if the progressive potential of peer observation is to be maximized then it is essential that academic staff are able to identify where such spaces exist, understand how such spaces might be best exploited and appreciate the need to work collectively to open out the spaces within which progressive work can take place. In a climate in which the structural pressures of academic capitalism (Slaughter and Leslie 1997) are intensifying and the emphasis is increasingly on private modes of provision, the need to work in progressive and more public ways becomes even more critical.

Experiencing Peer Observation – Pitfalls and Potentialities

In this section, the perspectives of academic staff at the University of Lincoln are explored and discussed in relation to the university's Peer Observation of Teaching Scheme which was established in 2002. In so doing, the authors seek to illustrate the tensions which have been identified in the literature and which relate to key features of peer observation as a process. The scheme was intended to be undertaken by all academic staff. Participation was monitored both by departments and formally through the university's quality procedures whereby course programme leaders were asked to confirm whether or not all staff had undertaken peer observation. The process was based on an annual cycle; a key feature was the principle that the observee chose their observer, which can be related to Gosling's (2005) collaborative model described above. Departments were encouraged to establish Peer Observation Scheme co-ordinators to oversee processes locally and to encourage engagement.

In 2008, as part of a commitment to evaluate and revise the scheme in light of the evaluation outcomes, it was decided to conduct a survey of the scheme with regard to participation and operation at a local level. Following collection and analysis of the results, the purpose was then to improve and develop the scheme, specifically for its potential to enhance practice both locally and across the university. Two separate questionnaires were sent out and completed online: one to heads of departments and one to academic teaching staff. The data here draws on results from the questionnaire completed by academic teaching staff, which contained both closed questions and free text responses. Just over 30 per cent of staff responded (152). Academic staff were asked how the scheme was managed in their department. They were also asked questions relating to scheme awareness, their experience of it, managing participation and non-participation, practice relating to the selection of observers and broader opinions about the impact and value of the scheme. A report was written where a small number of possible directions were presented for consideration and discussion (Morris and Saunders 2009).

Among respondents, participation in the scheme was generally high, but may arguably be higher among respondents than non-respondents. Seventy-four per cent of respondents indicated that they had participated in the scheme as an observer and 85 per cent had participated in the scheme as an observee. Sixteen per cent of respondents indicated that they had not been observed within the scheme in the previous 12 months. Of those who had been involved, the vast majority had undertaken one or two sessions as observers (56 per cent) or as observees (70 per cent). However, in a small number of cases the process had clearly become more substantial, with five or more sessions being reported by some observers and observees. Practice between departments could vary considerably, particularly in the way that staff were made aware of the scheme and encouraged to engage with it. Where a department had a Peer Observation Scheme co-ordinator, there did appear to be correspondingly higher levels of engagement. As is often the case, a key success factor appeared to derive from the personal interests and motivations of one individual; where this factor was not present then more limited participation was likely.

A number of questions sought to ascertain colleagues' perceptions of the effectiveness and impact of the scheme, both at a personal level and, more widely, in their curriculum area. A cluster of questions focused on these issues generated the following results.

It is clear from the rated responses that a significant proportion of colleagues see a benefit from the scheme, both for themselves personally and across their wider curriculum areas, although there is also a significant number who 'neither agree nor disagree': a result which might suggest that there is some uncertainty, ambivalence and/or fence-sitting. Interestingly, within the 113 free text responses, 51 per cent commented on the scheme in a positive way, 33 per cent were negative and 16 per cent were read as either neutral or ambivalent. 'It is what you make of it', one respondent commented. The most common benefits identified related to the space for personal reflection, collegial discussion around practice, and the particular benefit of having another person offer feedback and critique. There was also recognition that, too often, good and committed teaching passes by unacknowledged and that, in a world dominated by Research Excellence Frameworks, commitment to good teaching can be overlooked. Peer observation provided an opportunity to redress that imbalance and colleagues valued a focus on this aspect of their work (it is, after all, what the majority of them spend most of their time doing) and an affirmation that their teaching was sound. One respondent commented

> I find peer observation to be very worthwhile both for observer and for observee IF the reason for being observed comes from some need/desire on the part of one of the participants rather than as a necessity to say that it has been done for some administrative reason. Being observed when trying out a new teaching method or in order to assess whether some aspect of teaching practice is successful or not is empowering. Watching someone else's teaching I find to be MORE useful however. It allows the observer to be exposed to novel ideas which can be incorporated into one's own teaching. Even when one only recognizes one's own practices then this can also be affirming.

Where there were criticisms of the scheme, or concerns about its lack of impact, a number of issues were identified. As has been indicated, much hinged on the extent to which the scheme was understood, effectively managed and valued at a local or departmental level. In a working environment characterized by multiple and competing demands, high workloads and pressing deadlines, often what gets done is what is signalled as being important. Where these signals were absent in relation to peer observation, it was correspondingly easier for the scheme to be left purely to the personal motivation of individual colleagues. At the same time, respondents were concerned about the scheme being too embedded within the bureaucratic structures of the university. While there was a recognition that some of the key principles of the scheme gave the observed ownership of the process, there were also concerns that peer observation formed part of a managerialist accountability agenda which was more concerned with quality than development. A typical comment offered by one respondent asserted 'It is vital that ownership is retained by the observed and the observer, and does not become a management tool for assessment'. Other common concerns related to the linked issues of scheme bureaucracy, the lack of time to undertake the process properly and the perception that participation was sometimes tokenistic.

Almost all of these issues reflect those identified in the literature presented earlier in this chapter. They highlight what seem like endemic dilemmas; for example, between the desire to keep the institution at arm's length from the process and allowing individuals to determine their own approaches, while also wanting the process to be valued, promoted and encouraged through institutional support. There can be, sometimes, a fine line between encouragement and coercion.

These dilemmas cannot easily be resolved. The question remains as to how productive is it to try to reconcile them. Rather, it is more useful to highlight the wider issue that emerged from the survey, specifically relating to what appeared to be a lack of understanding of the purpose, philosophy and values underpinning the peer observation scheme. For example, several respondents believed the scheme should be clearly located within a quality assurance model. They saw the scheme as designed to identify and remedy bad teaching and believed the overall approach should be both more systematic and standardized, with clear links to the appraisal process. Others recognized the notion of observer–observee ownership as a central tenet, and valued this. However, some questioned how robust the process was, indicating that it was relatively easy to not engage, either by avoiding participation altogether or negotiating a 'get it over and done with' approach with the chosen observer. This lack of understanding and ambivalence is perhaps confirmed by the high proportion of survey respondents who answered 'neither agree nor disagree' to all the questions presented in Table 1. These results resonate with the findings of a study which Kell and Annetts (2009) carried out on the perceived clarity, value and ownership of another peer review of teaching scheme, which led them to develop an approach where there was a closer match to the specific culture, needs, values and staff within one specific department.

Beyond Peer Observation

As has been indicated, the issues raised by the study at Lincoln are not unique. They mirror many of the benefits and problems that have been identified in peer observation schemes elsewhere (Shortland 2004, Peel 2005). As a result of some of these issues Gosling and Mason O'Connor,

Table 7.1 Results of peer observation scheme impact questionnaire

Statement	Strongly agree	Agree	Neither agree nor disagree	Dis-agree	Disagree strongly
The scheme has been useful in developing teaching practice in the department	8	32	37	18	5
I have, personally, found the scheme useful for improving my teaching practice	14	30	31	21	4
I believe the scheme is useful for improving my colleagues' teaching practice	8	44	31	13	4
I am satisfied with the way the scheme works at the University	5	30	32	28	5

Responses expressed as a percentage of total replies.

through the presentation of a series of case studies, make the case for going 'beyond peer observation' in favour of 'peer-supported review' (Gosling and Mason O'Connor 2009: 8). The relinquishing of the word observation is significant. The term conveys an unequal relationship and arguably links, in some form, the process of observing with that of making a judgement. Furthermore, the observer role is essentially passive in relation to the learning processes taking place. The observer remains external to the process – on the outside, objective, neutral. Gosling and Mason O'Connors' (2009) preference for the word review begins to rebalance the relationship, with the reviewer taking a more active role, indeed responsibility, for the process. Peer-supported review is presented as a conversation or dialogue in which both reviewer and reviewee (terms which may not be appropriate, given the argument being presented here) are engaged in interrogating some aspect of professional practice. Crucially, both participants are seen as learning from the process; either equally, or perhaps the reviewer even more so. What is significant is that the role of reviewer as expert is explicitly rejected. Teaching is recognized as being an embedded cultural practice (Boud 1999) and learning as complex and contextual (Prosser and Trigwell 1999) and thus, understood as a problematic process in which it is acknowledged that it is difficult to make claims about what is known about what works, where and under what circumstances. The challenge is to deconstruct as a precursor to developing an enhanced understanding.

Notwithstanding some of the issues described earlier, the peer-supported review model has considerable potential and represents a significant advance on many of the more managerialist models of peer observation that are common across the sector. However, the question remains as to whether it remains, fundamentally, a tweaking of peer observation and, as such, fails to embrace the radicalism required to address many of the criticisms levelled at it. While recognizing the progressive potential of peer-supported review, there are two key limitations which ensure it can act as no more than a staging post to something more fundamental and potentially transformatory. First, it seems likely that peer-supported review models are intended to work within the same paradigm within which peer-observation schemes currently function. Peer-supported review focuses more explicitly on development, but continues to nod in the direction of quality assurance systems. As such, it is likely to possess many of the features of peer observation. For example, although models may vary, the most common approach is likely to be a paired reviewee–reviewer model (or some very limited variation on a theme). Moreover, the intention to make clear that peer-supported review is *not* part of a performance management system is likely to reinforce the notion that all discussions and records are the property of the reviewee. Only the reviewee can choose whether to use the evidence generated for some other purpose, such as an appraisal or a promotion process. Although this appears to set peer-supported review against the managerialist agenda (through asserting the primacy of reviewee ownership), it effectively connects it by working within the same framework and playing by the same rules. The aim must not be to work to mitigate the impact of managerialism, but to transcend it – to establish and work within an alternative frame of reference.

This links to the second concern with peer-supported review, which is the tendency of these processes to focus on the micro, or technical, elements of teaching, that is on the detail of teaching practices. This focus is often driven by a conviction that something is wrong in one's teaching, and that it needs to be improved, indeed fixed. Such is the complexity of teaching that there is an almost infinite number of issues that might be the focus of a micro study of teaching practices, but the use of questioning techniques, or the provision of a particular form of feedback offer illustrative examples. There is no problem with the focus of reviews on these issues. The issues are important and a legitimate topic of reflective practice. However, there is a tendency within peer observation and peer-supported review for this to be the main element involved. Because such reviews are small scale, there is a tendency that they only ever focus on the micro. This is partly a practical response, but it is also a comfortable one. A focus on fixing a technical problem allows us to avoid more contentious issues.

The current argument is that any process of reflective practice must address the big questions, as well as the small ones. There is therefore a need to connect the micro to big and more controversial issues, and in so doing link our practices to wider questions relating to the purposes of education. What is education for? Who decides? Who benefits and who doesn't? How and why? How is my practice shaped by these big questions, and in turn, how can my practice reframe these questions and the answers they generate? Walker, in discussing her work with colleagues in educational action research, points to 'how a reconstructed professionalism in university teaching might be realised through a collaborative and reflexive professional dialogue regarding the ends and purposes of learning' (Walker 2001: 1) and how this might 'speak back' to a limited 'discourse which fails to centre the purposes of higher education teaching' (Walker 2001: 1). This opening up and reconstruction follows on from the points made in Chapter 1. Walker goes further in saying that: 'Indeed, lecturers in universities might be seen as having a professional duty to adopt an explicitly oppositional stance to policies that prioritise the external goods of the institution or militate against the internal goods of learning' (Walker 2001: 3).

The isolating focus on teaching in this way also, to some degree, plays into the hands of those who hope to manage and direct academic activity for specific purposes (income generation, research output or student satisfaction, for example). The activity of teaching is packaged and commodified in this sense and seen as something that can be captured and re-packaged although not, it is argued here, before it is reduced. Enhancement activity such as peer observation and peer review then becomes a mechanism for making something better at an individual level rather than making something better understood and shared at a collective level. There is an implicit encouragement that teaching is viewed as something neutral, while the context for teaching in higher education is neglected, and the tensions and dissonance in terms of teaching, research and the quality agenda are overlooked. Thus, the context in which academic labour takes place is, at best, ignored and, at worst, becomes invisible (Fanghanel and Trowler 2008).

Conclusion: Moving Beyond the Beyond – Making Teaching Public

Peer-supported review schemes are important and can have value. It is vital that HE teachers work to ensure that they embrace many of the guiding principles that Gosling and Mason O'Connor (2009) identify. However, it is also important to recognize that such approaches represent no more than a pushing at the boundaries of a progressive, but necessarily limited, approach to teaching. The argument here is that teachers and lecturers should be seeking to transcend these limitations, not just working within existing institutional paradigms, but helping to create new ones in which teaching becomes genuinely public. This involves, at one and the same time, teachers asserting control and ownership of their teaching (and thereby reclaiming it from the those who have sought to control teaching in the name of accountability), while also laying it open to others – students, peers and the public.

How might this look? The first point to assert is that this is not seen as a system, or a process, but as a movement – a movement of teachers that is committed to celebrating teaching and its transformatory potential. What is being suggested here takes place outside institutional frameworks. What is being proposed is untainted by bureaucracy because there is no bureaucracy. While institutional frameworks are inevitable, and academics must work within them, this movement sits outside those frameworks. As such, it represents a move towards teachers reclaiming their teaching through a reconstructed discourse around teaching, learning and the purposes of a higher education. Teaching needs to be intellectualized and any attempts to enhance what HE teachers do needs to be 'congruent with the lifeworld of academics' (McLean 2008: 151) in that it includes critical inquiry, reflective practice and the use of evidence. This, it is stated, could help to 'forge another discourse with which teachers will identify because it deals with the actualities of teaching and with goals for students that express a renewal of the critical and transformative role of the university' (McLean 2008: 151).

Trowler explores to what extent academic staff have been captured by the new higher education (NHE) discourse and its managerialist roots and emphasis on private provision and considers 'what factors condition their ability to displace, negotiate, reconstruct and create alternative repertoires' (Trowler 2001: 184). He points to the real potential for individuals to be 'empowered to resist the NHE discourse through the influence of various conditioning structures and through the agency incorporated in communities of practice operating within activity systems' (Trowler 2001: 196). Thus, the idea of communities of practice can be seen to be where knowledge and skill are recognized as socially constructed and distributed. From this, perhaps, there is hope that it is possible for staff to be engaged in constructing alternative, perhaps oppositional and more public, discourses around what constitutes good teaching. However, staff may, in fact, need to 'be "captured" by an alternative discourse' (Trowler 2001: 196).

As academics, we need to adopt critical theoretical positions which locate discourse in relation to power and resources and identify social inequities in terms of their effects to do whatever we can to render challengeable any one way of seeing the world. (Trowler 2001: 197)

Higher education has long been seen as a seat for and of resistance; at the time of writing, student and staff reaction to the Browne Report (2010) and the future financing of the university system pay testimony to this. Taylor (1999) argues that within higher education there is evidence of a growing respect for ambivalence and a valuing of scepticism. There is, therefore, the potential for academic staff to become players rather than pawns in the on-going processes of change. There is no pretence that this is easy. On the contrary, to work not only within and against prevailing systems, but also outside them, is always challenging. Each situation and each context needs to be navigated by those facing their own specific challenges and there can be no blueprint applicable to all. However, this complexity is not a weakness, but a strength. The strength derives from the quality of the dialogues about teaching when teaching practices are opened up to critical scrutiny. In this way, our teaching is problematized and deconstructed. The growing tendency (rampant in the Ofsted-driven school and FE sectors) to provide choreographed teaching to a universal design is explicitly rejected.

The key therefore is to take control of our teaching as a collective group of practitioners, while being willing to crack open our own teaching and to make it truly public. It is perhaps part of greater conversation where academics can find their voice and be able to articulate the sense of value for the university, given the marketization of the university sector where colleagues have become rivals (Rochford 2006). In so doing, there is a challenge to both the quack accountability of the marketeers and managerialists and also the fallaciousness of the 'teacher knows best' quasi-professionals. Nothing needs to be confidential, because confidentiality is only necessary in a system underpinned by surveillance and sanctions. This is real democratic practice in which the focus is not on individual performance, but where all HE teachers take collective responsibility for practice.

Our argument is that collective responsibility for teaching and learning emerges when, in the sense intended by Gramsci (1971), all academics recognize that they are both learner and teacher. Learning is enhanced when teaching is opened up and critiqued. This is not a process that takes place occasionally, once a year or every two years, to make sure a box is ticked, but is on-going and continuous. Nor is it a process in which two people lock themselves away and then exchange confidential notes in hushed tones – the dialogue needs to be much broader than that, genuinely involving peers and students in the process. Finally, and perhaps most importantly, this must not be a process that focuses only on the micro – the apparently technical adjustments to teaching required secure improvement. The micro in teaching is obviously important, and this is not an argument that it should be ignored. But its emergence as the sole focus of observations has more to do with Ofsted-style lesson grading ('thank you – your lesson was judged "satisfactory", this is what you should have done to make it "good"') and the pressure for conformity than with a genuine concern about enhancing learning. What is important here is that HE teachers are engaging in a broader critique of their teaching, in which day to day practice is located within much wider considerations relating to the purposes of education and its potential to either reproduce or transform. In making this case, the argument is being located within the need for a new approach to a teaching critique drawing on the principles of critical pedagogy (Freire 1972, McLean 2008).

What is being proposed sits outside existing frameworks. It is partly born out of a recognition that when living in difficult times, radical solutions are required. The current trajectory of HE policy towards an increasingly private provision threatens to unravel many of the central features of what many believe to be the core principles of a university education. There needs to be a stand taken that is in opposition to the potential Ofsted-ization of higher education envisaged by Browne (2010) and a move to celebrate all that is fundamental to a university education. This requires teachers and lecturers to expose the quack accountability of the market for the sham that it is. But this can only be done when teachers take control of their practice and open it up to real critique from those engaged in the same learning and teaching practice – by making both teaching and its observation a public exercise. In so doing, our work as teachers is not just democratic practice in action, but becomes part of the wider democratic values of our society.

Chapter 8

Public Technology: Challenging the Commodification of Knowledge

Julian Beckton

Introduction

Throughout the twentieth century, there has been a tension between the public provision of higher education – the perception of education as a public good – and the private provision, with the marketization and the commodification of education. As was seen in Chapter 3, by the start of the twenty-first century, the balance between provision as public and provision as private had swung heavily in the direction of the private. Now, however, there is a growing dissatisfaction with the concept of a university education as a private commodity bought by students primarily, if not solely, as an investment in their own future. Teaching in public is the notion that what students and teachers do should be engaged with the wider community that the university serves and critiques. The purpose of this chapter is to elucidate how this concept can be implemented.

The argument presented here is that the uncritical adoption of technology by those working in universities has, in the past, accentuated the tendency to commodify university education. Conditions have thus been created in which higher knowledge can be effectively privatized by creating spaces, such as virtual learning environments, that require institutions to invest in commercial products which serve to keep the public out. More subtly, other products require subscription to ostensibly free Web 2.0 services which harvest commercially valuable personal data which is then sold on to other services. This is a process inimical to the promotion of teaching in public since it renders the university a site of both capitalist production and of significant consumption. The position taken here is that higher knowledge is inherently a public good; the chapter suggests that it is possible to identify similarities between the conditions that gave rise to the nineteenth-century Luddite uprisings and the situation that modern academics find themselves in. While machine-breaking is not a course of action available to academics, the chapter goes on to suggest more positive ways in which technology can be adapted to serve a progressive, critical agenda that promotes student learning and social justice, and begins to reconfigure university education as a joint project between students, academic staff and the wider public.

The Commodification of Teaching

Teaching is, historically at least, a relatively private activity. It is true that the teacher and students share an experience of learning, but this is rarely extended beyond the classroom or lecture hall. Because teaching is not, generally, a public activity, it is often characterized inaccurately as a process in which information is transferred from the teacher to the learner, although this transmission model has been largely discredited by educational researchers in favour of what are sometimes described as constructivist models, which place greater emphasis on the student engaging in activities that promote learning (Biggs 2003, Laurillard 2002). This distinction is of interest in any discussion of the role of technology in higher education because, if teaching and learning are things that can be transmitted, there is an implication that they are effectively products, in the way that a piece of music or a holiday is a product. They have a start, an end and features in common with similar products. This is the conceptualization that has led to the growth of the inappropriate New Public Management attitudes to higher education as described in Chapters 1 and 4.

If teaching is a product, then technology can be seen as an opportunity to commodify university teaching; that is, in Marxist terms, to give it an exchange value beyond its use value. One result of this understanding of teaching has been the growth of claims that technology is going to have as profound (and negative) an effect on university education as it has had on the music and travel industries (Simmons 2001, Morgan 2010). Noble, for example, argues that by placing courses on-line, university administrations are 'now in a position to hire less skilled, and hence cheaper workers to deliver the technically prepackaged course' (Noble 2001: 32).

Universities' Use of Technology

Universities are a significant consumer of technology and many applications have been developed to service the needs of higher education. Perhaps the most pervasive of these applications has been the Virtual Learning

Environment (VLE). One study suggested that more than 95 per cent of universities have at least one VLE (Education for Change Ltd, The Research Partnership *et al.* 2005). Turnitin, a self-described plagiarism detection service developed by iParadigms, has over 9,500 institutional subscriptions, according to their own documentation (iParadigms LLC 2010).

Other examples of technologies produced to meet the needs of higher education include electronic voting systems for use in lecture theatres and lecture capture systems which record and make lecturers' performances available to students. On the administrative side, there exist student management systems and curriculum management systems. Finally, while not specifically designed for higher education, data analysis software packages such as NVivo and SPSS enjoy significant custom from the higher education sector. Higher education is also a significant consumer of office suites: word processors, spreadsheets, e-mail and presentation software that handle what might be described as the business side of any organization. Interestingly, many of these products have also been adapted for teaching.

The use of these products presents some problems for the university, which is itself a significant producer not only of knowledge, but of complexity (Barnett 2000). The ways in which these proprietary technologies are used serve to undermine its role as a producer of knowledge and to effectively discourage attempts at teaching in public. First, such technologies are often supplied under licence conditions that limit their use to members of the university, and thus maximize the sense of the university as being separate from society, rather than an integral part of it (you cannot read a Microsoft Word document if you do not have access to Microsoft Word). In effect, they privatize university education. In the case of the office products, this is mitigated somewhat by their ubiquity but, even here, different versions of word processed documents can present problems for tutors receiving student submissions produced in versions of the software that they are unable to read.

Secondly, these technologies open up spaces for capital to exploit the university, not only by creating a debate around ownership of intellectual property, but also by creating a sense of expectation among academics and students, along the lines of 'We're not a proper university if we don't have Blackboard or NVivo', or whatever product happens to be currently fashionable. Certainly, access to such technology can be and is used to market the university to potential students (Cornford and Pollock 2003) but again, the use of these technologies is inimical to attempts to teach in public, first because the public is largely unfamiliar with them, and, secondly, because in many cases a username and password, only available to members of the university community, is required to access them.

Thirdly, many of these technologies have themselves begun to influence university practices. Information technology, as the name implies, deals in information. Information is not, however, synonymous with knowledge, and the consequences can be unfortunate.

> the curriculum is reorganised as a sequence of knowledge gobbets (Bytesize as it is on the BBC revision website) which can be transferred as 'credits' and combined in novel ways with no guarantee of internal coherence – they are made 'readable' in the jargon of the Bologna Declaration. (Ball 2004: 5)

There are works that advocate precisely this kind of chunking of knowledge as a technique for managing change in higher education (Ford *et al.* 1996), and this kind of approach is becoming evident in the way VLEs are being used to provide 'lecture notes'. The emphasis here is on managing change, not necessarily on improving learning, although there is often quite a high level of student demand for this kind of service (Rolfe 2002); this is unsurprising if students are treated as consumers who are to be provided with knowledge in return for their tuition fees. As Ball (2004) suggests, chunking is a rather incoherent approach to pedagogy, but the danger for attempts to teach in public is that the chunks of knowledge themselves become private commodities, inaccessible to those who might be able to develop them by building them, or using them to build their own understandings of a new subject.

Finally, there are regulations concerning the use of technology, often arising from a quite proper concern to extend opportunity. As pointed out in Chapter 6, the Disability Discrimination Act (1995) in the UK states that no one should be denied access to a service by reason of a disability. In theory, academic staff providing electronic learning content should ensure that it is available in formats that are accessible by any student, irrespective of any potential disability. It is also the case that not having access to a computer connected to the Internet is, to all intents and purposes, a disability since the student cannot access electronic materials. Again in the UK, the Data Protection Act (Home Office 1998) requires that data about individuals is registered centrally and that individuals can request to see that data. These requirements are not in themselves unreasonable, but they do add to the workload of teachers and administrators wishing to take advantage of technology. Furthermore, technological products are often marketed as a solution to generic problems, taking no account of individual preferences. Even without the regulatory framework, which in many cases is largely ignored (Chapter 6), technology requires that its users constantly adapt it to their own, or their students' needs.

Given these difficulties, it is appropriate to ask why proprietary technologies have been relatively successful in universities. One likely reason is their claim to make life easier for users; there is undoubtedly something in this argument, especially where the software is conceptually similar to the task it is facilitating. A good example of this is Microsoft Word, where users are presented with a blank white screen and a keyboard, thus effectively mimicking a typewriter. Similarly, e-mail resembles traditional mail services. A user posts messages and receives them in an inbox, conceptually similar to a letterbox. The more successful Virtual Learning Environments appear to have learned this lesson so, for example, Blackboard offers spaces in which tutors can post learning materials, assignments, contact information, course announcements and so forth. Blackboard also allows individual course tutors to completely redesign their sites, although research by the author found that academics rarely take advantage of this facility (Beckton and Penney 2011). It is also the case that there are concerns about student privacy. Certainly, universities do have a legal responsibility under the Data Protection Act to keep personal data about students confidential.

Nearly all the commercial technologies designed for university teaching and learning support this provision by only permitting access through a password, a selling point for many applications. There is no doubt that this is an essential service, but it is, paradoxically, inimical to attempts to teach in public. After all an academic opinion is not personal data. As discussed below, academics are finding ways to overcome this difficulty. A final reason for the success of such systems is that technology, as Cornford and Pollock (2003) note, can be used as a marketing tool to attract students. It is hard to imagine a modern university that would not provide computer laboratories, Internet access, library catalogues and, increasingly, e-journal and e-book provision, along with software for creating assignments which, beyond the obvious word processing tools, might include quantitative analysis software, computer-aided design packages, video and audio production software and others appropriate to the disciplinary profile of the institution.

All these are an example of the way capital has successfully used technology as a mode of colonizing human activity, in order to maximize value from human labour. Initially, it appears that the adoption of these technologies reduces costs. It is not a novel observation that Virtual Learning

Environments are very effective at transferring the cost of printing from the institution to the student, although that is a very small-scale example of this kind of colonization. Equally, if students' opinions are hidden from a wider public, the university can avoid the costs of litigation under the Data Protection Act (1998). More serious is the fact that over-reliance on technology means that students cannot attend university unless they are prepared to make a significant investment in technology, as well as a regular re-investment in assorted upgrades. Academics too are obliged to subscribe to corporate values in their work. Cornford and Pollock (2003) have argued that the adoption of technology almost always changes working practices. Such practices are always informed by a particular philosophical standpoint, not so much 'we've always done it this way', but 'we've always done it this way because. . .' This point is discussed in more detail in the next section. Returning to the theoretical discussion of technology as a colonizing force, it can be seen that even those products that are sometimes described as Web 2.0 will eventually lead to the alienation of academics from their discipline. Google, for example, offers software that provides much of the functionality that commercial software does, for free, ostensibly offering universities a significant saving and thus an attractive proposition in times of public sector retrenchment:

> Having signed up for a Gmail account, a user can publish websites with Blogger, manage groups and mailing lists with Google Groups, video-conference with Google Talk, write collaboratively with Google Docs, track topics with Google Alerts, manage syndicated feeds with Google Reader, share video with You Tube, post images with Picassa [*sic*] and do whatever it is that Google Wave is supposed to do. (Groom and Lamb 2010: 54)

Groom and Lamb (2010), however, point out that such software is not as free as it might appear. In the first place, they draw attention to concerns over privacy. While the corporations behind Web 2.0 products might be largely benevolent, the fact remains that users of these services, including universities, are effectively handing over enormous amounts of data to a third party. Secondly, the business models of nearly all of the corporations are predicated on advertising, which means that the values of the corporations that are their customers inevitably take precedence over the values of educators and learners. These values are essentially monetary, but money is merely a social form (Neary and Taylor 1998) of the value that is being extracted from the labour of academics and students. That labour is commodified into chunks of information which can be sold and controlled, often through intellectual property rights.

Lessig (2004) argues that over-enthusiastic protection of intellectual property can privatize ideas that were once in the public domain and, as such, were themselves an encouragement. Intellectual property is an important right for the protection of creative artists' work but paradoxically it can, if used inappropriately, lead to a significant stifling of creativity. In *Free Culture*, Lessig (2004: 15) gives the example of the Disney Corporation, which jealously protects its interpretations of folk tales (such as Cinderella and the Sorcerer's Apprentice) from attempts by other artists at re-interpretation, seemingly oblivious to the fact that its own work was based on re-interpretations of stories that are freely available in the public domain. Boyle (2008) sees our intellectual property system as an attempt to solve a variety of public goods problems. Intellectual property rights are essentially incentives that encourage the writer to write, the inventor to invent, the investor to invest and the corporation to sell the property. Essentially, they are mechanisms that create legal entities that can be traded in various markets. Such entities are thus private goods, in that the public can only access them through exchange mechanisms, such as money or barter. The question then becomes, to what extent is university teaching a private as opposed to a public good? This is far from clear. If it is a private good, then it has a duty to protect its own commercial interests. If it is a public good, then it has a moral obligation to make the knowledge that it has developed through public funding freely available to the public. Again, that is not a position that is likely to be welcomed by those anxious to sell hardware and software to universities and their students.

Nevertheless, whether they like it or not, a legal entity that can be sold or traded can also be given away, or more accurately licensed for use by others; usually, although not necessarily, free of charge. If the original producer owns the copyright they are in a position to specify the terms under which it is used. This is the philosophy behind the Creative Commons movement (Creative Commons 2011). Through Creative Commons licences, academics can share their work with others on terms that they decide, although, as noted in Chapter 9, this does not in itself reduce institutions' reliance on capital funding. There is something of an irony in the fact that funding models in the UK put great pressure on academics to publish and that, as part of this process, they are almost always required to transfer the copyright to publishers. There is some evidence of resistance to this. For example, Martin Weller, Professor of Education at the Open University, has stated that he will only publish his research in peer-reviewed Open Access journals (those that make work freely available for others to use) and likewise, that he will only peer review work for such journals (Weller 2010). As well as research, there is a movement to develop Open Educational Resources, materials that can be freely adapted for use in Virtual Learning Environments; a critical analysis of these can be found in Chapter 9.

Luddites in the Academy?

It would be absurd to deny that there are powerful social and economic influences encouraging universities to adopt particular technologies but, as discussed above, technology can be, and is being exploited by universities, or more properly by those working and studying in them, to develop a more socially just praxis. Holloway (2005) made a useful distinction between *potestas* (power over) and *potentia* (power to) and develops an argument that as human beings we will alienate ourselves from our own activity if we do not develop our own *potentia*. In other words, in a capitalist environment, university teachers who allow the use of technology to be imposed upon them will ultimately, as Noble (2001) argues, lose control over their own intellectual output:

> Teachers as labour are drawn into a production process designed for the efficient creation of instructional commodities, and hence become subject to all the pressures that have befallen production workers in other industries undergoing rapid technological transformation from above . . . their activity is being restructured via the technology, in order to reduce their autonomy, independence and control over their work. (Noble 2001: 32)

This should not be seen as a reactionary proto-Luddite cry to smash the machines, tempting though that sometimes may be! As Jones (2006) argues, the Luddites were themselves skilled technologists, who were actually mounting a social protest against the misappropriation of their livelihood through the use of cheaper technologies. These technologies produced what they regarded as an inferior product, in the sense that it did not benefit from the care and attention of a craft worker. A modern Luddite argument may be that machine-made education may be of a standard quality, and may reduce or even eliminate production flaws, but has no inherent ability to inspire the individual. In other words, the context of the Luddite uprisings is being replicated in the modern university. Technology is often seen as providing opportunities for organizations, including universities, to reduce costs in much the same way that nineteenth-century mill owners saw the introduction of stocking frames as a way of extracting more value from the labour of their operators. A contemporary version of this can be found in a description of what universities can learn from e-business. Buller (2008) explained how Cisco Systems exploited technological capabilities to save $2.2 billion:

> They leveraged additional value from all areas of the business; Customer care, workforce optimization, supply chain improvements and staff development/additional services via e-Learning provision. Technology has impacted on processes across the business to such an extent that customer orders placed via the web can be routed to outsourced manufacturers with the finished products being delivered to the customer without Cisco itself touching the actual product. (Buller 2008: 37)

One might therefore wonder what Cisco's role in the enterprise actually is, and this passage reflects a very real fear among academics that they themselves will be rendered redundant by technology. It is not, of course, technology itself that is the threat, but the way in which it is used to extract greater quantities of surplus value from academic labour.

The original Luddites are often characterized, however unjustly, as unthinking anti-technology reactionaries, but their supporters began an intellectual tradition, sometimes described as neo-Luddism (Jones 2006), that has continued ever since. Compare, for example, these three extracts: from Lord Byron's maiden speech to the House of Lords; the Communist Manifesto; and Donna Haraway's *Cyborg Manifesto*:

> However, we may rejoice in any improvement in the arts which may be beneficial to mankind, we must not allow mankind to be sacrificed to improvements in mechanism. (Byron 1812, Speech to the House of Lords, quoted in Jones 2006: 96)
>
> Owing to the extensive use of machinery and to division of labour, the work of the proletarians has lost all individual character and consequently all charm for the workman. (Marx 1888: 15)
>
> Technologies and scientific discoveries can be partially understood as formalizations, i.e., as frozen moments of the fluid social interactions constituting them, but they should also be viewed as instruments for enforcing meaning. (Haraway 1991: 164)

What runs through these arguments is not so much a fear that machines will replace people, but that they will in some sense diminish what it is to be human. The value of teaching in public is that it reinforces the wider connection with society, and counters these rather isolationist tendencies of technology.

In the educational context, efforts to extract the human element from the teaching and learning transaction have been around for considerable time. Noble (2001) describes the rapid growth of correspondence schools in the USA during the first half of the twentieth century, which offered what we would now call 'distance learning'. These schools promoted themselves as widening access to the university for those who could not, for financial or social reasons, attend campuses themselves. Theoretically at least, this is very much in the spirit of teaching in public. However, the reality was less idealistic. Most of these schools offered little or no support to their students, and indeed relied for their continuing existence on what became known as 'dropout money', essentially the fees collected from students who did not continue with their studies (in some cases as many as 80 per cent) (Noble 2001). This less than successful record did not prevent US universities leaping onto the correspondence course bandwagon, even though in many cases they did not even offer academic credit to the few students who did manage to complete them.

The foregoing should not be read as an attack on the idea of distance learning itself. Clearly, along with the notion of teaching in public, this does have the potential to provide access to educational opportunities to those who are otherwise unable to attend university. Indeed, the Open University, a UK institution set up in the 1960s to offer distance learning courses (as discussed in Chapter 3), and which now makes extensive use of digital and networked technology, reported a significant increase in applications during summer 2010 from disappointed A level students who had failed to secure places at conventional universities (Ross 2010). The significance of the movement towards distance learning is that it indicates the extent to which the degree (however delivered), rather than the university experience, has come to be seen as the product. The degree has become a commodity that can be exchanged for future higher earning power.

Although distance learning is a different order of educational experience from a conventional campus-based education, the techniques of distance learning are increasingly being deployed on the conventional campus in order to save money. This is taking the form of the provision of lecture notes, digitized readings and other learning content made available through

VLEs. There is little evidence that students use technology for anything learning-related other than accessing resources. A 2007 study found that the 'VLE was not used principally as a means of communication; even discussion boards served more as a resource/logistical function than as a communicative one' (Heaton-Shrestha *et al.* 2007: 460).

This is essentially the transmission argument discussed earlier in this chapter. If knowledge can be transmitted, it can be bought and sold. However, what is being stored ready for transmission is not knowledge, but information. Information is valuable, in many cases indispensable to knowing, but it cannot itself become knowledge without the 'active intervention of the theoretical imagination' (Roszak 1986: 109). Students learn not by receiving information, but by relating it to other information from their personal, professional and academic lives, building ideas around it, and exposing these ideas to criticism from others. One of the strengths of digital technology is that it allows the widespread sharing of ideas, and this is perhaps one way in which academics can follow the path of the Luddites through, for example, creating more research-like curricula, as argued in Chapter 5.

Even the strongest advocates of technologically-advanced learning appear to recognize that teaching that takes place in public has some value. For example, Buller's argument above is not that universities should become purely private e-Learning based institutions, but that, with regard to standardizing infrastructure and developing common business practices, they 'can learn from the best practices of e-business' (Buller 2008: 47). If this is so, then it is not hard to see how it might 'enforce' – as Haraway (1991) terms it – a meaning of education as a commodity. The students in the e-university are producers only in the sense that factory workers are producers. Students take knowledge (raw material) that they are given by the expert (the teacher) and reproduce something for that same expert, that the quality of their re-workings might be judged. The work the student produces in this environment is defined not by any sense of the student as an individual, but by the requirements of the syllabus. Clearly, technology has the capacity to package, re-format and deliver this 'raw material' but, if that is the case as with the example of Cisco Systems above, one might be forgiven for wondering what the university's role in the educational transaction is.

One might thus infer that the argument that the implementation of technology is business-like in the sense that its adoption will increase quality is based more on optimism than evidence. Certainly, there are administrative functions within the university that will greatly benefit from the approaches described by Buller (2008), but the teaching function is profoundly different. Groom and Lamb (2010) recall that as recently as 2004,

> The difficulties in migrating learning materials from one system to another, or even from one version to another were so severe that urgent activity was dedicated to defining interoperability standards . . . [which] were mind-bendingly complex and almost impossible to justify to the bemused educators expected to adopt them. (Groom and Lamb 2010: 52)

Groom and Lamb (2010) go on to describe the development of participatory approaches including social bookmarking, podcasting, online video and blogging that have collectively become known as Web 2.0, and it is in these areas that there lies some hope for the application of the theoretical imagination and for some practical examples of how teaching might take advantage of technology so that it can become a more open, public activity.

Public Teaching: Wikipedia and the Academic Commons

There are reasons to think that some of the neo-Luddite concerns expressed earlier arise from attempts to automate the practices associated with teaching in private, rather than from inherent features of the technology. There are a number of features of the traditional classroom that militate against a more public approach to teaching. It is further arguable that the confines of the classroom, the syllabus and the end of term assessment reinforce the notion of learning as the relatively unproblematic acquisition of authenticated knowledge rather than the complex, iterative process it actually is. First, in traditional forms of assessment, the student is typically writing for an audience of one: the person they believe will assess their work, and so they see no reason to consider any other audience. Second, their work is bounded by the time and place in which it is created, that is the environment created by a given class cohort, and thus students are unlikely ever to return to it. Even if knowledge is created this way, it is unlikely to be further developed. Thirdly, objectives for learning are limited by the set curriculum, with no reason for students to attempt to go beyond them and explore different aspects of the topic. Lastly, the students' work has no impact outside the class, making it difficult for them to see any worth in what they are doing beyond its potential to secure them a grade, and ultimately a qualification. A tool such as Wikipedia, which has come in for a great deal of criticism from academics for its many inaccuracies, may prove to have real value in changing the learning process, if the nature of the learning process is rethought.

Martha Groom, at the University of Washington Bothell in the USA, has experimented with asking students on two of her courses to submit articles to Wikipedia (Groom and Brockhaus 2008). Her findings are that students valued the public peer review process that Wikipedia offers, even when other editors pointed out that their work was derivative, and even if other users of Wikipedia subsequently deleted it. (Deletion is a slightly misleading term when discussing Wikipedia. All edits are actually preserved and can be discovered through the page history.) Students were much more cautious about checking the value of references, and the work was further developed as other readers contributed to the debate or requested further information. The message for those who wish to use technology to promote teaching in public is that it is important to prepare the students, both conceptually and technically, for learning in public. In spite of claims about 'digital natives' (Prensky 2001), Groom felt that it was worth explaining to students what Wikipedia was, and how it worked. There were also technical issues about the privacy of students which were resolved by asking them to create pseudonymous accounts, learning the markup language used by Wikipedia and making students understand that writing for an encyclopaedia requires a different style from a more traditional academic essay. Nevertheless, Groom and Brockhaus (2008) argue that the investment required pays off dramatically in students' much greater understanding of how knowledge is created.

A further example of teaching and public is the Academic Commons developed by CUNY (City University of New York), a mash-up of WordPress, MediaWiki, and BuddyPress into what has been described as an 'appealing and highly sustainable environment' (Groom and Lamb 2010: 56). The website (CUNY 2011) is a public site which facilitates the open and free interchange of students' and academics' knowledge and ideas, allowing them to publish them in a forum which anyone can access and is therefore an excellent example of teaching in public; in fact other institutions have adopted WordPress to take a broadly similar approach. In the United States, Mary Washington University has developed a sophisticated publishing platform for the entire university community which, as well as providing blogs, has extended to providing course sites, spaces for group interactions, clubs and societies (Mary Washington University 2011). Again, this is largely available to public users. Similarly, universities in the United Kingdom are beginning to look at this kind of provision (Hughes 2009), providing blogging platforms based on WordPress.

This kind of model is susceptible to the arguments made by Groom and Lamb (2010) that Web 2.0 products such as WordPress are just as much the products of corporations as Blackboard, Microsoft Office and Turnitin and are thus primarily driven by their values. However, there is an important difference in that Automattic, the corporation behind WordPress, derives most of its profit from its hosted service. Users can, if they wish, download the software for free and maintain it themselves, thus ensuring that they use it in a way that matches their own values. Of course, Automattic provides additional services such as spam filtering, which organizations are charged for. An important benefit offered by this model is that the educational technologists behind it are forced to collaborate with a wider developer community; this ability to draw on a wider community can result in considerable savings on consultancy and licensing fees, while at the same time building a pool of expertise among an institution's own staff.

Conclusion

This chapter has demonstrated some practical ways in which higher education institutions can make learning spaces that are open, public and free from overtly commercial interests, and given some examples of how teachers can take advantage of social technologies to make their work public. Teaching in public is not, though, entirely unproblematic as universities employ a wide range of staff primarily for their disciplinary skills, rather than for their skills in using technology. This raises a question of how far it is reasonable to expect people to use Web 2.0 services. The description by Groom and Lamb (2010) of Google services, quoted above, reveals that the functions rely not only on users having a Google account, but on their making regular use of it. It also relies on their being prepared to engage with the various functions sufficiently to be at least comfortable with using them.

For all users, even those with the relevant skills, technology, as mediated by capital, presents an undoubted threat to higher education through its tendency to commodify knowledge. However, informed by an approach to higher education based on teaching in public, technology has the potential to challenge this commodification because the students, as much as their teachers, are the producers of their learning and as such can decide its exchange value (Neary and Winn 2009). There remain therefore reasons for optimism. Noble's (2001) rather gloomy prognostications have not been entirely borne out, since academics have proved it is possible to use technology for their own ends. This chapter has explored two ways in which academics and students can regain control over their work, while retaining its quality.

The use of Wikipedia is an excellent example of how a sharing model works, since the students take from Wikipedia the space in which to work and the peer review process and, in return, provide content for the project. This content can then be used to inform future work in the same area. In this way, the educative process of supporting students in producing publicly accessible information offers a direct challenge to the commodification of knowledge and contributes to a process of teaching in public. Similarly, the Academic Commons opens the work of university to a wider public especially, and importantly, through the use of the Creative Commons licensing model. Academics do not abandon their intellectual property rights in their ideas, but they do license others to use them, thus facilitating the development of those ideas while resisting the commodification of that knowledge. Hence, both Wikipedia and Creative Commons have a significant contribution to make to teaching in public.

In summary, capital will, by its very nature, always exploit technology in ways that maximize value from academic labour, (for example, through the use of VLEs to chunk and commodify learning content or the use of e-portfolios to package skills). This process will tend to alienate academics from their discipline, as they are forced to become adept in the new technologies. Yet, capital has also rendered technology ubiquitous outside the academy. It cannot be ignored. So the argument is made that academics must embrace technology or be left behind. But to argue thus is to misread the nature of both academic work and technology. The former deals with ideas that are free and uncommodifiable and the latter in information which is not. The latter is not sentient, but is infinitely adaptable to human purpose. The challenge then is not to follow capital in a futile race to keep up, but to resist its influence by the spreading and sharing of ideas through our own uses of technology, by teaching in public. Teachers and researchers should, therefore, share work and ideas since, in order to share, there must be someone to share with – a wider public.

Chapter 9

Open Education: From the Freedom of Things to the Freedom of People

Joss Winn

Introduction

Marx declared that '[t]he wealth of those societies in which the capitalist mode of production prevails, presents itself as "an immense accumulation of commodities," its unit being a single commodity. Our investigation must therefore begin with the analysis of a commodity' (Marx 1976: 125). This chapter offers a critical analysis of Open Education, a growing international movement of educators and educational institutions who, through the use of the Internet, seek to provide universal access to knowledge. This analysis focuses particularly on Open Educational Resources (OER), the current, dominant form of Open Education, and attempts to understand the purpose and production of this public good within the immense accumulation of commodities that characterizes the creation of value – also termed wealth – in capitalist society.

It is acknowledged that Open Education is a potentially radical form of public education and, in spite of the differences in meaning of public and open (which are not the focus of this chapter), Open Education can be understood as a public good or, rather, a form of social wealth. Here, the use of the term social wealth draws from Marx and refers to an understanding of value that is intrinsically related to a historically specific mode of production, capitalism (Postone 1993, Wood 2002). Understood as a form of social wealth in capitalist society, Open Education can be subjected to a critique from the standpoint of critical political economy which recognizes that social wealth is a historically specific form of value, created through specific relations among people, to which Marx refers as 'a refined and civilised method of exploitation' (Marx 1976: 486). In this view, social wealth is derived from labour that is dominated by particular social structures. As Postone makes clear,

Within the framework of Marx's analysis, the form of social domination that characterizes capitalism is not ultimately a function of private property, of the ownership by the capitalists of the surplus product and the means of production: rather, it is grounded in the value form of wealth itself, a form of social wealth that confronts living labor (the workers) as a structurally alien and dominant form of power. (Postone 1993: 30)

Taking this view of social wealth, being open or public does not offer an adequate way out of the capitalist form of social domination. We must examine aspects of Open Education as a public good in capitalist society from the perspective of a critique of value as the form of social wealth in capitalist society. The latter is derived from the domination of people by alien structures, which leads us to question the notion that what is public is necessarily good. The issue then becomes, can Open Education create a form of value that helps us overcome those alien structures? If not, can it point us towards an emancipatory social practice that does create a new form of social wealth? In order to answer this question, the first section of this chapter situates Open Education, not within a history of technology which is relatively straightforward, but within the history of neo-liberal education policy in the UK over the last 30 years. Open Educational Resources are then analysed using Marx's critique of value in order to understand better whether Open Education points towards a different form of social wealth.

The Public are Our First Students

In 2007, the Open Society Institute and the Shuttleworth Foundation convened a meeting in Cape Town, where a number of leading Open Education proponents sought to find ways to 'deepen and accelerate their efforts through collaboration' (CTOED 2007). An outcome of this meeting was the Cape Town Open Education Declaration (CTOED), which described Open Education as an emerging movement that 'combines the established tradition of sharing good ideas with fellow educators and the collaborative, interactive culture of the Internet' (CTOED 2007). The Declaration begins

We are on the cusp of a global revolution in teaching and learning. Educators worldwide are developing a vast pool of educational resources on the Internet, open and free for all to use. These educators are creating a world where each and every person on earth can access and contribute to the sum of all human knowledge. They are also planting the seeds of a new pedagogy where educators and learners create, shape and evolve knowledge together, deepening their skills and understanding as they go. (CTOED 2007)

It is understandable that the authors should begin their Declaration by celebrating what had so far been achieved. Indeed, over the last decade or so, proponents worldwide have attracted millions of pounds from philanthropic and state funding. Although still relatively few in number, individual educators and their institutions have created a discernible movement that has produced tens of thousands of educational materials, often entire courses, and made them available to anyone with access to the Internet (Winn 2010). Today, there are international consortia, conferences, NGOs and an increasing number of government reports that promote the opening of education.

The Declaration is not a manifesto that defines the Open Education movement, but is an attempt by a small number of influential individuals to build the movement through a unifying vision, which anyone can sign up to; at the end of 2010, over 2,100 individuals and 220 organizations had done so. Significantly, the authors of the Declaration acknowledge that it is heavily focused on Open Educational Resources (OER), the aspect of Open Education that continues to receive the greatest amount of effort and funding.

Open Educational Resources (OER) refers to the 'educational materials and resources offered freely and openly for anyone to use and under some licenses to re-mix, improve and redistribute' (Wikipedia contributors 2011). Typically, those resources include both learning resources and tools by which those resources are created, managed and disseminated. They are defined as open by the application of a permissive licence, such as those developed by Creative Commons (Creative Commons 2011). At the heart of the Declaration are three strategies aimed at increasing the reach and impact of OERs. Their implementation will require changes in the relationship between teachers and learners and in their practices; changes in the creation, use and distribution of educational resources and changes in policy to support the open, participatory culture of the Open Education movement.

The Declaration's emphasis on OER is not surprising. For a number of years, there have been efforts to create Re-usable Learning Objects (RLO), digital teaching and learning materials that are produced and shared through an adherence to formal technological standards so they can be disaggregated and reconstituted for re-use over time and by other educators (Freisen 2003). In contrast, OERs can be understood as less formally identified in terms of their composition and adherence to technological standards, yet more formally identified through the application of Creative Commons or other permissive licences; the latter act as methods of both protecting the Intellectual Property Rights (IPR) of the creator (an individual or institution) and liberalizing the potential re-use of the materials.

One of the reasons why OERs remain the dominant mode of expression of Open Education is that the creation and licensed distribution of these teaching and learning materials has been very successful in attracting philanthropic and state funding over the last ten years. For example, in 2009, MIT received over $1.8m for its OpenCourseWare project, which has systematically published OERs for over 2,000 of MIT's courses since 2001 (Wiley 2009). This high profile project has raised the profile of OERs and similar projects have followed elsewhere. In 2008, the UK Higher Education Funding Council (HEFCE) provided £4.7m of funding to the Joint Information and Systems Committee (JISC) and the Higher Education Academy (HEA) to 'make a significant amount of existing learning resources freely available online, licensed in such a way to enable them to be used and re-purposed worldwide' (JISC 2009b). Similarly, £5m was provided in 2010 to 'build on and expand the work of the pilot phase around the release of OER material, and commence research and technical work examining the discovery and use of OER - specifically by academics' (JISC 2010).

It is important to remember that proponents of Open Education are advocating that all university courses should be made publicly available for re-use. In the author's experience, the process of designing, creating and publishing OERs for public re-use affects the way in which teachers conceptualize both their course and the public as students (Winn 2010). Hence, Open Education has the potential to reform not only the way that teachers teach and students learn, but also teachers' perception of the student and the role of universities as institutions where knowledge is somehow produced. Arguably, Open Education goes beyond Burawoy's assertion, which Neary and Morris highlight in Chapter 1 of this book, that 'students are our first public' (Burawoy 2004: 1608) and turns this idea on its head: for Open Education, the public are our first students.

The Open Education movement has not gone unnoticed by government. In the UK, the funding for the pilot phase of OER projects was first mentioned by the then Minister for Higher Education David Lammy, during a speech (Lammy 2009) where he launched *The Edgeless University* (DEMOS 2009). This report argued for a 'rebirth' of universities, no longer as simply harbours of knowledge, but as users of online tools and open access as a means to survive in a changing environment. Thus, Open Education is advocated by the government both as a way to respond to changes that technology is imposing on institutions and as a way to further liberalize the higher education sector rationalized by the rhetoric of access, democratization and choice.

Open Education within the Neo-Liberal Transformation of Higher Education

The Edgeless University report (DEMOS 2009) posited technology as both a problem and solution for universities. Advocates of Open Education saw this as an opportunity to further their vision of 'a world where each and every person on earth can access and contribute to the sum of all human knowledge' (CTOED 2007), yet this view neglects to situate the role of technology, and in particular, Open Education, within the history of educational reform in the UK over the last three decades. Since 1978, there have been successive policy changes within UK higher education, which can be identified as points along a trajectory of neo-liberal reform. Finlayson and Hayward (2010) have argued that between 1978 and 1997, Conservative government policy led to

- an expansion of the university system, leading to resource scarcity
- the deliberate imposition of complex conditions of resource competition between institutions
- the adoption by all but a small number of elite institutions of a corporate management structure appropriate to these conditions.

The advent of the Labour government in 1997 marked a shift from the years of Tory attrition to the promotion of the knowledge economy, within which universities were primarily conceived as engines for economic growth. That is, '[c]onservative policy was about reducing the economic input, while Labour sought to increase their economic output' (Finlayson and Hayward 2010: 2). Whereas the Conservative government had sought to impose corporate structures of management on universities as a matter of efficiency, the Labour government set them to work, fuelling the engine of the knowledge economy with intellectual property produced by a massive programme of widening participation of human capital.

In their analysis, Finlayson and Hayward (2010) identified four rationales for such reforms of higher education: expansion, efficiency, economic accountability (value for money) and political accountability (democratization or widening participation). The values of expansion, efficiency and accountability were embedded in successive government-commissioned reports, which led to their practical realization and implementation through changes in legislation (for example, Jarratt's 1985 *Report of the Steering Committee for Efficiency Studies in Universities* and the *Education Reform Act* (DES 1988)). These values themselves must also be located within their historical context at the end of the 1970s, a period that witnessed the move from Keynesian welfarism to neo-liberal privatization, from Fordism to post-Fordism and a corresponding shift in the West away from manufacturing towards services and the knowledge economy. It is along this historical trajectory, when the heteronomy of neo-liberalism has become the new common-sense (Stevenson and Tooms 2010), that we should try to understand the development of Open Education, a term originally used in the 1960s and 1970s to refer to changes in classroom organization and pedagogy but now used largely to refer to a resource-centric mode of production and consumption of information.

It is beyond the scope of this chapter to situate the Open Education movement of the last ten years within the historical context of educational reform. However, for it to succeed in its ambitions it is necessary for the proponents of Open Education to develop a greater sense of self-reflexivity, to ask how it is of its time and to recognize the structural constraints and imperatives within which they are working. For example, almost all of the funding that has been directed towards Open Education has been around the development of OERs, either from private philanthropic organizations in the US, such as the Mellon Foundation and Hewlett Foundation or, in the UK, government funding like that administered by HEFCE (Stacey 2010). Most recently, the US government announced a $2bn funding programme over four years for OERs to develop and make innovative use of a variety of evidence-based learning materials, including cutting-edge shared courses and open educational resources. These resources would be available online for free, greatly expanding learning opportunities for students and workers. (United States Department of Labor 2011)

To what extent, we might ask, are these funders serving their own specific interests? Is Open Education being used as a method of compensating for a decline in the welfare state? Is government advocacy of OER a way of tackling resource scarcity in an expanding system of higher education? To what extent is Open Education a critical response to neo-liberal reforms of education (Nelson and Watt 2004, DeAngelis and Harvie 2009) or, as Lammy (2009) makes clear, is it first and foremost meant to serve the knowledge economy and the increasing liberalization of higher education? If 'education is a political activity, framed within a political environment' (Stevenson and Tooms 2010: 6), how do we frame Open Education as a political activity within a political environment?

Similarly, to locate Open Education within a history of the use of technology in education might also tell us something about the overall trajectory within which Open Education exists. Throughout the history of capitalism, technology has served to 'improve' the efficiency of production and no less so than in the production of the knowledge economy (Noble 1998). As it will be argued below, Open Education in its dominant, institutional OER form can be understood as the application of technological innovation and efficiencies to create greater value out of academic labour an entirely capitalist, not a revolutionary endeavour.

The Commodification of Open Education and the Role of Academic Labour

This section shows how Marx's critical social theory of capital based upon the categories of commodity, labour and value remains apposite for an analysis of Open Education today and in doing so, how our understanding of the public good is defined by the alien structures that create social wealth in capitalist society. According to Marx, capital is a historically specific form of social mediation through commodities whose source of value is human labour. The categories of commodity, labour and value are central to Marx's theory of capital as *the* hegemonic logic of modernity. Recent Marxist writers (Wood 2002, Clarke 1991a, Postone 1993) have shown the extent of capitalism's imperatives and constraints, and write about the history of capitalism as driven by an imperative or 'unfreedom', that is 'the unfolding of an immanent necessity' (Postone 2009: 32). As Neary elaborates in the final chapter of this book, the education system, like all other social institutions, should be understood as contained by and in many ways complicit in the persistence of this unfreedom. When its proponents refer to Open Education as a 'revolution in teaching and learning' (CTOED 2007), we should question whether Open Education is an emancipatory practice and ask how the imperatives and constraints of capitalism manifest themselves within it. A preliminary attempt to answer these questions can be found in Marx's categories of the commodity, labour and value by revealing their form in the Open Education movement.

For Marx, the categories of labour and value have dual characteristics which are embodied in the commodity. In a capitalist society, the commodity mediates the way worker and employer, friends, family, teachers and students relate to one another. Every thing (commodity) has the dual characteristic of use-value and exchange-value. Its use value is not only the material, qualitative usefulness of the thing (such as an OER that can be used to teach or learn something), but also the bearer of its exchange value (its dynamic quantitative relation) (Marx 1976). All societies throughout history have understood the utility of things (use value) but it is unique to capitalist societies that the exchange value of a commodity becomes the reason why things are produced (Marx 1976). Exchange value is an abstraction, a form of equivalence and a defining characteristic of all commodities. According to this view, the value of an OER to the institution that releases it is not simply in its usefulness but in its relative equivalence to the exchange value of other commodities. It is this real, yet, abstract, constantly changing, value embedded in the potential for exchange that is common to all commodities.

The measure of this real abstraction (its value) is to be found not in the commodity's usefulness, but in the dual characteristics of labour: concrete labour (productive, purposeful human activity) and abstract labour (the objectified expenditure of labour measured against the total labour power of society). Marx describes abstract labour as the common 'congealed quantities of homogeneous human labour' (Marx 1976: 128), a commodity itself, whose value is measured by the socially necessary labour-time to produce any use value under the normal conditions of production and the average skill and intensity of labour prevalent in society (Marx 1976). In capitalism, social relations, mediated by the circulation of commodities, puts out of sight and out of mind the concrete labour expended to create the usefulness of the object so that we relate to one another through the exchange of things, whose source and substance of value is found in the social equivalence of abstract labour. Finally, Marx's theory of surplus value refers to the dynamic force of capitalism which is the imperative to accumulate value through exchange; that is, buying in order to sell. Technology, machines and commodities, can transfer their value but only labour-power provides the opportunity to create more value as its value must be less than that which it valorizes in the production process. The form in which surplus value is generally realized is profit in the form of money which is then circulated in exchange for more commodities and so on (Marx 1976).

The Value of the OER Commodity

In the Marxist view, the Open Educational Resource is a commodity, a digital file, text book, pedagogical tool or series of lectures, which has both a use value and exchange value. The use value of an OER is in how we can teach with it and what we can learn from it. However, according to Marx, it is not enough for an object to simply have a use value in capitalist society, it must also have an exchange value, which is how the value of OERs can be expressed. The value of the OER commodity is defined by the ability to share (exchange) the resource for public re-use. Arguably, it is for this reason that sharing is so central to the self-identity of the Open Education movement. It is the process by which the movement's value becomes apparent and, potentially, by which institutions can accumulate surplus value.

Educational resources have always been created by teachers, but the imperative to share them is what defines Open Education. Technologies such as the Internet and licences such as Creative Commons are employed to help realize and safe-guard the value of the educational resource and can be used both to liberate and protect the OER commodity. The Internet provides a medium for exchange and the Creative Commons licence guarantees the attributed, unfettered exchange from producer to consumer, overcoming the bottleneck of one-to-one negotiation over the appropriate use of the resource. Through the use of Creative Commons licences as a legal standard for exchange, the circulation of the OER commodity on the Internet can occur at great velocity (Winn 2011).

The concrete labour of the person who produces an OER is the mental and physical energy exerted in the process of designing, writing, building and publishing the resource itself. In capitalist society, employers are not primarily interested in employees as complex, social individuals, but in the contribution that their labour-power can make to the value of, in this case, the university. Employees are remunerated for the time spent expending their energy, receiving less than their overall value to the institution (Marx 1976). Employees are a source of value for the university in a number of ways, including providing quality assured teaching, attracting research income and enhancing the reputation of the institution. The creation of OERs therefore exists only within the capitalist value accumulation process.

In capitalist society, employers are compelled to ensure that employees are as productive as possible within the limits of time and space. The value of the OER, therefore, is that a single teaching resource is a depository of value for exchange outside of the traditional time and space of the physical classroom. The publishing of the OER on the Internet initiates an act of exchange which may realize surplus value for the institution in several ways; this is evident from the constantly recurring discussions about sustainability within the Open Education movement (McGill *et al.* 2008). How can OERs keep producing value over time? If OERs cannot create value over time or, in other words, if there is no sustainable business case for OERs, then can institutions continue to justify their production?

Conjuring Value Out of MIT's OpenCourseWare

MIT's OpenCourseWare (OCW) initiative is the single largest institutional provision of OERs to date, offering teaching and learning materials for over 2,000 of its courses. This initiative provides a good example of how Open Education, currently dominated by the OER commodity form, is contributing to the predictable course of the capitalist expansion of value. Through the use of technology, MIT has expanded its presence in the educational market by attracting private philanthropic funds to create a competitive advantage, which has yet to be surpassed by any other single institution. In this case, technology has been used to improve the labour of MIT academics as a source of value, who produce lecture notes and recordings of lectures which are then published on MIT's website. In this process, value has been created by MIT through the novel application of science and technology, which did not exist prior to the inception of OCW in 2001. Over ten years, 78 per cent of the OCW initiative has been paid for by external, mostly philanthropic, income (d'Oliveira and Lerman 2009). In 2009, this valorization process attracted $1,836,000 of private philanthropic funding, donations and commercial referrals, contributing 51 per cent of the annual operating costs of the OCW initiative, the other 49 per cent being contributed by MIT (d'Oliveira and Lerman 2009). Through the production of OERs on such a massive scale, MIT has released into circulation a significant amount of capital which enhances the value of its brand as educator and innovator. Through the OCW initiative, additional value has been created by MIT's staff, who remain the source and substance of the value-creating process. Even though the OERs are non-commercially licensed and require attribution in order to re-use them, the production of this value-creating property can be understood within the 'perpetual labour process that we know better as communication' (Söderberg 2007: 72). Understood in this way, the commodification of MIT's courses occurs long before the application of a novel licence and distribution via the Internet. OCW is simply 'a stage in the metamorphosis of the labour process' (Söderberg 2007: 71).

Following this initial expansion of the value of OCW and MIT's leadership position in Open Education, and with the private philanthropic funding that has supported it due to run out, new streams of funding based on donations and technical innovation are being considered to enhance the value of the materials provided (d'Oliveira and Lerman 2009). Innovation in this area of education has made the market for OER competitive and for MIT to retain its major share of web traffic, it needs to refresh its offering on a regular basis and seek to expand its footprint in the educational market. Proposed methods of achieving this are, naturally, technological: the use of social media, mobile platforms and a 'click to enroll' system of distance learning (Wiley 2009). More recently, reflecting on the tenth anniversary of OCW, one of the founders of the initiative underlined their objective for the next ten years.

> Our ambition is to increase the impact of OCW by an order of magnitude,' says Professor Dick Yue, who chaired the committee that proposed OCW and also advises the program. 'If we've reached 100 million people in our first ten years, we want to reach a billion in the next ten. If a million educators used our content in their classrooms so far, we hope to help 10 million use the content in our next decade.' (MIT 2011a)

The plan to expand the OCW initiative ten-fold to reach a billion people in the next ten years has four strands, each based around the objective of a quantitative expansion of MIT's capital in the global OER commodity circuit: placing OCW everywhere; reaching key audiences; creating communities of open learning and empowering educators worldwide (MIT 2011b). In this respect, technology, such as the Internet, has had both an intensive and extensive effect. It allowed MIT to intensify the productivity of its academics through the duplication of digital resources and to extend the reach and value of the MIT brand through the distribution of OCW. The economic imperative to expand can be understood as a compulsion enforced by an increasingly competitive market for OER (Wood 2002).

MIT's statement concerning the need to find new ways to create value out of their OCW initiative is a good example of how value is temporally determined and quickly diminishes as the production of OERs becomes generalized through the efforts of other universities. Seen as part of MIT's entire portfolio, the contribution of OCW follows a well-defined path of capitalist expansion, value creation and destruction and highlights the need for constant innovation in a competitive environment. It also points to the potential crisis of OER as an institutional commodity form, through the diminution of academic labour, which is capitalism's primary source of value, and the declining value of the generalized OER commodity form, which can only be counteracted through constant technological innovation (Wendling 2009).

The analysis of MIT is not intended to imply criticism of the OCW team at MIT, who are, no doubt, working on the understanding that the initiative is a public good. In terms of creating socially useful wealth, it is indeed a public good. The suggestion here is to show how seemingly good and public initiatives such as OCW are subject to the structural discipline of capitalism and compound its social relations through the exploitation of labour and the valorization of the commodity form. The sustainability of such initiatives remains primarily dependent not on any measure of their contribution to the public good, but rather on their ability to attract the commodity of money by enhancing the reputation of the institution, recruiting staff and students, demonstrating efficiencies, furthering innovation, improving the student experience and supporting other institutional activities such as staff development and the quality assurance process (McGill *et al.* 2008). In the light of these institutional benefits, it is worth considering the Open Education movement's failure to provide an adequate critique of the institution as a form of company and regulator of wage-work, while it celebrates the expanding circulation of a form of institutional value.

The University as a Personified Subject

As Neocleous (2003) has shown, in modern capitalism, the worker is objectified, as the commodity of labour serves to transform the company into a personified subject, with greater rights and fewer responsibilities under the law than people themselves. As the neo-liberal university increasingly adopts corporate forms, objectives and practices, so the role of research and teaching is to improve the persona of the university. Like many other US universities, MIT awards tenure to a tiny handful of elite academics in their field (Lin 2010) thus rewarding, but also retaining through the incentive of tenure, staff who bring international prestige to MIT. The employment of prestigious researchers diverts effort and attention from individuals' achievements and reputations and focuses on the achievements of the institution. This is measured by its overall reputation, which is rewarded by increased government funding, commercial partnerships and philanthropic donations. This, in turn, attracts a greater number of better staff and students, who join the university in order to enjoy the benefits of this reward. Yet, once absorbed into the labour process, these individuals serve the social character of the institution, which is constantly being monitored and evaluated through a system of league tables in which

> the process of personification of capital ... is the flip side of a process in which human persons come to be treated as commodities – the worker, as human subject, sells labour as an object. As relations of production are reified so things are personified – human subjects become objects and objects become subjects – an irrational, 'bewitched, distorted and upside-down world' in which 'Monsieur le Capital' takes the form of a social character – a *dramatis personae* on the economic stage, no less. (Neocleous 2003: 159)

To what extent the Open Education movement can counteract this personification of educational institutions and the subtle objectification of their staff and students is still open to question. The overwhelming trend so far, however, is for OER to be seen as sustainable only to the extent that it can attract private and state funding which serves the reputational character of the respective universities. Yet, as Marx and more recently Postone (1993) have argued, the creation of this temporally determined form of value is achieved through the domination of people by time, structuring our lives and mediating our social relations. The increased use of technology is, and always has been, capitalism's principal technique of improving the input ratio of labour-power, measured by time, to the output of value, which is in itself temporal and therefore in constant need of expansion. And so the imperative of conjuring value out of labour continues upon its treadmill.

The Freedom of People, Not Things

Clarke maintains that

> [t]he working class is not simply the object of domination of the 'instrumental rationality' of capitalism. However alienated may be the forms of social labour under capitalism, the fact nevertheless remains that the creative powers of co-operative labour remain the only source of social wealth, and of the surplus value appropriated by the capitalist class. (Clarke 1991a: 327)

Education is at the heart of the contradiction of capitalist domination in that the working class, through its creative labour, is the sole source of wealth; capitalism must at the same time develop this creativity through education and restrain it through the discipline of wage labour. This contradiction is no less apparent in the Open Educational Resources movement as institutions and educators seek to demonstrate and sustain the value of their resources, and therefore the value of themselves. Furthermore, the state has assumed its role of promoting Open Education as a source of social wealth and institutional value. This has the additional effect of increasing the marketization of higher education by liberalizing the productive output of teaching staff and shaping the overall movement of Open Education into one that is tied to private and state funding and on-going institutional valorization processes. Through the useful sharing of knowledge, OER has the potential to be a source of social power, but remains constrained by the dominant structures of social wealth and complicit in the valorization process of teaching and learning.

This critical analysis presents the circulation of Open Educational Resources as a misguided concern for the freedom of things over the freedom of people, a concern that is based on a liberal view of economics, where value is attached to things rather than labour being understood as the actual source of value. Marx understood this important distinction and criticized 'the modern bagmen of free trade' (Marx 1976, 153) who see the exchange relation as the source of value, rather than the social relation of private property and wage labour (Marx 1976, Rubin 1979). Marx acknowledges the dual characteristics of the commodity being fundamentally an expression of the dual characteristics of labour and, in so doing, provides an emancipatory social theory that could lead to a really emancipatory social practice of Open Education (Clarke 1991a). If the emphasis of the Open Education movement can be moved away from the institutional processes of OER production and exchange towards a critique of research, teaching and learning as capitalist forms of labour, it might be possible to assert the movement as a critical form of social power rather than wealth.

Political action, including education, must therefore recognize that the potential to bring about such a change lies not in the freedom of things, but in the freedom of people from labour, capital's sole source of value and hence its contradiction. In this view, Open Education's revolutionary potential is in its as yet under-acknowledged re-conceptualization of what it means to work as a researcher, teacher and student. In this view, the project for Open Education is not the liberation of resources but the liberation of teachers from the work of teaching and the liberation of students from the work of learning. Elsewhere, this has been more fully elaborated as a 'pedagogy of excess' (Neary and Hagyard 2010), where teachers and students develop an understanding of the present as history and so become more than their prescribed roles through a radical, self-reflexive, intellectual and practical process, which interrupts the logic of capitalism (Neary 2010, Neary and Hagyard 2010). As a social movement, the Open Education movement's contribution could be to re-conceive education not merely in yet another commodified form but in the production of knowledge at the level of society through the abolition of teaching and learning as commodified forms of labour that mediate social relations and dominate our lives.

Chapter 10

Beyond Teaching in Public: The University as a Form of Social Knowing

Mike Neary

This chapter brings together ideas and practices that constitute the concept of teaching in public, to consider the possibilities of a new form of higher education based on a redefined notion of public. Previous chapters have stressed the importance of maintaining a historical perspective in terms of the radical history of higher education and illustrated the ways in which that history can be used to inform and support progressive alternatives to the current privatized model. A part of the history of higher education is the way in which the state has emerged as an increasing form of control and regulation of universities, based on the imperatives of what has become a highly marketized society. It is, therefore, important to conceptualize the relationship between the state and the market in order to rethink the notion of public and, in the context of higher education, the concept of teaching in public.

This volume makes the point that, while it is important to provide a coherent theory of the relationship between the state and the market in relation to higher education, it is important to ground that theory in the everyday practice of teachers and students in universities. These relationships are not simply about enhancing quality and the student experience, but they are always deeply political. The book describes how teaching and learning activities can be arranged both between students and teachers, and between teachers and other teachers, in ways that suggest real alternatives to the managerialist notions of quality assurance and enhancement. It exposes the limits of the methodologies on which the protocols and practices of managerialism are based, and urges university teachers to find their own critical discourse to frame alternative progressive teaching practices. One of these protocols is the increasing reliance on technology as a means of delivery teaching and learning. Chapters in this book examined the limits of technologically driven solutions for pedagogical practices that fail to connect with the underlying logics out of which these new digitalized machines are derived. Utilizing the conceptual framework of critical political economy, the book reveals the extent to which technology is based on the imperatives of capitalist work and, as such, is designed to replicate rather than replace the logic of the market and the consumer society, with all of its inequalities and exclusive practices.

The aim of this final chapter is to connect the key themes that have been used within the book to delineate the concept of teaching in public and to examine the extent to which the concept of public is a useful critical idea through which to recover higher education as a progressive intellectual project (Nixon 2011, Pesch 2006). It is clear from earlier chapters that there has always been a tension between the public and private provision of higher education and that, over the last three decades, the balance has swung increasingly towards private provision. The point will be made in this chapter that the concepts of the private and the public are not antithetical, but are complementary forms of regulation in a marketized society based on the productive process of value creation (Clarke 1991a, Polanyi 1975). For this reason, it is not possible to properly engage in a debate about the future form and trajectory of higher education without locating that debate in a much broader analysis of the relationship between the market and the state. This chapter therefore begins by setting out key features of the nature and form of market-state relations as a necessary basis for understanding the role and potentiality of the university of the future. In particular, it draws on the tradition of critical political economy to make the case for a new conceptualization of the university as a public institution.

The concept of the private and the public, in the ways in which they are usually formulated, are the ideological building blocks of liberal fundamentalism (Mill 1970, Clarke 1991a, Polanyi 1975, Pesch 2006). Any attempt to get beyond the liberal forms of regulation are treated with contempt by liberal intellectuals (Zizek 2002). The problem of how to escape the liberal fundamentalist framework in a marketized society has been explored throughout this volume, by looking at the very specific practical ways in which teachers are attempting to create progressive teaching practices. The approach to the concept of publicness adopted in this chapter is grounded in classical political economy, which makes a clear distinction between the private and the public spheres.

For classical political economy, the public sphere is identified as the way in which political power is organized across society. This organization of political power is referred to as the state. The private sphere relates primarily to the ways in which everyday social life is dominated by marketized and commercial activities that are organized and regulated across society as part of a generalized economic system. In capitalist society, there is a clear connection between the different ways in which the political power of the state is used to ensure the logical imperatives of the economic sphere. In this chapter, the focus on publicness is through an exposition of theories of the state, with a recognition of the role of the university in building the modern nation state; that is, the importance of the relationship between the production of knowledge and the organization of political power. The importance of this relationship is largely ignored in the academic literature on theories of the state.

Any attempt to blur the distinction between the private and the public, without first grounding them as categories of political economy, simply produces a complexity that gives an impressionistic account of the matters under review. This chapter critically engages with the work of one of the most influential authors in the field of education writing in this genre, Stephen Ball, who provides an empirically rich but theoretically flawed impressionistic account of policy transformations in education. Ball attempts to reconceptualize the nature of the capitalist state by recasting the relationship between the private and the public using notions of hybridity, inter-twining, bumping, over-crowding and heterarchy. This obfuscates rather than enlightens any practical political action. This chapter establishes an engagement with Ball through a critical review of the theorizations of Jessop (2002), who has become an influential intellectual source for Ball and for other academics with a progressive agenda for the development of education policy.

A different framework on which to base a progressive project of higher education can be conceived, which can describe the private and the public, not as discrete forms of economic and political regulation, but rather as complementary forms of a universal and totalizing matrix which is defined, after Clarke (1991a), as the capital relation. The unique feature of the capital relation is that it contains a non-empirical as well as an empirical sphere of human sociability (Sohn-Rethel 1978). The combination of the non-empirical as well as the empirical form of social activity allows the creation of an entirely novel way of conceptualizing higher education, as a form of general intellectual activity not at the level of institutionalized higher education – the university of knowledge – but as knowledge at the level of society, or the knowing society.

The core political idea on which to base the university at the level of society is that capitalism has indeed improved the creativity and productive powers of humanity, but those powers have been used to alienate and oppress the direct producers of that knowledge and science (Postone 1993).

The important political question then becomes how to re-appropriate knowledge and science so that the population which has produced this knowledge becomes the project and not the resource for a new progressive political programme (Bonefeld 1997). Thus, there is a need to re-compose the university so that it becomes not another form of political regulation but a new form of radical political science.

Educational Research and Theories of the State

Ball has written over a prolonged period a number of important accounts of the transformations in education policy in the UK, mainly with specific reference to schools but also to higher education (Ball 1990, 1994, 2006, 2007, 2008, Bowe *et al.* 1992, Gewirtz *et al.* 1995) . A key issue for Ball is the relationship between the public and the private sector and how new forms of state regulation are re-composing new forms of educational provision. The strength of his work is the rigour and comprehensiveness of his empirical research and his willingness to engage in a state-centric account of changes in education policy.

Ball's work includes research into the politics and policy-making of education in relation to the national curriculum and special needs provision, as well as work on parental choice in the context of a marketized schools system. He refers to his work as 'policy sociology', drawing on the research methods of social science, a preoccupation with the concept of social class and the conceptual frameworks of critical social theory, including post-structuralism. Although his work is mainly about school-based education, he has written specifically about the relationship between the private and public sectors in education in ways that provide a model against which teaching in public might be conceived. While his conclusions may not be supported here, his work is framed in such a way as to provide a very useful practical and conceptual structure against which to set out the idea of teaching in public. The strength of his work is the strong sociological framework he brings to his research. The limitation is the theoretical model within which his state theory is based which, in the world of mainstream political science, is referred to as regulation theory. Ball relies heavily on the work of Jessop, which Ball describes as a 'set of tools' and a combination of 'economic geography and political sociology' (Ball 2007: 3). Ball, curiously, does not mention Jessop's position as the doyen of a particular version of Marxist state theory, and its origins in the writings of a particular style of political science (Meiksins Wood 1998, Clarke 1991b).

Key to Jessop's Marxist theory of the state is the way in which he formulates one of the central tenets of Karl Marx's mature social theory: the law of value. The relevance of the law of value for a discussion of private and public in the higher education sector is that the controversy surrounding the law of value provides a framework within which different models for state regulation are devised, and the context against which struggles against that regulation are framed. This controversy was particularly prevalent among social scientists in the 1970s and has re-emerged in the recent period in response to the latest instalment of capitalist crisis. A significant issue for political economy since the eighteenth century has been to establish the substance of the source of surplus value or, in other words, what makes something valuable in a world in which the absolute power of kings has been replaced by the relativistic law of private property (Dinerstein and Neary 2002).

Marx's major contribution to political economy is not that labour is the source of value, that point was already understood by political economists (Smith 2008, Ricardo 1971), but that both value and measurement of value are derived from the way in which capitalist work is organized and controlled at the level of society. In capitalist society, the value that forms the substance of labour was described by Marx as use value and exchange value. Use value is the usefulness of things. Exchange value is both the reason why things are produced and the measure of their usefulness; useful things are made not simply because they are useful, but in order to be exchanged. The measure of a thing's value is determined by the amount of social labour which goes into making it. This is not the direct amount of human energy expended on making a useful thing but rather the amount of labour expended as a proportion of the total amount of social labour available at the level of society. Marx refers to this as socially necessary labour time (Marx 1976). This notion of social labour enabled Marx to explain how exchange value, as a social measure and therefore a non-empirical substance, dominates the empirical world of everyday life.

In Marx's social theory, the relationship between the empirical and the non-empirical is defined as a theory of social form, which is why the concepts in Marx's analysis of capital are referred to as the money-form and the value-form. This version of Marxism as a theory of social form is completely avoided by liberal social scientists who are able to recognize the social world only in its divided forms: either as the empirical realm (sociology, political science, economics) or the non-empirical realm (philosophy, postmodernism) (Bonefeld and Holloway 1991). The strength of Marx's social theory, making it the most fully developed social theory of all, is its ability to conceptualize both the empirical and non-empirical levels at the same time (Sohn-Rethel 1978).

The explanation is complex, and the law of value is, therefore, a controversial matter in Marxist social science. Since the 1970s, regulationist theorists have sought to reconcile Marxist economic analysis with developments in the twentieth century (R. Boyer 1990) by arguing that value is an economic category that needs to be supported by extra-economic forms of political activity (Meiksins Wood 1998). For Jessop (2002), as one of the leading regulation theorists, the production of value provides the structural framework within which accumulation of surplus value takes place, but it does not shape the political ways in which accumulation is achieved. This, Jessop (2002) argues, is the result of factors that lie outside the value form itself.

Jessop maintains that the law of value determines the shape and size of capitalist development although it does not fully determine the course of economic accumulation (Jessop 2002). As he puts it, 'although the basic parameters of capitalism are defined by the value form, this form alone is an inadequate guide to its nature and dynamics' (Jessop 2002: 159). He looks for solutions to this practical and theoretical problem in the concepts of 'accumulation strategy' and 'hegemonic projects'. For Jessop (2002) capitalist accumulation is the contingent outcome of the dialectical relationship between structures and strategies, with structures derived not only through the value form, but also through the 'emergent properties of social interaction' (Jessop 2002: 169). These structures are transformed by accumulation strategies, which involve readjusting the balance of class forces through ideological and political practices. For Jessop, the state exists as an external power imposing a form of regulatory authority onto these competing factors, including and supported by a particular 'hegemonic project' as part of an 'accumulation strategy' (Clarke 1991b: 50).

Ball (2007) seeks to enrich and inform Jessop's model by describing the new messy and complex forms of state regulation as they apply to education policy. He does this by identifying new types of institutions, as well as newly emerging policies of governance and meta-governance, all of which involve new discursive strategies and hegemonic projects within which intellectuals play a key role. In this process, Ball argues, the boundaries between the state and the market, between the public and the private and the left and right of the political spectrum are attenuated, so as to support the 'neo-liberal market fantasy' (Ball 2007: 10) that the market operates autonomously from the state and its political frameworks, made real by the introduction of increased private sector provision and new forms of state education.

Following Jessop's theory of the state, Ball (2008) describes this form of regulation as the polycentric and the post-modern state, the key characteristic of which is 'a shift in the centre of gravity around which policy circles move' (Jessop 1998: 32, cited in Ball 2008: 747). As Ball (2008) argues, the new forms of state regulation are based on new types of experimental and strategic governance, with new networks and policy communities. He is keen to emphasize that the state does not give up its capacity to steer policy and that this is, in fact, a new form of modality of state power, and indeed a new form of state. Ball is clear, however, about its political limits – the achievement of political ends by political means, involving governing through governance to produce what he refers to as changes in the English education state. The result is a new form of accumulation strategy made up of businesses, quangos, other non-government organizations as well as the energy of entrepreneurs and venture philanthropists, which has produced a blurring of the public and private divide and the rise of networks over bureaucracies (Ball 2008). Ball is keen to argue that this is not a hollowing out of the state, or any kind of weakening of the state's capacity to steer policy. Rather, it is a filling in (Taylor 2000) of the state in a situation where the core executive retains substantial authoritative control over policy. While Ball is keen to maintain the centrality of the state as the driver of education policy, this blurring between the public and the private that he describes is not a sound basis for the construction of a reconstituted notion of the public on which an alternative model of higher education, organized around the notion of teaching in public, might be based. In the next section, the limits of this methodology and its consequences for progressive political pedagogic practice in universities will be discussed.

The Weird Non-empirical World of Capitalism

As has been shown, Ball's reinterpretation of the education state is based on Jessop's particular, politicized theory of the capitalist state and on an economistic reading of Marx's labour theory of value. This version of Marx's law of value has been subject to much critique, as has the political strategy on which it is based (Meiksins Wood 1998). The first part of this section will provide a critical exposition of Jessop's Marxist theory of the state through a re-interpretation of Marx's mature theory and then examine its political implications for the development of a progressive form of higher education.

The key point to elaborate is that the concept of publicness and, therefore, teaching in public in the context of higher education is not a matter that can be left to the discretion of the state. The state itself is an expression of the problem that we are attempting to resolve. The issues surrounding the concept of public in the progressive forms that we are discussing can only be resolved by struggling in and against the capitalist state and, in terms of teaching in public, struggling in and against the university. This is not, however, a struggle against the university as such but rather against what the university has become: a form of the capital relation. In order to deal with that question, we have to explore in more detail the nature of the state in capitalism.

There is another version of Marx for which value is the organizing principle for the whole society, including its repressions and the basis for forms of resistance. This version of Marx is based on a revolutionary critique of Marxism through a re-interpretation of Karl Marx's mature social theory. The approach was developed in the UK the 1970s and the 1980s through the journal *Capital and Class* and elaborated further in the *The State Debate* (Clarke 1991b, Holloway and Picciotto 1991) and *Open Marxism* (Bonefeld *et al.* 1992). This debate was much influenced by the work of *Autonomia* (Negri 1984, Wright 2002) in Italy in the 1970s and 1980s and further developed more recently through critical appraisals of Marx's social theory (Postone 1993). In this approach, the defining principle of Marx's social theory is the notion of social form.

The essence of Marx's revolutionary theory of production lies in his theory of surplus value, which provides the conditions through which the social world can be progressively transformed. According to Marx's theory of value, labour is the source and substance of all value in a society dominated, uniquely, by the production of surplus value. In capitalist society, surplus value is produced by the quantitative expansion of human energy in the process of industrial production. While the value of labour (human energy) is the value of all things (commodities), the value which labour produces is not fully recognized in the financial reward paid to workers (wages). The difference between the value of the reward and the value that is produced by workers constitutes surplus value. In this way, both value and surplus value are social, non-empirical, abstract measures, as well as abstract forms of social regulation and control.

The physical limitations of human labour, and the continuing resistance of workers to the imperatives of waged work, mean that human labour is removed by the representatives of capital from the process of production and replaced by technology and science. For the labour that remains, work is intensified physically and enhanced intellectually – with a clear distinction between mental and manual work. As labour is the source and substance of all value, this joint process of the expulsion and enhancement of labour is profound. On one side, the expulsion of labour from the process of production means that the production of surplus value breaks down, resulting in dramatic declines in profitability. On the other side, the release of labour from the production process provides the opportunity for labour – and, therefore, for society as a whole – to develop its full creative capacity in ways that are antithetical to the logic of capitalist production. Both scenarios, singularly and together, spell crisis and catastrophe for capitalist society (Marx 2005).

In practice, capital has sought to restrict the development of discarded labour through the politics of oppression and the imposition of scarcity, poverty and violence. The politics of oppression has been met by resistance and struggle throughout the period in which history has been constituted as history (Meiksins Wood 2002) and forms the basis for the description of all history as being the history of class struggle (Marx 2004). The peculiarity of capital is that these imperatives of the politics of production are impersonal and indirect, enforced through the abstract law of value which exists as the political power of the state (public) and the economic power of money (private) , each of which constitute the abstract power of the capital relation (Postone 1993, Clarke 1991a). In this sense, the state is a form of the capital relation: the struggle between capital and labour. In capital relation theory, the forms of the state, either in its polycentric and/or postmodern forms are not rational strategic responses to the crisis of capitalism, as they are for Ball, Jessop and regulation theorists in general, but are the forms in which struggle is constituted (Clarke 1991b, Holloway and Picciotto 1991).

It is important to stress that in this model the economic and political spheres are complementary forms of the capitalist relations of production and cannot be 'conceptualised independently of one another' (Clarke 1991b: 37). These forms are developed and challenged as the process of the reproduction of capitalism develops through the containment of the intensification of struggle (Clarke 1991b). Any progressive political project needs to recognize this complementarity and understand that any political project that seeks to challenge capitalist in the fragmented forms in which it is constituted is doomed to failure (Wainwright *et al.* 1979).

Clarke provides a devastating critique of Jessop's theory of the state, framed around his:

> failure to grasp the fact that the class struggle, and at another level the activity of the state, is not a means of *resolving* the contradictions of capitalist accumulation, but is an *expression* of those contradictions. In this

sense, there can be no such thing as an 'accumulation strategy', because there is no agent, not even the state, which can stand above the process of accumulation to give it unity and coherence by resolving the contradictions inherent in capitalist accumulation. The state cannot stand about value relations, for the simple reason that the state is inserted in such relations as one moment of the class struggle over the reproduction of capitalist relations of production. (Clarke 1991b: 51)

For Clarke, the fundamental contradiction of capitalism is that capital:

In reproducing itself also reproduces the working class, but it does reproduce the working class as its passive servant, it reproduces the working class as the barrier to its own reproduction. This is the fundamental contradiction of the capitalist mode of production, whose concrete unfolding constitutes the history of capitalism. (Clarke 1991b: 190)

The revolutionary and counter-intuitive strength of Clarke's interpretation of Marx is the way in which he recognizes that 'capital sets up barriers to its own reproduction that can only be broken down through its successful conduct of the class struggle' (Clarke 1991b: 92–3). While capital seeks to make use of the state, 'the state is not a functional agency that can resolve these contradictions. It is rather a complementary form through which capital attempts to pursue the class character in a vain attempt to suspend its contradictory character' (Clarke 1991b: 193). In other words, 'the state is not simply a tool of capital, it is an arena of class struggle' (Clarke 1991b: 195). If the political class struggle goes beyond the limits set by the expanded reproduction of capital, the result is the breakdown of the material reproduction of society (Clarke 1991b: 195). It is clear that Jessop's inability to

provide an adequate account of the contradictory unity of the process of capitalist reproduction means that it is the state that has to carry the burden of establishing the unity and coherence of the 'social formation' which it is not able to do. (Clarke 1991b: 49)

The political consequences of Jessop's Marxism-lite, and of Ball's account of state theory, are not simply academic, but promote attitudes and activities that are unlikely to challenge in a fundamental way the logic of capitalist power, leading to accommodation and appeasement and, ultimately, failure and defeat. This lack of any real critical capacity is evident from

Ball's limited suggestions as to how the world of education might deal with its current predicament.

A similar form of practical paralysis can be found in Jessop's analysis. Jessop (2008) applies his theoretical framework to the current role, nature and purposes of universities and the ways in which they are governed in the context of a globalized market system. In this work, hegemonic projects have become 'hegemonic economic imaginaries' (Jessop 2008: 15) through the prism of what he refers to as 'cultural political economy': extra economic activities that include discourse analysis, semiotics, semantics, rhetoric and performance or 'the social production of intersubjecive meaning' (Jessop 2008: 15). Cultural political economy tries to make what it defines as the hyper-complexity of the natural and social world amenable to sociopolitical and economic analysis through the construction of a series of meaningful economic and extra-economic subsets that can be identified by their numerous regulations and strategies. In this way, it is possible to identify each subset as a discrete economic imaginary with its own operational and constitutive force. Jessop (2008) reveals the most prominent of these economic imaginaries as the knowledge-based economy and charts its rise as a main motivation for the development of educational policy at the national and international level, as well as its particular implications for higher education as a set of practices that impacts directly on economic competitiveness, calling for a realignment of the university, business and the state in a new paradigm of 'academic capitalism'.

Conveniently for our purposes, Jessop (2008) uses Ball (2007) in this analysis as one of his main points of reference. While Jessop's (2008) interpretation offers a neat analysis of the current predicament of higher education, it is a world away from teaching practice, nor does it provides any of the negative consequences on universities nor does it suggest any strategy or hegemonic project, even at the level of its own cultural, discursive, rhetorical or performative framework, by which the current dominant orthodoxy might be challenged. Cultural political economy does allow for challenge, indeed a key aspect of hegemonic imaginaries is that they are the outcome of struggle between different sets of actors: trades unions, interest groups, think tanks, social movements, world institutions (OECD and the World Bank), political parties and the mass media (Jessop 2008). It is, however, essentially an extraneous descriptive account of policy-making, with no critical dynamic within the theoretical framework itself (Meiksins Wood 1998).

For Clarke and his collaborators, the form of the capitalist state is not the result of hegemonic projects, imaginary or otherwise, but is the real outcome of class struggle within an historical and logical framework. This theoretical model identifies the significance of a revolutionary subject operating immanently within the form of the capital relation, wherein each capitalist institution or category is the outcome of struggle and is subject to transformation. This position has been described as *In and Against the State* (London Edinburgh Weekend Return Group 1980).

Writing in the UK in the 1970s, the London Edinburgh Weekend Return Group (1980) were seeking to find ways to counteract attempts by the government to dismantle the welfare state. Their book sought to provide everyday examples of the practical resistance of public sector workers, in the context of a theoretical conceptualization of the capitalist state as a form of the capital relation. The Edinburgh Weekend Return Group (1980) identified a number of strategies of resistance, including defining the problem in political rather than merely economic terms, as well as alternative forms of organization, overcoming individualization and defining problems in terms of the progressive logic of the lessons learnt from the working-class struggle. Following the inspiration of *In and Against the State* (London Edinburgh Weekend Return Group 1980), teaching in public seeks to focus this radical approach to institutional change, at the level of higher education institutions, but in a way that deals with higher education not simply as an instrument of the capitalist state, but as a form of the capital relation.

The significance of this account for a reconstituted notion of the public is that it demands that the possibility of institutional and social transformation lies in the hands of the workers on whose labour the social world is constituted. It now becomes possible to conceive the university as a particular social and institutional form of the capital relation that has itself been derived out of class struggle and is, therefore, susceptible to further progressive transformations. In what follows, the analysis of immanent struggle will be extended 'in and against' the university to include intellectual work and academic labour, so as to ground the concept of teaching in public in radical and alternative forms of higher education.

The University as a Political Category

While Marxist social science has done much to advance state theory, it has done very little to advance the development of how we conceive of the university as a political theoretical concept and, therefore, to provide the basis for a progressive political project about the production of knowledge in a post-capitalist society. In other words, it is important to consider the university as a previously unacknowledged part of state theory with an important role to play in the way in which political power is organized at the level of society. The university has a role in nation-state building (Readings 1996), but this has not been acknowledged in discussions relating to Marxist theories of the state nor as a form of radical political science. In order to conceive another theory and practice for a progressive university, it is necessary to understand the university as the relationship between its institutional (empirical) and social (non-empirical) forms.

The Speculative University

The non-empirical world was well known to the inventors of the modern university who sought to establish the legitimacy for higher learning through the practice of political philosophy; that is, the power of abstraction. The idea of the university as a non-empirical form was derived from the philosophy out of which the modern European university was born in Berlin at the beginning of the nineteenth century. The founders of the University of Berlin (Hegel, Humboldt, Schleiermacher and Fichte) were on a mission to design the university on the basis of their idealistic political philosophies (Lyotard 2005). The problem was how to reconcile the metaphysics associated with these ideals with the mechanics of constructing a civilized nation-state; 'science for the sake of science' against the 'spiritual and moral training of the nation' (Lyotard 2005: 32). This conundrum was resolved not by grounding the pursuit of knowledge in a narrow nationalism, nor indeed in any particular purpose, but in a system of philosophical speculation (Lyotard 2005).

For the new university, legitimacy was neither to be found in the preoccupation of scientists, nor populist science, nor usefulness, nor crude notions of the will of the people, nor serving the interests of the state and civil society, nor through the idea that humanity finds dignity and freedom through knowledge nor in the pure positivism and functionalism of the pursuit of knowledge for its own sake. For the German Idealists, the speculative university was to be legitimated through its ability to be 'the knowledge of all knowledge': an 'encyclopaedia' of speculative discourse, within which knowledge was to be valued not in terms of its own particular 'truth-value', but in terms of its relation to what society knows about itself as a universal whole (Lyotard 2005: 34 –5) or knowledge at the level of society.

Within the philosophy expounded by the German Idealist, this system of encyclopaedic knowing was conjured up and made subject through the notion of the 'Spirit' or 'Life' (Lyotard 2005: 35). Through the 'Life of the Spirit', knowledge is not only able to name and to know itself, but is also able to provide recognition and legitimacy for the institutions through which knowledge itself exists, the nation state and the university. The speculative university writes its own narrative history in which it sits as the embodiment, the institutionalized subject of its own enchanted and enlightened ideals (Lyotard 2005).

The new university appeared protected by the progressive nature of its optimistic abstract speculations linked to the process of European nation building. However, this idealistic project was undermined, first when the project of nation-making turned against itself to become a process of nation-destroying in the form of two massively destructive global wars, and secondly, when advances in revolutionary science challenged the very scientific principles on which speculative science is based (Kuhn 1962). Lyotard described this crisis of metaphysics as the post-modern condition, with severe implications for the modern university, for whom progress and metaphysics have been its defining characteristic: 'the crisis of metaphysical philosophy and of the university institution which has in the past relied on it' (Lyotard 2005: xxiv). Lyotard describes how the metaphysical has been undermined by its own scientific conventions and the collapse of the principle of progress, on which this historical trajectory was pre-supposed. In other words, science has turned against itself, and emerged as postmodernism, or non-science (Kay and Mott 1982). In the world of the post-modern, speculation has become scepticism, that looks for reassurance in positivism, performativity, proofs and profit (Lyotard 2005). Faced with this predicament the speculative university is unable to defend itself from the pragmatics of the business university and the newly emerging knowledge economy.

Rebuilding the University

The question now becomes: is it possible to ground the speculative university in a way that will recover its lost legitimacy? In this section, it will be argued that it is not enough simply to make claims for higher education based on a new ethic of notions of civic responsibility (Deem *et al.* 2007), civic republicanism (Fuller 2001), cosmopolitanism (Nixon 2011) or increasing forms of democratization (Delanty 2001). Rather, it is necessary to argue much more fundamentally about the nature of higher education or about the idea of the university as a practical (empirical) and philosophical (non-empirical) problem. This will be done by seeking to ground the political philosophy on which the modern European university was founded through an engagement with Marx's mature social theory and the ways in which Marx's revolutionary social theory is being used to frame, in a real (empirical) context: teaching and learning at the University of Lincoln.

The most devastating critique of political philosophy is the work of Karl Marx. Through his work on critical political economy, Marx grounded the political philosophy developed by the German Idealists in the real world history of class struggle, written through the categories of critical political economy (Clarke 1991a, Postone 1993). While Marx did not develop a systematic theory of higher education (Small 2005), he did write about knowledge as a form of abstraction or a system of knowing. While the German Idealist projected the 'Life of the Spirit' through the life of the conscious mind, Marx grounded the development of knowledge in the productive processes of capitalist production. Marx argued that through the improvement of capitalist production processes human society had become exponentially more creative and productive, but that human knowledge had been used to oppress and alienate the direct producers of knowledge. The purpose of communism, he maintained, is to re-appropriate for humanity that which had been produced in an alienated form.

Marx (2005) discusses this process in the *Grundrisse* through the notion of the 'general intellect' and 'general social knowledge'

> Nature builds no machines, no locomotives, railways, electric telegraphs, self-acting mules etc. These are products of human industry; natural material transformed into organs of the human will over nature, or of human participation in nature, or of human participation in nature. They are organs of the human brain, created by the human hand, the power of knowledge objectified. The development of fixed capital (machinery) indicates to what extent general social knowledge has become a direct force of production, and to what degree, hence, the conditions of the process of social life itself have come under the control of the general intellect and been transformed in accordance with it. (Marx 2005: 706)

In our marketized society, the 'general intellect' and 'general social knowledge' have been appropriated by the expansive process of capitalist production and turned against the individuals, academics and students, who produced that knowledge. The logic of the expansive process of capitalist production is used as the justification for the continuing destruction of the social, cultural, natural, animal and human world. In capitalist society, the main manifestation of this form of appropriation has become the university and the system of knowledge creation it supports.

Is it possible then to re-conceive what Marx described as the 'general intellect' and 'general social knowledge', to see the university not as a particular institutional form of the capital relation, the university of knowledge, but as a new social form at the level of the general and the social: in a grounded notion of the knowing society? As a general social form, the university becomes the limit of what we know about ourselves as a society, that is knowledge at the level of society, with the capacity to expand what we know as science – natural and social, the humanities, arts and culture: and to do this exponentially, limited only by our own capacity and our need to know.

It is important to defend what has been achieved by the public university and the most progressive aspects of higher education. But, the public sphere is only one side of a complementary process – the other side being the private sphere – both of which have emerged through class struggle to maintain the capital relation. Therefore, there can be no real future in the notion of the public and publicness as it is currently conceived. A really progressive project must attempt to reclaim knowledge at the level of society for the social individuals that produced it and, in so doing, dissolve the contemporary corporate university and reconstitute the university in another more progressive form.

The contributors to this volume have created an outline for how we might go about re-defining the idea of the university and with it the meaning and purpose of higher education. While the writers in this volume do not get beyond the current limits of the institutional form of the university, each in its own way demonstrates the nature of those limits and, in some cases, ways in which those limits might be deconstructed. In that sense, work in this volume might be said to be written 'in and against' the current social form of higher education and is engaged in a struggle over the idea of the university. Both the Student Consultants on Teaching project and Student as Producer politicize the current state of higher education and find ways to re-define the relationship between teachers and students in the production of learning events and knowledge. The chapter on the historical development of higher education in the nineteenth century shows the ways in which radical ideas for an alternative way of learning were developed as a challenge to the mainstream provision so as to provide an inspiration for the invention of new forms of social knowing. The history of higher education in the twentieth century, up to the current provision, demonstrates the role of the state in reducing the radical parameters of higher education into forms of teaching and learning that can be controlled and regulated in accordance with market principles. The chapters on the impact of new machines in the labour process and new forms of digital technology for teaching and learning demonstrates the danger of assuming that what appears to be a progressive new practice can be yet another form of de-humanizing regulation and control. The work on the law of value around the commodification of higher education through the provision of new technologies and open educational resources points us in the direction of critical political economy as a way of articulating a more radical discourse on teaching and learning that is based in everyday pedagogic practice. The chapter on peer observation argues for the importance of such a critique to expose the limits of managerialism.

This book is written in a moment of crisis for higher education. This crisis is part of the much wider crisis that extends to our whole marketized society and its inability to reproduce itself. The key point about this book is that the debate about whether the private sector or the public realm constitutes the more progressive basis for the development of higher education is a sterile argument. The private (economic) and the public (state) are complementary forms of the capital relation, which are the expression of the contradiction that lies at the core of capitalist production, which can only ever exist as crisis and catastrophe.

We have, in other words, to think much harder about how to create a progressive and sustainable future. The argument set out here is that in order to do this we need to raise the debate about the future of the university and of the society out of which it is derived to the level of society. This means de-constructing the knowledge economy and replacing it with the idea of a knowing society. In the current crisis, ways of knowing have been reduced to forms of knowledge to be transformed into money in the marketized economy. In a situation where the market economy has once again shown itself to be unsustainable, ways of knowing reduced to the knowledge economy lose all capacity for resilience and are unable to confront the crisis and the catastrophe. In this moment, the demand for a more general level of knowing becomes irresistible, and knowing reduced to the level of the economy is replaced by knowledge at the only level at which the origins of the crisis can be revealed and comprehensively addressed: knowledge at the level of society. It is this knowledge at the level of society that we refer to as the knowing society. The university that we need to create is not another institutional form of higher education, the University of Knowledge. It is, rather, the unbounded limit of what we know about ourselves, that is higher and higher education, which can emerge in any number of sustainable and life enhancing forms.

References

Academic Earth (2011), Online courses from the world's top scholars, [online] www.academicearth.org (accessed 21 February 2011).

Allen, M. and Ainley, P. (2007), *Education Make You Fick, Innit – What's Gone Wrong in England's Schools, Colleges and Universities and How to Start Putting it Right*. London: Tufnell Press.

Alonso, C. S. (2003), 'European Union: the threat to education', *IV Online Magazine*, 35, 4 November, [online] www.internationalviewpoint.org/spip.php?rubrique16 (accessed 4 May 2011).

Amin, S. (2009), 'Seize the crisis!', *Monthly Review*, 61(7), pp. 1–16.

Archer, B. (2009), *Reaping the Whirlwind: The Financial Crisis and What it Means for the Labour Movement*, A Socialist Studies Pamphlet. London: Socialist Studies.

Arnold, M. (1853), *Poems*. London: Longmans.

Arnot, M. and Reay, D. (2007), 'A sociology of pedagogic voice: power, inequality and pupil consultation', *Discourse: Studies in the Cultural Politics of Education*, 28(3), pp. 311–25.

Arnstein, S. R. (1969), 'A ladder of citizen participation in the USA', *Journal of the American Institute of Planners*, 35(4), pp. 216–24.

Baggs, C. (2006), 'Radical reading? Working class libraries in the nineteenth and early twentieth centuries', in A. Black and P. Hoare (eds), *The Cambridge History of Libraries in Great Britain and Ireland*, Vol. III, 1850–2000. Cambridge: Cambridge University Press, pp. 169–79.

Ball, S. (1990), *Politics and Policy Making in Education: Explorations in Policy Sociology*. London and New York: Routledge.

—. (1994), *Education Reform: A Critical and Post-Structural Approach*. Buckingham and Philadelphia: Open University Press.

—. (2004), 'Education for sale! The commodification of everything', Department of Education and Professional Studies Annual Lecture, Institute of Education, London pp. 1–29.

—. (2006), *Education Policy and Social Class: The Selected Works of Stephen J. Ball*. London and New York: Routledge.

—. (2007), *Education Plc: Understanding Private Sector Participation in Public Sector Education*. Abingdon and New York: Routledge.

—. (2008), 'New philanthropy, new networks and new governance in education', *Political Studies*, 56(4), pp. 747–65.

Barnes, S. V. (1994), 'Crossing the invisible line: establishing co-education at the University of Manchester and Northwestern University', *History of Education*, 23(1), pp. 35–58.

Barnett, R. (2000), 'University knowledge in an age of supercomplexity', *Higher Education*, 40(4), pp. 409–22.

—. (2007), *A Will to Learn: Being a Student in an Age of Uncertainty*. Maidenhead: McGraw-Hill/Open University Press.

Becher, T. and Trowler, P. R. (2001), *Academic Tribes and Territories*, 2nd edn. Buckingham: SRHE and Open University Press.

Beckton, J. and Penney, E. (2011), 'Peer observation of on-line teaching in a distance learning environment', paper presented to the Blackboard Users' Group Conference, pp. 6–7 January 2011, Durham, [online] http://eprints.lincoln. ac.uk/3953/1/PeerObservationteaching.pdf (accessed 11 April 2011).

BECTA (2008), *Harnessing Technology: Next Generation Learning*, [online] www. dc10plus.net/resources/documents/Becta's_harnessing_technology08_summary.pdf (accessed 15 March 2011).

Bell, L., Stevenson, H. and Neary, M. (eds) (2009), *The Future of Higher Education: Policy, Pedagogy and the Student Experience*. London: Continuum Books.

Beloff, M. (1968), *The Plate Glass Universities*. London: Secker and Warburg.

Beresford, P. (2008), 'Service user values for social work and social care', in A. Barnard, N. Horner and J. Wild (eds), *The Value Base of Social Work and Social Care: An Active Learning Handbook*. Berkshire: McGrawHill and Open University Press, pp. 83–94.

Biggs, J. (2003), *Teaching for Quality Learning at University: What the Student Does*. Maidenhead: Society for Research into Higher Education and Open University Press.

Bijker, W. E. (1989), *The Social Construction of Technological Systems: New Directions in the Sociology and History of Technology*. Cambridge, MA: MIT.

BIS (2010), *UK National Plan for Digital Participation*, [online] www.bis.gov.uk/ assets/biscore/corporate/docs/p/plan-digital-participation.pdf (accessed 15 March 2011).

Black, A. (2006), 'The people's university: models of public library history', in A. Black and P. Hoare (eds), *The Cambridge History of Libraries in Great Britain and Ireland*, Vol. III, 1850–2000. Cambridge: Cambridge University Press, pp. 24–39.

Black, A. and Hoare, P. (eds) (2006), *The Cambridge History of Libraries in Great Britain and Ireland*, Vol. III, 1850–2000. Cambridge: Cambridge University Press.

Blackmore, P. and Cousin, G. (2003), 'Linking teaching and research through research-based learning', *Educational Developments*, 4(4), pp. 24–7.

Boggs, A. (2010), 'Understanding the origins and state of play in UK university governance', *The New Collection*, 5, pp. 1–8.

Boldyreff, C., Capiluppi, A., Knowles T. and Munro, J. (2009), 'Undergraduate research opportunities in OSS', in C. Boldyreff, K. Crowston, B. Lundell and A. Wasserman (eds), *Open Source Ecosystems: Diverse Communities Interacting*. Berlin: Springer, pp. 340–50.

Bonefeld, W. (1997), 'Notes on anti-semitism', *Common Sense*, 21, pp. 60–76.

Bonefeld, W. and Holloway, J. (1991), *Post Fordism and Social Form: A Marxist Debate on the Post-Fordist State (Capital and Class)*. Basingstoke: Palgrave Macmillan.

Bonefeld, W., Gunn, R. and Psychopedis, K. (eds) (1992), *Open Marxism: Dialectics and History*, Vol. 1. London: Pluto Press.

Boud, D. (1999), 'Situating academic development in professional work: using peer learning', *International Journal of Academic Development*, 4, pp. 3–10.

Bovill, C. (2009), 'Students as co-creators of curricula: changing the relationship between tutor and student in higher education', in iPED Research Network (eds), *4th International Conference iPED2009: Proceedings Researching Beyond Boundaries: Academic Communities without Borders*, pp. 14–15 September 2009. Coventry: Coventry University, pp. 130–31.

Bowe, R., Ball, S. and Gold, A. (1992), *Reforming Education and Changing Schools: Case Studies in Policy Sociology*. London and New York: Routledge.

Boyer Commission (1998), *Reinventing Undergraduate Education: A Blueprint for America's Research Universities*. Stony Brook, NY: Carnegie Foundation for the Advancement of Teaching.

Boyer, E. L. (1990), *Scholarship Reconsidered: Priorities for the Professoriate*. Princeton, NJ: Carnegie Foundation for the Advancement of Teaching.

Boyer, R. (1990), *The Regulation School: A Critical Introduction*. New York: Columbia University Press.

Boyle, J. (2008), *The Public Domain: Enclosing the Commons of the Mind*. New Haven and London: Yale University Press.

BPP Holdings (2011), [online] www.bpp.com (accessed 25 May 2011).

Brenner, R. and Probsting, M. (2008), *The Credit Crunch: A Marxist Analysis*. London: The League for the Fifth International.

Briggs, A. and Macartney, A. (1984), *Toynbee Hall. The First Hundred Years*. London: Routledge and Kegan Paul.

Broers, A. (2005), 'University courses for tomorrow', third annual Higher Education Policy Institute lecture, Royal Institution, London, 24 November, [online] www.hepi.ac.uk/483-1202/Third-HEPI-Annual-Lecture.html (accessed 27 April 2011).

Brookfield, S. (1995), *Becoming a Critically Reflective Teacher*. San Francisco, CA: Jossey Bass.

Brown, H. and Barrett, S. (2008), 'Practice with service-users, carers and their communities', in S. Fraser and S. Matthews (eds), *The Critical Practitioner in Social Work and Health Care*. London: Sage Publications, pp. 43–59.

Brown, P., Halsey, A., Lauder, H. and Wells, A. (1997), 'The transformation of education and society: an introduction', in A. Halsey, H. Lauder, P. Brown and A. Wells (eds), *Education: Culture, Economy and Society*. Oxford: Oxford University Press, pp. 1–44.

Browne, J. (2010), *Securing a Sustainable Future for Higher Education. An Independent Review of Higher Education Funding and Student Finance* (The Browne Report), [online] http://hereview.independent.gov.uk/hereview/report (accessed 15 March 2011).

Buller, W. (2008), 'Learning from e-business', in J. Boys and P. Ford (eds), *The e-Revolution and Post-Compulsory Education*. Abingdon: Routledge, pp. 33–48.

Burawoy, M. (2004), 'Public Sociologies: Contradictions, Dilemmas, and Possibilities', *Social Forces*, 82(4), pp. 1603–18.

—. (2005a), 'The Critical Turn to Public Sociology' *Critical Sociology*, 31(3), pp. 313–26, [online] http://burawoy.berkeley.edu/PS/Critical%20Sociology/The%20Critical%20Turn%20to%20Public%20Sociology.pdf (accessed 4 May 2011).

—. (2005b), 'For public sociology', *American Sociological Review*, 70(1), pp. 4–28.

—. (2007), 'For public sociology', in D. Clawson, R. Zussman, J. Misra, N. Gerstel, R. Stokes, D. L. Anderton and M. Burawoy (eds), Public Sociology: Fifteen Eminent Sociologists Debate Politics and the Profession in the Twenty-First Century. Berkeley, CA: University of California Press, pp. 23–66.

Calhoun, C. (ed.) (1992), *Habermas and the Public Sphere*. Cambridge, MA: MIT Press.

Callinicos, A. (2006), *Universities in a Neo-Liberal World*. London: Bookmark Publications.

Capiluppi, A. and Knowles T. (2008), 'Maintenance and evolution of free/libre/open source software', paper presented to the *International Conference on Software Maintenance*, 28 September to 4 October, Beijing.

Chamberlin, R. (1996), *Survival: The Rise, Fall and Rise of the Guildford Institute of the University of Surrey*. Godalming: Piton Publishing House Ltd.

Charnley, H., Roddam, G. and Wistow, J. (2009), 'Working with service users and carers', in R. Adams, L. Dominelli and M. Payne (eds), *Social Work: Themes, Issues and Critical Debates*, 3rd edn. Basingstoke: Palgrave Macmillan, pp. 193–208.

Clarke, S. (1991a), *Marx, Marginalism and Modern Sociology*, 2nd edn. Baskingstoke: Macmillan.

—. (1991b), 'The state debate', in S. Clarke (ed.), *The State Debate*. Basingstoke: Macmillan, pp. 1–61.

Clegg, S. (2009), 'Forms of knowing and academic development practice', *Studies in Higher Education*, 34(4), pp. 403–16.

Cohen, S. A. and MacVicar, M. L. A. (1976), 'Establishing an undergraduate research program in physics: how it was done', *American Journal of Physics*, 44(3), pp. 199–203.

Coleman, J. (1997), 'Social capital in the creation of human capital', in A. Halsey, H. Lauder, P. Brown and A. Wells (eds), *Education: Culture, Economy and Society*. Oxford: Oxford University Press, pp. 80–95.

Coles, J. (2003), Review of *A Ministry of Enthusiasm: Centenary Essays on the Workers' Educational Association* (review number 356), [online] www.history.ac.uk/reviews/review/356 (accessed 27 April 2011).

Committee on Higher Education (1963), *Higher Education Report of the Committee Appointed by the Prime Minister under the Chairmanship of Lord Robbins 1961–1963* (The Robbins Report). London: HMSO Cmnd 2154.

Cook-Sather, A. (2002), 'Authorizing students' perspectives: toward trust, dialogue, and change in education', *Educational Researcher*, 31(4), pp. 3–14.

—. (2008), ' "What you get is looking in a mirror, only better": inviting students to reflect (on) college teaching', *Reflective Practice*, 9(4), pp. 473–83.

—. (2009), 'From traditional accountability to shared responsibility: the benefits and challenges of student consultants gathering midcourse feedback in college classrooms', *Assessment and Evaluation in Higher Education*, 34(2), pp. 231–41.

Cornford, J. and Pollock, N. (2003), *Putting the University Online: Information Technology and Organisational Change*. Buckingham: SRHE and Open University Press.

Cosh, J. (1999), 'Peer observation: a reflective model', *ELT Journal*, 53(1), pp. 22–7.

Cousin, G. (2008), 'New forms of transactional curriculum inquiry', in R. Land, J. H.F. Meyer and J. Smith (eds), *Threshold Concepts in the Disciplines*. Rotterdam and Taipei: Sense Publications, pp. 261–72.

—. (2010), 'Neither teacher-centred nor student-centred: threshold concepts and research partnerships', *Journal of Learning Development in Higher Education*, 2.

Crawford, K. (2009), 'Continuing professional development in higher education: tensions and debates in a changing environment', in L. Bell., H. Stevenson and M. Neary (eds), *The Future of Higher Education: Policy, Pedagogy and the Student Experience*. London: Continuum Books, pp. 69–82.

Creative Commons (2011), 'About', [online] http://creativecommons.org/about (accessed 30 March 2011).

Creighton, M. (1902), *Thoughts on Education*. London: Longmans, Green, and Co.

CTOED (Cape Town Open Education Declaration) (2007), [online] www.capetowndeclaration.org (accessed 1 March 2011).

CUNY (2011), 'CUNY Academic Commons', [online] http://commons.gc.cuny.edu (accessed 30 March 2011).

d'Oliveira, C. and Lerman, S. (2009), 'OpenCourseWare: Working Through Financial Challenges', *MIT Faculty Newsletter*, 22(1), September/October, [online] http://web.mit.edu/fnl/volume/221/d%27oliveira_lerman.html (accessed 1st March 2011).

De Angelis, M. and Harvie, D. (2009), ' "Cognitive capitalism" and the rat race: how capital measures immaterial labour in British universities', *Historical Materialism*, 17(3), pp. 3–30.

Deal, M. (2007), 'Aversive disablism: subtle prejudice towards disabled people', *Disability & Society*, 22(1), pp. 93–107.

Deem, R. (1998), ' "New Managerialism" and higher education: the management of performances and cultures in universities in the United Kingdom', *International Studies in Sociology of Education*, 8(1), pp. 47–70.

—. (2001), 'Globalisation, new managerialism, academic capitalism and entrepreneurialism in universities: is the local dimension still important?', *Comparative Education*, 37(1), pp. 7–20.

Deem, R., Hillyard, S. and Reed, M. (2007), *Knowledge, Education and New Managerialism*. Oxford: Oxford University Press.

—. (2008), *Knowledge, Higher Education, and the New Managerialism: The Changing Management of UK Universities*. Oxford: Open University Press.

Delanty, G. (1998), 'The idea of the university in the global era: from knowledge as an end to the end of knowledge?' *Social Epistemology*, 12(1), pp. 3–25.

—. (2001), *Challenging Knowledge: The University in the Knowledge Society*. Buckingham: SRHE and Open University Press.

—. (2003), 'Ideologies of the knowledge society and the cultural contradictions of higher education', *Policy Futures in Education*, 1(1), pp. 71–82.

DEMOS (2009), *The Edgeless University*, [online] www.demos.co.uk/publications/the-edgeless-university (accessed 11 October 2010).

DES (Department of Education and Science) (1988), *Education Reform Act*. London: HMSO.

—. (1992), *Further and Higher Education Act*. London: HMSO.

DfEE (Department for Education and Employment) (1995), *Disability Discrimination Act*. London: HMSO.

—. (1998), *The Learning Age*. London: HMSO.

—. (2001), *Special Educational Needs Disability Act* (SENDA). London: HMSO.

DfES (Department for Education and Skills) (2003), *The Future of Higher Education*. Norwich: The Stationery Office.

Digby, A. and Searby, P. (1981), *Children, School and Society in Nineteenth-Century England*. London: Macmillan.

Dinerstein, A. and Neary, M. (eds) (2002), *The Labour Debate: An Investigation into the Theory and Reality of Capitalist Work*. London and New York: Ashgate.

DWP (Department of Work and Pensions) (2010), *Single Equality Act*. Norwich: The Stationery Office.

Eastwood, D. (2009), *Introduction to Urban Regeneration: Making a Difference*. Newcastle upon, Tyne: HEFCE, Northumbria University.

Education for Change Ltd, The Research Partnership and Social Informatics Research Unit, University of Birmingham (2005), *Study of Environments to Support e-Learning in UK Further and Higher Education*. London: JISC.

Edwards, C. (2011), 'Investigation of the relevance of the notion of a threshold concept within generic learning development work', *Journal of Learning Development in Higher Education*, 3.

Elliott, L. and Atkinson, D. (2008), *The Gods That Failed: How Blind Faith in Markets Has Cost Us Our Future*. London: Bodley Head.

Elton, L. (2005). 'Scholarship and the research and teaching nexus', in R. Barnett (ed.), *Reshaping the University: New Relationships between Research, Scholarship and Teaching*. Maidenhead: McGraw-Hill/Open University Press.

Epstein, D. and Boden, R. (2006), 'Managing the research imagination? Globalisation and research in higher education', *Globalisation, Societies and Education*, 4(2), pp. 223–36.

Evans, M. (2004), *Killing Thinking: The Death of Universities*. London: Continuum Books.

Fanghanel, J. and Trowler, P. (2008), 'Exploring academic identities and practices in a competitive enhancement context: a UK-based case study', *European Journal of Education*, 43(3), pp. 301–13.

Fejes, A. (2005), 'The Bologna process – governing higher education in Europe through standardisation', paper presented to the third conference on *Knowledge and Politics: The Bologna Process and the Shaping of the Future Knowledge Societies*, University of Bergen, May pp. 18–20.

Field, J. (2002), 'Governing the ungovernable: why lifelong learning policies promise so much yet deliver so little', in R. Edwards, N. Miller, N. Small and A. Tait (eds), *Supporting Lifelong Learning, Vol. 3: Making Policy Work*. London: Routledge, pp. 201–16.

Fielding, M. (2001), 'Students as radical agents of change', *Journal of Educational Change*, 2(2), pp. 123–41.

Finlayson, G. and Hayward, D. (2010), 'Education towards hetereonomy: a critical analysis of the reform of UK universities since 1978', [online] www.sussex.ac.uk/Users/jgf21/eth final version.pdf (accessed 18 October 2010).

Fitch, J. G. (1883), *Lectures on Teaching*. Cambridge: Cambridge University Press.

Ford, P., Goodyear, P., Heseltine, R., Lewis, R., Darby, J., Graves, J., Satorius, P., Harwood, D. and King, T. (1996), *Managing Change in Higher Education: A Learning Environment Architecture*. Buckingham: Open University Press.

Forster, G. and Bell, A. (2006), 'The subscription libraries and their members', in A. Black and P. Hoare (eds), *The Cambridge History of Libraries in Great Britain and Ireland*, Vol. III, 1850–2000. Cambridge: Cambridge University Press, pp. 147–68.

Foster, J. B. and Magdoff, F. (2009), *The Great Financial Crisis: Causes and Consequences*. New York: Monthly Review Press.

Foucault, M. (1980), *Power/Knowledge. Selected Interviews and Other Writings 1972–1977*. Brighton: Harvester Press.

—. (1988), *Madness and Civilization: A History of Insanity in the Age of Reason*. New York: Vintage.

Freire, P. (1972), *Pedagogy of the Oppressed*. Harmondsworth: Penguin.

Freisen, N. (2003), 'Three objections to learning objects and e-Learning standards', [online] http://learningspaces.org/n/papers/objections.html (accessed 1 March 2011).

Fuller, S. (2001), *Knowledge Management Foundations*. Boston, Oxford and New Dehli: KMCI Press.

Fuller, T. (1989), *The Voice of Liberal Learning: Michael Oakeshott on Education*. Yale: Yale University Press.

Fulton, O. (1981), *Access to Higher Education*. Guildford: Society for Research into Higher Education.

Gamble, A. (2009), The *Spectre at the Feast: Capitalist Crisis and the Politics of Recession*. Basingstoke and New York: Palgrave Macmillan.

Gardner, P. (2007), 'Literacy, learning and education', in C. Williams (ed.), *A Companion to Nineteenth-Century Britain*. Oxford: Blackwell Publishing, The Historical Association, pp. 353–68.

Gewirtz, S., Ball, S. and Bowe, R. (1995), *Markets, Choice and Equity in Education*. Buckingham and Philadelphia: Open University Press.

Gill, A. M. (1968), 'The Leicester school board', in B. Simon (ed.), *Education in Leicestershire, 1540–1940*. Leicester: Leicester University Press.

Goldman, L. (1995), *Dons and Workers: Oxford and Adult Education Since 1850*. Oxford: Clarendon Press.

—. (2003), 'The first students in the WEA: individual enlightenment and collective advance', in R. Roberts (ed.), *A Ministry of Enthusiasm: Centenary Essays on the Workers' Educational Association*, London: Pluto Press.

Gombrich, R. (2000), 'British higher education in the last twenty years: the murder of a profession', lecture given to the Graduate Institute of Policy Studies, Tokyo, 7 January.

Goodman, J. and Grosvenor, I. (2009), 'Educational research – history of education a curious case?', *Oxford Review of Education*, 35(5), pp. 601–16.

Gosling, D. (2005), *Peer Observation of Teaching*, SEDA paper 128. Birmingham: SEDA.

Gosling, D. and Mason O'Connor, K. (eds) (2009), *Beyond the Peer Observation of Teaching*, SEDA paper 124. London: SEDA.

Gramsci, A. (1971), *Selections from the Prison Notebooks*. London: Lawrence and Wishart.

Groom, J. and Lamb, B. (2010), 'Never mind the Edupunks or, the Great Word Count Swindle', *Educause Review*, 45(4), pp. 50–8.

Groom, M. and Brockhaus, A. (2008), 'Using Wikipedia to Re-envision the Term Paper', [online] www.educause.edu/node/162770 (accessed 21 July 2010).

Hagyard, A. (2009), 'Student intelligence: challenging received wisdom in student surveys', in L. Bell., H. Stevenson and M. Neary (eds), *The Future of Higher Education: Policy, Pedagogy and the Student Experience*. London: Continuum Books, pp. 112–25.

Halsey, A. (1997), 'Trends in access and equity in higher education: Britain in international perspective', in A. Halsey, H. Lauder, P. Brown, and A. Wells (eds), *Education: Culture, Economy and Society*. Oxford: Oxford University Press, pp. 638–45.

—. (2006), 'The European University', in H. Lauder, P. Brown, J. Dillabough and A. Halsey (eds), *Education, Globalization and Social Change*. Oxford: Oxford University Press, pp, pp. 854–65.

Halsey, A., Lauder, H., Brown, P. and Wells, A. (eds) (1997), *Education: Culture, Economy and Society*. Oxford: Oxford University Press.

Hammersley-Fletcher, L. and Orsmond, P. (2004), 'Evaluating our peers: is peer observation a meaningful process?', *Studies in Higher Education*, 29(4), pp. 489–503.

—. (2005), 'Reflecting on reflective practices within peer observation', *Studies in Higher Education*, 30(2), pp. 213–24.

Haraway, D. (1991), *Simians, Cyborgs and Women: The Reinvention of Nature*. London: Free Association Books.

Harrison, J. F. C. (1961), *Learning and Living, 1790–1960*. London: Routledge and Kegan Paul.

—. (1971), *Underground Education in the Nineteenth Century*, Mansbridge Memorial Lecture. Leeds: Leeds University Press.

Harvey, L. (2004), 'The power of accreditation: views of academics', *Journal of Higher Education Policy and Management*, 26(2), pp. 207–23.

Harvey, L. and Green, D. (1993), 'Defining quality', *Assessment and Evaluation in Higher Education*, 18(1), pp. 9–34.

Hattie, J. and Marsh, H. (1996), 'The relationship between research and teaching: a meta-analysis', *Review of Educational Research*, 66(4), pp. 507–42.

HEA (Higher Education Academy) (2006), 'The UK professional standards framework for teaching and supporting learning in higher education', [online] www.heacademy.ac.uk/assets/York/documents/ourwork/rewardandrecog/ProfessionalStandardsFramework.pdf (accessed 15 March 2011).

Healey, M. and Jenkins, A. (2009), *Developing Undergraduate Research and Inquiry*. York: Higher Education Academy.

Heaton-Shrestha, C., Gipps, C., Edirisingha, P. and Linsey, T. (2007), 'Learning and e-Learning in HE: the relationship between student learning style and VLE use', *Research Papers in Education*, 22(4), pp. 443–64.

HEFCE (Higher Education Funding Council for England) (2005), *Strategy for e-Learning*. [online] www.hefce.ac.uk/pubs/hefce/2005/05_12 (accessed 16 March 2011).

—. (2006a), 'Higher Education Funding Council for England. A brief history', [online] www.hefce.ac.uk/aboutus/history/history.htm (accessed 10 February 2011).

—. (2006b), 'Widening particpation', [online] www.hefce.ac.uk/widen (accessed 11 February 2011).

—. (2006c), *Teaching Quality Enhancement Fund: Funding Arrangements 2006–07 to 2008–09*, [online] www.hefce.ac.uk/pubs/hefce/2006/06_11 (accessed 6 March 2011).

—. (2009a), *Enhancing Teaching and Learning Through the Use of Technology*, [online] www.hefce.ac.uk/pubs/hefce/2005/05_12 (accessed 25 March 2011).

—. (2009b), 'Teaching Quality Enhancement Fund (TQEF)', [online] www.hefce. ac.uk/learning/enhance/tqef.asp (accessed 25 May 2011).

Hewitt, M. (2006), 'Extending the public library 1850–1930', in A. Black and P. Hoare (eds), *The Cambridge History of Libraries in Great Britain and Ireland*, Vol. III, 1850–2000. Cambridge: Cambridge University Press, pp. 72–81.

Hoare, P. (2003), 'The operatives' libraries of Nottingham: a radical community's own initiative', *Library History*, 19, pp. 173–84.

—. (2006), 'The libraries of the ancient universities to the 1960s', in A. Black and P. Hoare (eds), *The Cambridge History of Libraries in Great Britain and Ireland*, Vol. III, 1850–2000. Cambridge: Cambridge University Press, pp. 321–56.

—. (2010), 'Evidence from Thomas Greenwood's *British Library Year Book, 1900–1901*', pers. comm., 31 August 2010.

Holloway, J. (2005), *Change the World Without Taking Power*. Ann Arbor, MI: Pluto Press.

Holloway, J. and Picciotto, S. (1991), 'Capital, Crisis and the State', in S. Clarke (ed.), *The State Debate*. London: Macmillan, pp. 109–41.

Home Office (1998), *Data Protection Act 1998*. London: HMSO.

Huber, V. A. (1843), *The English Universities*, Vol. II, Part I. London: William Pickering.

Hughes, A. (2009), *Higher Education in a Web 2.0 World*. London: Committee of Inquiry into the Changing Learner Experience.

Humboldt, W. von (1970), 'On the spirit and organisational framework of intellectual institutions in Berlin', *Minerva*, 8, pp. 242–67.

Hunter, A-B., Laursen, S. L. and Seymour, E. (2007), 'Becoming a scientist: the role of undergraduate research in students' cognitive, personal, and professional development', *Science Education*, 91(1), pp. 36–74.

Hunter, S. and Ritchie, P. (2007), 'Introduction – with, not to: models of co-production in social welfare', in S. Hunter and P. Ritchie (eds), *Co-Production and Personalisation in Social Care: Changing Relationships in the Provision of Social Care*. London: Jessica Kingsley, pp. 9–18.

Inkster, I. (1976), 'The social context of an educational movement: a revisionist approach to the English Mechanics' Institutes, 1820–1850', *Oxford Review of Education*, 2(3), pp. 277–307.

Innes, J. (2006), 'Libraries in context: social, cultural and intellectual background', in G. Mandelbrote and K. A. Manley (eds), *The Cambridge History of Libraries in Britain and Ireland*, Vol. II 1640–1850. Cambridge: Cambridge University Press, pp. 285–300.

iParadigms LLC (2010), 'Company questions and answers', [online] http://turnitin.com/resources/documentation/turnitin/sales/turnitin_qa.pdf (accessed 9 December 2010).

iTunes University (2011), [online] www.apple.com/education/itunes-u (accessed 21 February 2011).

Jarratt, A. (1985), *Report of the Steering Committee for Efficiency Studies in Universities.* London: CVCP.

Jenkins, A. (2004), *A Guide to the Research Evidence on Teaching-Research Relations.* York: Higher Education Academy.

Jenkins, A. and Healey, M. (2005), *Institutional Strategies to Link Teaching and Research.* York: Higher Education Academy.

Jenkins, A., Healey, M. and Zetter, R. (2007), *Linking Teaching and Research in Departments and Disciplines.* York: Higher Education Academy.

Jepson, N. A. (1973), *The Beginnings of English University Adult Education – Policy and Problems. A Critical Study of the Early Cambridge and Oxford University Extension Lecture Movements between 1873 and 1907.* London: Michael Joseph.

Jessop, B. (2002), *The Future of the Capitalist State.* Cambridge: Polity Press.

—. (2008), 'A cultural political economy of competitiveness and its implications for higher education', in B. Jessop, N. Fairclough and R. Wodak (eds), *Education and the Knowledge-Based Economy in Europe.* Rotterdam and Tapei: Sense.

Jewell, E. and Brew, M. (2010), *Undergraduate Research Experience Programs in Australian Universities,* [online] www.mq.edu.au/ltc/altc/ug_research/files/Brew_MQFellowship_UGprograms_report2010.pdf (accessed 6 March 2011).

JISC (2008), *Great Expectations of ICT: How Higher Education Institutions are Measuring Up,* [online] www.jisc.ac.uk/publications/research/2008/greatexpectations.aspx (accessed 16 March 2011).

—. (2009a), *CIBER Report - Information Behaviour of the Researcher of the Future,* [online] www.jisc.ac.uk/media/documents/programmes/reppres/gg_final_keynote_11012008.pdf (accessed 25 March 2011).

—. (2009b), 'Open educational resources programme - phase 1', [online] www.jisc.ac.uk/ /link.aspx?_id=FC3EA2576C484B99A47DD4AFE925D900&_z=z (accessed 11 October 2010).

—. (2010), 'Open educational resources programme – phase 2', [online] www.jisc.ac.uk/oer (accessed 11 October 2010).

Jones, D. (1977), *The Making of the Educational System, 1851–81.* London: Routledge and Kegan Paul.

Jones, S. E. (2006), *Against Technology: From the Luddites to Neo-Luddism.* London: Routledge.

Kay, G. and Mott, J. (1982), *Political Order and the Law of Labour.* London: Macmillan.

Kell, C. and Annetts, S. (2009), 'Peer review of teaching: embedded practice or policy-holding complancency?', *Innovations in Education and Teaching International,* 46(1), pp. 61–70.

Kelly, T. (1992), *A History of Adult Education in Great Britain,* 3rd edn. Liverpool: Liverpool University Press.

Kogan, M. (1975), *Educational Policy-Making: A Study of Interest Groups and Parliament.* London: George Allen and Unwin Ltd.

Kreisberg, S. (1992), *Transforming Power: Domination, Empowerment and Education.* Albany, NY: University of New York Press.

Kuhn, T. (1962), *The Structure of Scientific Revolutions.* Chicago: Chicago University Press.

Lambert, R. (2003), *Lambert Review of Business-University Collaboration: Final Report.* Norwich: HMSO, [online] www.eua.be/eua/jsp/en/upload/lambert_review_final_450.1151581102387.pdf (accessed 4 May 2011).

Lammy, D. (2009), 'The Edgeless University', [online] http://webarchive.nation-alarchives.gov.uk/+/http://www.dius.gov.uk/news_and_speeches/speeches/david_lammy/edgeless_university (accessed 11 October 2010).

Laurent, J. (1984), 'Science, society and politics in late nineteenth century England: a further look at Mechanics' Institutes', *Social Studies of Science*, 14(4), pp. 585–619.

Laurillard, D. (2002), *Rethinking University Teaching: A Conversational Framework for the Effective Use of Learning Technologies.* London: Routledge Falmer.

Leadbeater, C. (2000), *Living on Thin Air.* London: Penguin.

Lesnick, A. and Cook-Sather, A. (2010), 'Building civic capacity on campus through a radically inclusive teaching and learning initiative', *Innovative Higher Education*, 35(1), pp. 3–17.

Lessig, L. (2004), *Free Culture: How Big Media Uses Technology and the Law to Lock Down Culture and Control Creativity.* New York, NY: Penguin Press.

Levidow, L. (2002), 'Marketising higher education: neo-liberal strategies and coun-ter strategies', in K. Robins and F. Webster (eds), *The Virtual University? Knowl-edge, Markets and Management.* Oxford: Oxford University Press, pp. 247–48.

Levy, P. (2008), ' "I feel like a grown up person": first year undergraduates' expe-riences of inquiry and research,' paper presented to CILASS Third Monday Research Seminar Series, University of Sheffield, 17 November, [online] www.slideshare.net/cilass.slideshare/third-mondays-research-seminars-philippa-levy-november-2008-presentation (accessed 6 March 2011).

Lin, J. (2010), 'Unraveling tenure at MIT', *The Tech*, 130(28), [online] http://tech.mit.edu/V130/N28/tenure.html (accessed 1 March 2011).

LJMU (2010), 'A brief history of LJMU', [online] www.ljmu.ac.uk/AboutUs_City/history.htm (accessed 11 March 2011).

Lock, G. and Lorenz, C. (2007), 'Revisiting the University Front', *Studies in the Philosophy of Education*, 26(5), pp. 405–18.

London Edinburgh Weekend Return Group (1980), *In and Against the State.* London: Pluto Press.

London University (2008), 'University of London external system – 150th', [online] www.londonexternal.ac.uk/150/index.shtml (accessed 27 April 2011).

—. (2010), 'Our history', [online] www.londoninternational.ac.uk/about_us/history.shtml (accessed 27 April 2011).

Lyotard, J.-F. (2005), *The Postmodern Condition: A Report on Knowledge.* Manchester: Manchester University Press.

Mandelbrote, G. and Manley, K. A. (eds) (2006), *The Cambridge History of Libraries in Britain and Ireland*, Vol.II 1640–1850. Cambridge: Cambridge University Press.

Mansbridge, A. (1920), *An Adventure in Working Class Education. Being the Study of the Workers' Educational Association, 1903–1915.* London: Longmans Green and Co.

Marks, A. (2005), 'Changing spatial and synchronous structures in the history and culture of learning', *Higher Education*, 50(4), pp. 613–30.

Marx, K. (1888), *Manifesto of the Communist Party*. London: W. Reeves.

—. (1976), *Capital*, Vol 1. Harmondsworth: Penguin.

—. (2005), *Grundrisse: Foundations of the Critique of Political Economy*, trans. M. Nicolaus, London and New York: Penguin Classics.

Mary Washington University (2011), 'UMW blogs', [online] http://umwblogs.org (accessed 30 March 2011).

McCord, N. and Purdue, B. (2007), *British History, 1815–1914*. Oxford: Oxford University Press.

McCulloch, A. (2009), 'The student as co-producer: learning from public administration about the student-university relationship', *Studies in Higher Education* 34(2), pp. 171–83.

McCulloch, G. (2010), 'A people's history of education: Brian Simon, the British Communist Party and *Studies in the History of Education 1780–1870*', *History of Education*, 39(4), pp. 437–57.

McGill, L. and Currier, S. and Duncan, C. and Douglas, P. (2008), 'Good intentions: improving the evidence base in support of sharing learning materials', [online] http://ie-repository.jisc.ac.uk/265 (accessed 1 March 2011).

McKibbin, R. (2006), 'The destruction of the public sphere: Brown v. Cameron', *London Review of Books*, 28(1), pp. 3–6.

McLean, M. (2006), *Pedagogy and the University: Critical Theory and Practice* (hardback). London: Continuum Books.

—. (2008), *Pedagogy and the University: Critical Theory and Practice* (paperback). London: Continuum Books.

McQuillan, M. (2010), 'False Economy', [online] www.thelondongraduateschool. co.uk/wp-content/uploads/2010/11/False_Economy1.pdf (accessed 4 May 2011).

McSherry, C. (2001), *Who Owns Academic Work? Battling for Control of Intellectual Property*. Cambridge, MA: Harvard University Press.

McWilliam, E. (2002), 'Against professional development', *Educational Philosophy and Theory*, 34(3), pp. 289–99.

Meacham, S. (1987), *Toynbee Hall and Social Reform 1880–1914*. New Haven: Yale University Press.

Meiksins, W. E. (1998), *The Retreat from Class: A New 'True' Socialism*. London and New York: Verso Classics.

—. (2002), *The Origins of Capitalism: Aa Longer View*. London and New York: Verso.

Mill, J. S. (1970), *Principles of Political Economy with Some of Their Applications to Social Philosophy*, Books iv and v. Harmondsworth: Penguin Classics.

MIT (2011a), 'MIT OpenCourseWare celebrates 10th anniversary', [online] http://ocw.mit.edu/about/media-coverage/press-releases/tenth-anniversary (accessed 1 March 2011).

—. (2011b), 'The next decade of open sharing: reaching one billion minds', [online] http://ocw.mit.edu/about/next-decade/initiatives (accessed 1 March 2011).

Morgan, J. (2010), 'Universities are blind to open-learning train set to smash up their models', *Times Higher Education Supplement*, 23 September 2001.

Morley, L. (2003), *Quality and Power in Higher Education*. Maidenhead: SHRE/OUP.

Morris, A. and Saunders, G. (2009), 'University of Lincoln peer observation of teaching scheme: review and evaluation', unpublished internal report, Centre for Educational Research and Development, University of Lincoln.

Mullaly, B. (2002), *Challenging Oppression: A Critical Social Work Approach.* London: Jessica Kingsley.

Munby, Z. (2003), 'Women's involvement in the WEA and women's education', in S. K. Roberts (ed.), *A Ministry of Enthusiasm: Centenary Essays on the Workers' Educational Association.* London: Pluto Press, pp. 215–37.

Naidoo, R. (2003), 'Repositioning higher education as a global commodity: opportunities and challenges for future sociology of education work', *British Journal of Sociology of Education*, 24(2), pp. 249–59.

Naidoo, R. and Jamieson, I. (2006), 'Empowering Participants or Corroding Learning? Towards a Research Agenda on the Impact of Student Consumerism in Higher Education', in H. Lauder, P. Brown, J. Dillabough and A. Halsey (eds), *Education, Globalization and Social Change.* Oxford: Oxford University Press, pp. 875–84.

NCIHE (National Committee of Inquiry into Higher Education) (1997), *Higher Education in the Learning Society. Report of the National Committee of Inquiry into Higher Education* (The Dearing Report). London: HMSO.

Neary, M. (2010), 'Student as producer: a pedagogy for the avant-garde; or, how do revolutionary teachers teach?', *Learning Exchange*, 1(1).

Neary, M. and Hagyard, A. (2010), 'Pedagogy of excess: an alternative political economy of student life', in M. Molesworth, R. Scullion and E. Nixon (eds), *The Marketisation of Higher Education and the Student as Consumer.* London: Routledge.

Neary, M. and Taylor, G. (1998), *Money and the Human Condition.* Basingstoke: Macmillan.

Neary, M. and Winn, J. (2009), 'The student as producer: reinventing the student experience in higher education', in L. Bell, H. Stevenson and M. Neary (eds), *The Future of Higher Education: Policy, Pedagogy and the Student Experience.* London: Continuum Books, pp. 126–38.

Neary, M., Harrison, A., Saunders, G., Parekh, N., Crellin, G. and Austin, S. (2010), *Learning Landscapes in Higher Education.* Lincoln: Centre for Education Research and Development, University of Lincoln.

Negri, A. (1984), *Marx Beyond Marx.* Massachusetts: Bergin and Garvey.

Nelson, C. and Watt, S. (2004), *Office Hours: Activism and Change in the Academy.* London: Taylor & Francis Ltd.

Neocleous, M. (2003), 'Staging power: Marx, Hobbes and the personification of capital', *Law and Critique*, 14(2), pp. 147–65.

Nixon, J. (2011), *Higher Education and the Public Good: Imagining the University.* London and New York: Continuum Books.

Noble, D. (1998), 'Digital diploma mill', *First Monday*, 3(1), [online] http://firstmonday.org/htbin/cgiwrap/bin/ojs/index.php/fm/article/view/569/490 (accessed 1 March 2011).

Noble, D. F. (2001), *Digital Diploma Mills: The Automation of Higher Education.* Delhi: Aakar Books.

Oakeshott, M. (1989), 'Education: The Engagement and its Frustration', in T. Fuller (ed.), *The Voice of Liberal Learning: Michael Oakeshott on Education.* New Haven: Yale University Press, pp. 90–1.

Oliver, M. (2009), *Understanding Disability. From Theory to Practice,* 2nd edn. London: Palgrave Macmillan.

O'Neill, O. S. (2002), 'A question of trust', Reith Lecture, *BBC Radio,* 4, 3 April to 1 May), [online] www.bbc.co.uk/radio4/reith2002 (accessed 9 September 2010).

Open University (2011), 'About the OU', [online] www8.open.ac.uk/about/main/the-ou-explained (accessed 10 March 2011).

Pashley, B. W. (1968), *University Extension Reconsidered.* Leicester: University of Leicester, Department of Adult Education.

Peel, D. (2005), 'Peer observation as a transformatory tool?' *Teaching in Higher Education,* 10(4), pp. 489–504.

Pesch, U. (2006), *The Predicament of Publicness.* Delft: Eburon Academic Publishers.

Peston, M. (1975), 'Towards an Economic Theory of Higher Education', in L. Dobson, T. Gear and A. Westoby (eds), *Management in Education: Some Techniques and Systems.* London: Ward Lock Educational in association with The Open University Press, pp. 189–99.

Polanyi, M. (1975), *The Great Transformation.* New York: Octagon Books.

Postone, M. (1993), *Time, Labor, and Social Domination. A Reinterpretation of Marx's Critical Theory.* Cambridge: Cambridge University Press.

—. (2009), 'Rethinking Marx's critical theory', in M. Postone, V. Murthy and Y. Kobayashi (eds), *History and Heteronomy: Critical Essays* (UTCP Booklet 12). Tokyo: UTCP, pp. 31–47.

Power, M. (1999), *The Audit Society: Rituals of Verification.* Oxford: Oxford University Press.

Pratt, J. (1997), *The Polytechnic Experiment.* Buckingham: Society for Research into Higher Education and Open University Press.

Prensky, M. (2001), 'Digital natives, digital immigrants part 1', *On the Horizon,* 9(5), pp. 1–6.

Pring, R. (2002), 'Performance management and control of the professions', in G. Trorey and C. Cullingford (eds), *Professional Development and Institutional Needs.* Aldershot: Ashgate Publishing Limited, pp. 15–33.

Prosser, M. and Trigwell, K. (1999), *Understanding Learning and Teaching: The Experience in Higher Education.* Buckingham: SRHE and Open University Press.

QAA (Quality Assurance Agency) (2000), *Handbook for Academic Review.* Gloucester: Quality Assurance Agency for Higher Education.

—. (2010), *Revised Code of Practice for Disabled Students,* [online] www.qaa.ac.uk/academicinfrastructure/codeOfPractice/section3/Section3Disabilities2010.asp (accessed 15 March 2011).

Ratcliffe, F. W. (2006), 'The civic universities and their libraries', in A. Black and P. Hoare (eds), *The Cambridge History of Libraries in Great Britain and Ireland,* Vol. III, 1850–2000. Cambridge: Cambridge University Press, pp. 357–76.

Readings, B. (1996), *The University in Ruins.* Cambridge, MA: Harvard University Press.

Ricardo, D. (1971), *Principles of Political Economy and Taxation*. Harmondsworth: Penguin.

Robinson, J. (2009), *Bluestockings*. London: Viking/Penguin Books.

Rochford, R. (2006), 'Is there *any* clear idea of a university?', *Journal of Higher Education Policy and Management*, 28(2), pp. 147–58.

Roderick, G. W. (1972), *Scientific and Technical Education in Nineteenth-Century England*. Newton Abbot: David and Charles.

Rogers, P. J. and Williams, B. (2006), 'Evaluation for practice improvement and organizational learning', in I. F. Shaw, J. C. Greene and M. M. Mark (eds), *The Sage Handbook of Evaluation*. London: Sage Publications, pp. 76–97.

Rolfe, H. (2002), 'Students' demands and expectations in an age of reduced financial support: The perspectives of lecturers in four English universities', *Journal of Higher Education Policy and Management*, 24(2), pp. 171–82.

Ross, T. (2010), 'University shortages force students into part-time degrees', *London Evening Standard*, News, 16 August 2010.

Roszak, T. (1986), *The Cult of Information: The Folklore of Computers and the True Art of Thinking*. New York: Pantheon Books.

Rubin, I. I. (1979), *A History of Economic Thought*. London: Pluto Press.

Rudduck, J. and Fielding, M. (2006), 'Student voice and the perils of popularity', *Educational Review*, 58(2), pp. 219–31.

Sanderson, M. (1972), *The Universities and British Industry 1950–1970*. London: Routledge and Kegan Paul.

—. (1991), *Education, Economic Change and Society in England 1780–1870*, 2nd edn. London: Macmillan.

Scott, J. C. (2006), 'The mission of the university: mediaeval to postmodern tranformations', *Journal of Higher Education*, 77(1), pp. 1–39.

Scott, P. (1989), 'Accountability, responsiveness and responsibility', in R. Glatter (ed.), *Educational Institutions and their Environments: Managing the Boundaries*. Milton Keynes: Open University Press.

—. (2008), 'Higher education and post modern societies', paper presented to the EUA Spring Conference, Barcelona, March 2008.

Seale, J. (2006), *e-Learning and Accessibility in Higher Education*. Oxon: Routledge.

—. (2009), *Digital Inclusion*. London: London Knowledge Lab, Institute of Education.

Shattock, M. (ed.) (2009), Entrepreneurialism in Universities and the Knowledge Economy: Diversification and Organisational Change in European Higher Education, Maidenhead and New York, Society for Research into Higher Education and Open University Press.

Shattock, M. and Berdahl, R. (1984) 'The British University Grants Committee 1919–83: changing relationships with government and the universities', *Higher Education*, 13(5), pp. 471–99.

Shevlin, M., Banyard, P., Davies, M. and Griffiths, M. (2000), 'The validity of student evaluation of teaching in higher education: love me, love my lectures?', *Assessment and Evaluation in Higher Education*, 25(4), pp. 397–405.

Shortland, S. (2004), 'Peer observation: a tool for staff development or compliance?', *Journal of Further and Higher Education*, 28(2), pp. 219–28.

Shulman, L. (2005), 'Going public with our teaching: an anthology of practice', [online] www.goingpublicwithteaching.org (accessed 15 January 2011).

Shutt, H. (2010) *Beyond the Profits System: Possibilities for a Post-Capitalist Era*. New York: Zed Books Ltd.

Silver, H. (2007), 'Higher education and social change: purpose in pursuit?', *History of Education*, 36(4–5), pp. 535–50.

Simmons, J. (2001) 'Educational technology and academic freedom', *Techne*, 5(3), pp. 82–95.

Simon, B. (1960), *Studies in the History of Education 1780–1870*. London: Lawrence and Wishart.

—. (1974), *Education and the Labour Movement 1870–1920*. London: Lawrence and Wishart.

—. (1994), *The State and Educational Change: Essays in the History of Education and Pedagogy*. London: Lawrence and Wishart.

Slaughter, S. and Leslie, L. (1997), *Academic Capitalism: Politics, Policies and the Entrepreneurial University*. Baltimore and London: Johns Hopkins University Press.

Small, R. (2005), *Marx and Education*. Aldershot and Burlington: Ashgate.

Smith, A. (2008), *The Wealth of Nations*. Oxford: Oxford World's Classics, Oxford University Press.

Söderberg, J. (2007), *Hacking Capitalism. The Free and Open Source Software Movement*. London: Routledge.

Sohn-Rethel, A. (1978), *Intellectual and Manual Labour*. London: Macmillan.

Solly, H. (1867), *Working Men's Social Clubs and Educational Institutes*. London: Working Men's Clubs and Institute Union.

Spronken-Smith, R. and Walker, R. (2010), 'Can inquiry-based learning strengthen the links between teaching and disciplinary research?', *Studies in Higher Education*, 35(6), pp. 723–40.

Stacey, P. (2010), 'Foundation funded OER vs. tax payer funded OER – a tale of two mandates', *Open ED 2010 Proceedings*. Barcelonea: UOC, OU, BYU, [online] http://hdl.handle.net/10609/5241 (accessed 1 March 2011).

Standish, P. (2005), 'Towards an economy of higher education', *Critical Quarterly*. 47(1–2), pp. 53–71.

Stephens, M. D. and Roderick, G. W. (eds) (1983), *Samuel Smiles and Nineteenth Century Self-Help in Education*. Nottingham: Nottingham Studies in the History of Adult Education, Department of Adult Education, University of Nottingham.

Stevenson, H. and Bell, L. (2009), 'Introduction – Universities in transition: themes in higher education policy', in L. Bell, H. Stevenson and M. Neary (eds), *The Future of Higher Education: Policy, Pedagogy and the Student Experience*. London: Continuum Books, pp. 1–14.

Stevenson, H. and Tooms, A. K. (2010), 'Connecting "up there" with "down here": thoughts on globalisation, neo-liberalism and leadership praxis', in A. H. Normore (ed.), *Global Perspectives on Educational Leadership Reform: The Development and Preparation of Leaders of Learning and Learners of Leadership*. Bingley: Emerald, pp. 3–21.

Streeting, W. and Wise, G. (2009), *Rethinking the Values of Higher Education – Consumption, Partnership, Community?*, Gloucester: The Quality Assurance Agency for Higher Education.

Sumner, R. J. (1990), 'Nineteenth century British working class adult education: a model for Australian colonial efforts', *Australian Journal of Adult and Community Education*, 30(1), pp. 4–12.

Tatton, D. (2003), 'Literature, cultural studies and the WEA', in S. K. Roberts (ed.), *A Ministry of Enthusiasm: Centenary Essays on the Workers' Educational Association*, London: Pluto Press, pp. 238–58.

Taylor, A. (2000), 'Hollowing out or filling in? Taskforces and the management of cross-cutting issues in British government', *British Journal of Politics and Industrial Relations*, 2(1), pp. 46–71.

Taylor, C. and Robinson, C. (2009), 'Student voice: theorising power and participation', *Pedagogy, Culture and Society*, 17(2), pp. 161–75.

Taylor, P. G. (1999), *Making Sense of Academic Life: Academics, Universities and Change*. Buckingham: Open University Press and Society for Research into Higher Education.

Thirlwall, C. (1850), *The Advantages of Literary and Scientific Institutions for All Classes*. London: Longman and Co.

Thompson, E. (1971), *Warwick University Limited*. London: Penguin Books.

Thomson, P. and Gunter, H. (2006), 'From "consulting pupils" to "pupils as researchers": a situated case narrative', *British Educational Research Journal*, 32(6), pp. 839–56.

Trowler, P. (2001), 'Captured by the discourse? The socially constitutive power of new higher education discourse in the UK', *Organization*, 8(2), pp. 183–201.

TUC/NUS (2006), *All Work and Low Pay*, [online] www.tuc.org.uk/extras/allworklowpay.pdf (accessed 4 May 2011).

Turner, C. M. (1966), 'The development of Mechanics' Institutes in Warwickshire, Worcestershire and Staffordshire, 1825–90', unpublished MEd thesis, University of Leicester.

UCISA (2008), 'Universities and Colleges Information Systems Association: Survey of technology-enhanced learning for higher education in the UK', [online] www.ucisa.ac.uk/sitecore/media%20library/groups/tlig/vle_surveys/TEL%20 survey%202008%20pdf (accessed 15 March 2011).

United States Department of Labor (2011), 'US Labor Department encourages applications for Trade Adjustment Assistance Community College and Career Training Grant Program', [online] www.dol.gov/opa/media/press/eta/eta20101436.htm (accessed 1 March, 2011).

University of Reading (2011), 'The University's History', [online] www.reading.ac.uk/about/about-history.aspx (accessed 18 May 2011).

van Dijk, J. (2006), 'Digital divide research, achievements and shortcomings', *Poetics*, 34(4–5), pp. 221–35.

Vernon, K. (2001), 'Calling the tune: British universities and the state, 1880–1914', *History of Education*, 30(3), pp. 251–71.

Vincent, D. (1981), *Bread, Knowledge and Freedom*. London: Europa Publications Ltd.

Wainwright, H., Rowbotham, S. and Segal, L. (1979), *Beyond the Fragments: Feminism and the Making of Socialism*. London: Merlin Books.

Walker, M. (2001), 'Higher education, critical professionalism and educational action research', paper presented at UCL Debates in Higher Education, 11 October 2001, [online] www.ucl.ac.uk/cishe/seminars/prev_debates.html (accessed 15 March 2011).

Walsh, H. J. (2009), 'The university movement in the North of England at the end of the nineteenth century', *Northern History*, XLVI(1), pp. 113–31.

Waterman, R. H. and Peters, T. J. (1982), *In Search of Excellence: Lessons from America's Best Run Companies*. New York: Harper and Row.

Webster, F. (2002), 'The information society revisited', in L. A. Lievrouw and S. Livingstone (eds), *Handbook of New Media*. London: Sage, pp. 255–66.

Weissenstein, R. L. (2010), 'Born with a mouse in their hand', *Bulletin* (Credit Suisse Magazine International), 2(May/June): pp. 57–60.

Weller, M. (2010), 'The return on peer review', [online] http://nogoodreason.typepad.co.uk/no_good_reason/2010/06/the-return-on-peer-review.html (accessed 8 October 2010).

Wendling, A. (2009), *Karl Marx on Technology and Alienation*. New York: Palgrave Macmillan.

West, E. (1963), 'A counterblast to Robbins', *STATIST*, pp. 1–5, [online] www.ncl.ac.uk/egwest/pdfs/counterblast.pdf (accessed 10 March 2011).

Wikipedia contributors (2011), 'Open educational resources', in *Wikipedia, The Free Encyclopedia*, [online] http://en.wikipedia.org/wiki/Open_educational_resources (accessed 1 March 2011).

Wiley, D. (2009), 'Update on MIT OCW finances – and click to enroll!', *Iterating Toward Openness*, [online] http://opencontent.org/blog/archives/1180 (accessed 1 March 2011).

Willetts, D. (2010), *The Pinch – How the Baby Boomers Stole Their Children's Future – and How They Can Give it Back*. London: Atlantic Books.

Williams, C. (ed.) (2007), *A Companion to Nineteenth-Century Britain*. Oxford: Blackwell Publishing, The Historical Association.

Williams, G. and Blackstone, T. (1983), *Response to Adversity: Higher Education in a Harsh Climate*. Guilford: The Society for Research in Higher Education.

Winn, J. (2010), 'ChemistryFM final report', [online] www.heacademy.ac.uk/assets/York/documents/ourwork/oer/OER_1_Lincoln_Final_Report.pdf (accessed 1 March 2011).

—. (2011), 'Wikileaks and the limits of protocol', in J. Mair, and R. L. Keeble (eds), *Face the Future – Tools for the Modern Media Age. The Internet and Journalism Today*. Bury St. Edmunds: Abramis Publishing, pp. 238–48.

Wodehouse, H. (1925), *A Survey of the History of Education*, 2nd edn. London: Edward Arnold and Co.

Wood, E. M. (2002), *The Origin of Capitalism. A Longer View*. London: Verso.

Wood, J. and Levy, P. (2008). 'Inquiry-based learning pedagogies in the arts and social sciences: purposes, conceptions and models of practice', paper presented to the Improving Student Learning Symposium, University of Durham, pp. 1–3 September.

Wright, S. (2002), *Storming Heaven: Class Composition and Struggles in Italian Autonomist Marxism*. London: Pluto Press.

Young, I. M. (1990), *Politics and the Justice of Difference*. Princeton, NJ: Princeton University Press.

Zabaleta, F. (2007), 'The use and misuse of student evaluations of teaching', *Teaching in Higher Education*, 12(1), pp. 55–76.

Zizek, S. (2002), *Revolution at the Gates: A Selection of Writing from February to October 1917*. London: Verso.

Index